THE
CROSS

THE POWER · THE PURPOSE · THE PASSION

Cathy Ciaramitaro

THE CROSS: The Power, the Purpose, the Passion

ISBN: 0-924748-65-6

UPC: 88571300035-2

Printed in the United States of America

© 2006 by Cathy Ciaramitaro

Milestones International Publishers
P.O. Box 104
Newburg, PA 17240
717-477-2230
303-503-7257
www.milestonesintl.com

4 5 6 7 8 9 10 11 / 09

Endorsements

"*The Cross* is for people who want radical change in their Christian lives. Cathy Ciaramitaro skillfully weaves her powerful testimony throughout the chapters of this book and demonstrates how a true understanding of the Cross of Christ can positively transform your life. If you are tired of quick fixes and desire a life-changing encounter with the risen Christ, read this book."

—Carol Kent, Speaker and Author
When I Lay My Issue Down
Becoming a Woman of Influence
Secret Longings of the Heart

As the alphabet is to our language; so is the Cross of Jesus to Christianity. Without it, Christianity makes no sense at all; and the more we are familiar with the Cross, the more we understand and appreciate our Christian faith. Pastor Cathy Ciaramitaro has done a masterful work in her comprehensive study of the Cross of Jesus and what it affords every believer and person in the world. As a pastor she is quite thorough in caring for the "sheep," and as a student of the Word she accurately brings the Cross back to the center focus of the church with a fresh anointing.

—Jim Clark, Apostolic Overseer
B.C.C.N. and Bethany World Prayer Center

The Cross is a must-read for most western world Christians. Many have reduced the action at Calvary as just an annual memorial day. Many acknowledge the Cross upon initial profession of their faith, but then leave it behind. Cathy Ciaramitaro hits the nail right on the head when she dares to expound that there is so much more. It is at the Cross where it all takes place; without understanding this, neither the fullness of Christ in us nor the love of God can be fully comprehended.

—Bill Wilson, Pastor
Metro Ministries

Cathy has her finger on the pulse of something in this book that needs to be heard by the entire body of Christ! She asks a question, "If Jesus provided a complete redemption, why is there so much additional labor, time, and pain invested in healing and delivering the church?" Could it be that we have fallen short of something the first century church grasped? Could we have missed the central driving revelation of the Cross? Little did Cathy know as she began her God-driven quest to study the Cross that she was, in fact, receiving a mandate to tear the veil off of the minds of a generation that is familiar with the Cross as a symbol, but know very little of its supernatural transformational power. Cathy had an encounter with the Cross. She could hear Jesus crying out, "It is finished," and in that moment realized it is finished for us as well! Cathy took this message to her own Windsor, Ontario, church alongside of her husband Rick, and testimonies began breaking forth as one life after another was miraculously delivered, healed, and changed by an encounter with this message. The Cross may very well be the central revelation at the heart of the end-time church. After running the circuit of 2,000 years of learning, the Christian movement may indeed end right where we started, alongside Paul who proclaimed, "God forbid that I should glory in anything but the cross...." This is not a book for the broken; it is a book for all of us. I encourage you to pray as you read so that you too can encounter the *power*, the *passion*, and the *purpose* of the Cross.

—Dr. Lance Wallnau, Author and Director
The Lancelearning Group

Acknowledgments

I wish to express my deep appreciation to all who have helped me with this project. First and foremost, I thank my Lord and Savior Jesus Christ for His work of the Cross. Secondly, I thank my husband Rick for his love, patience, and commitment to me. He has been a tremendous source of strength and encouragement.

I want to thank Chris Standeven and Marilyn Czachor who did wonderful research and helped at every turn. They are two awesome women of God who gave tremendous input and read and reread the manuscript. I also must give credit to Jim Clark for his helpful input and suggestions to the manuscript. Much thanks goes to Jeannie Rogers for her valuable advice and wisdom.

I want to thank my mother for her unending love for me through a difficult childhood. Without her support I don't know where I would be today.

I wish to thank all who have contributed testimonies: Robert Powell, a mighty man of God who has overcome so much; Bob MacIntyre, whose breakthrough has been a testimony to all who know him; and Mike and Jen Iacobelli who have received such transforming revelation of the Cross that has changed their lives.

My thanks go to David Meece, Carrie McDonnell, Gracia Burnham, Carol Kent, Bill Wilson, Nicky Cruz, and Renée Bondi, whom I had the privilege of interviewing and using their incredible stories. I also owe a debt of gratitude to Stephanie Morris, Brenda Harrison, Donna Hughes, Dwayne White, Marc Brule, and Dave Pistagnesi, all who contributed in various ways to this book. I want to thank my deceased sister Jennifer Bojahra who demonstrated fearless faith in the face of death, showing all who knew her the hope of heaven.

I also must give my appreciation to my publisher Jim Rill and my editor Jeanette Sprecher. Special thanks also to Jane Rucker who helped me through the initial process of refining the manuscript. All have been very helpful and gracious.

I also want to thank Pastors Larry and Melanie Stockstill, Carl and Gaynel Everet, and Bishop Tony Miller for their encouragement. You all have spoken into my life with prayer and support throughout my writing. I want to thank the Windsor Christian Fellowship Ladies Prayer Ministry, headed by Marjie Paolini, for their continual prayer support as I wrote and sought God on this book.

Blessings to you all!

Table of Contents

Introduction

The Very Power of God

M any times I had thought to write a book, but never until now had I been compelled to write one. In fact, I *had* to write this book; I felt I would be missing God's will if I didn't. This past year of my life has been an incredible journey that has taken me to levels of joy and peace that I never thought possible. I had believed that many of the incredible spiritual experiences I am now enjoying were reserved only for the next life, that the unsearchable treasures of heaven were for a distant time, seemingly always beyond reach.

As a leader in the body of Christ, pastoring for 23 years, my experience with Christians from many camps was that of defeat, struggle, and often joyless living. Many hide behind masks in an effort to cover up their hurts and disappointments, and they continually run from place to place in search of something that always seems elusive to them. Many are in disillusionment and discouragement from prayers that seem to have gone unanswered. Of the thousands of believers I have met, I know of only a few who found the secret of true love, peace, and joy, although I am sure there are many others out there.

This book is about what I discovered regarding this secret—the secret of understanding the Cross of Christ. What I learned transformed me from a struggling believer into one who truly has discovered how to live in unspeakable joy and victory every day. Am I perfect? No, far from it, but I now understand the most incredible truths of the Cross that have the power to keep me and fill me with all that God intended us all to have. What I have learned about the Cross is worth living and dying for, and it has so changed my mindsets, my heart, and my entire outlook on life. I can now truly rejoice in *all* things and know in my heart that our God is the most incredibly awesome, amazing God who daily overwhelms me with His immeasurable love. I can now honestly thank Him for *everything* that has ever happened in my life—even those things that caused me incredible pain—because they all led me to the truths of His Cross. And that is worth it all.

Most Christians lose their first love for Christ. I was no different; I had lost mine. Most Christians struggle in their prayer life. I did too. Most believers struggle under layers of guilt and condemnation, living in discouragement and under judgment. I did too. Many settle for an apathetic, comfortable, powerless life, knowing God is real and serving Him because of what they do know, but deep in their hearts the passion, the love, the peace, and the joy are absent. Many even backslide as a result.

I have spent a solid year studying the Cross, devouring the Word and books, and researching the Internet. I seek God diligently to reveal to me all that the Cross speaks to us. After being saved 34 years, I was amazed at how few people really understand its full meaning. Like many believers, I thought the Cross was the place we went to for salvation and then from there we went on to live out our Christian life. After all, Jesus is no longer on the cross; therefore, we no longer need it. I have learned that the Cross must be a daily part of our lives. As a result, I went from one who served God out of obedience and duty to one who serves Him because I am passionately in love with Him. I went from struggling in my prayer life to easily entering His Presence and struggling to *stop* praying! I went from occasional victories and joy to overwhelming victory and joy. Guilt and condemnation, which were once regular visitors to my mind, are now things of the past, and my love walk toward my husband, family, and others takes much less effort. I have found everything I need to live this life in the messages that the Cross reveals, and those messages were meant to empower us to live the Christian life that God intended.

Speaking on the Cross has become my passion, and as I have shared on it in my church and with others, its power has transformed many defeated believers into the men and women of God they were meant to be. The testimonies keep pouring in. We can read in 1 Corinthians that this message sounds foolish, but that to those who believe it is the very power of God!

I know very well how foolish the message of the cross sounds to those who are on the road to destruction. But we who are being saved recognize this message as the very power of God (1 Corinthians 1:18).

Introduction

The message of the Cross includes the suffering, death, and resurrection of Jesus Christ. You cannot separate them; they all are integrated into one event. Any one part without the others would have rendered it powerless. So when I refer to the Cross, I am referring to all that it entails. From my experience in the church, I am convinced that the majority of God's people are greatly lacking knowledge of *all* the truths of the Cross, limiting its power as a result.

As you read this book, I trust and pray that the truths revealed will open your eyes and heart to the greatest event that ever happened on planet Earth: *the Cross*.

Chapter One

A Passion for the Cross

As for me, God forbid that I should boast about anything except the cross of our Lord Jesus Christ. Because of that cross, my interest in this world died long ago, and the world's interest in me is also long dead (Galatians 6:14).

At the end of February of 2004 I began a journey that still today just keeps getting better and better. This journey has caused me to pursue the revelation of the Cross like never before. There is so much to unfold in the pages of this book, some of which is foundational and some of which is a deeper revelation of the purpose of the Cross than is commonly taught. First, though, let me start with the day that it all began for me.

Where Did My Passion Go?

I looked at my watch and was amazed to see that several hours had passed. I was a mess. I was still sobbing almost uncontrollably and felt that my insides would come out. Never had I felt such waves of emotion and horror and overwhelming amazement of love all at the same time. I felt like a lifetime of pain, disappointment, shame, and fear was being purged through my tears and anguish. I grieved over the memories of my life. Raised in a dysfunctional home with an abusive father and a mother who ended up marrying five times and divorcing four, I had lived a childhood of guilt and shame. Even though I knew my mother loved me, I grew up with the gnawing feeling that I was inferior, flawed, and rejected. The feeling that I was destined to failure resulted in wild and rebellious teenage years, giving my mother more heartache. I left home at age 14, did drugs, lived common law, and partied hard until the age of 18 when someone introduced me to the person of Jesus Christ.

When I surrendered myself to Him, I was radically changed and became passionate about my new faith. I witnessed to everything that moved and attended every Bible study and church service I could. In my early years as a Christian I led a youth group, ran a Christian coffee house, taught children's church, and even had a jail ministry. Faith and miracles came easily. I felt free from my life of rejection, inferiority, and loneliness; I had purpose, and I was determined to win every soul I could. Then, gradually, things began to change.

As major trials hit my life, I was tempted to turn my back on God, but I couldn't deny the miracles and power I had experienced from Him. Still, as I began to question His love, He seemed distant and my passion for Him waned. Then I met and married a wonderful Christian man, Jim, and we were determined to serve God together. Once again I began to grow spiritually. However, as life's trials continued to flood in, my security in God's love wavered again. I couldn't deny God—He was definitely real—but my heart became guarded. I finally concluded that I needed to take His promises by faith, confessing and trusting in them in spite of how I felt. This was not easy, but things slowly began to improve, the miracles continued, and God blessed. I grew confident in the fact that He was for me and not against me.

Three years after our marriage, Jim and I began pastoring a small church in Mississauga, Ontario, and things began to change again. The work of the ministry, the stress of dealing with imperfect people, and the challenges that come with leadership began to drain the life out of me. Looking back, I see how the deep roots of rejection embedded in my past began to resurface and loom like giants before me. I battled daily with the challenges of being a pastor's wife, facing judgment and criticism at every turn and feeling inadequate at best. Hardness of heart began to set in, and, even though I knew I had to love people, the walls around my heart hindered me. No one was going to get too close since I felt misjudged and was often under intense criticism. Yet, my biggest fear was disappointing those I was meant to help. I knew unforgiveness and bitterness were not options; love I must, but my feelings seemed remote. Duty and performance drove me while inside I felt cold. My passion for Him only surfaced occasionally when I really worked at it.

Then tragedy struck. My husband was killed in a car accident, and I became a widow at 35 years old with three daughters. When Jim died, I felt like someone had ripped my heart out. For the first time in my life I wanted to die. I learned the meaning of living one day at a time, forcing myself to get up in the mornings to go through each moment one step at a time. Again I was devastated, feeling like God had let me down. My knowledge of the Word enabled me to put up a good front and carry on, but when I was alone, I battled depression and the desire to live. I wrestled with an overwhelming sense of hopelessness, even though I knew that I had hope. It took over a year for the heaviness to lift. It was the most difficult time of my life.

I looked again at the clock. Another hour had passed, and my tears were still flowing. Once more my life loomed before me. I had remarried to a wonderful man of God, a pastor who was deserted by his wife and left with three sons. Rick and I both had a strong love and zeal to serve God and knew He had put us together. We loved each other, but the challenges of blending six children between the ages of 9 to 19 (we were the real Brady bunch) were taxing on me. Taking over the position of the senior pastor's wife of an already well-established large church

> *My passion for Him only surfaced occasionally when I really worked at it.*

also had major challenges for my confidence. Again the old fears of rejection, inferiority, and inadequacy began to rear their ugly heads. As a result of these fears, I withdrew and the walls around my heart got stronger while my love and passion continued in a downward decline.

Even though I loved God and only wanted to serve Him, my problem was that self-protection and self-preservation had crept in, making it difficult to serve Him wholeheartedly. I knew the right things to do and say, and I did care about the people, but I had begun to accept the lie that maybe this was just the way it was supposed to be. I knew many ministers who had left the race because of hurts and disappointments and I didn't want to be one of them, so I began to feel that I was a survivor. I was not tempted to backslide, but I wondered where the love, joy, and peace were that the Word promised.

As I left my memories and came back to the reality of the moment, I stared at the box of tissues on my coffee table through tear-streaked eyes. I was not surprised to see that I had used half of them, and I thanked God that I was all alone in the house.

My tears were for an overwhelming sense of God's love. I really felt like I had just gotten saved, even though it had been 33 years almost to the day when I had surrendered my life to Christ. Still crying and even wailing at times, I thought of earlier that day when I dropped my husband off at the airport as he left to minister in Red Deer, Alberta. I would be meeting him the following week, as I had to stay back and minister at our Sunday services and prepare for a speaking engagement at a ladies group in Toronto. Before Rick left he had asked me to go and see the movie, *The Passion of the Christ*. It had just been released that week and although I had seen it two days earlier, I had looked away for most of it. Rick felt I needed to watch it again and address it with our congregation on Sunday morning. I had reluctantly returned to the theater that afternoon and forced myself to sit through it, this time taking in every scene.

I cannot adequately describe what happened to me, but I left the theater shocked by what I had seen. I drove home to my empty house and within moments was an emotional wreck. I don't know why it impacted me as much as it did; perhaps because I am a visual person it may have been what I needed. All I knew is that something happened deep inside me that I can only attempt to explain. In hindsight, I see it as a catalyst for a mandate on my life to teach on the Cross that I had not recognized before. This book has been birthed from that calling, a calling that continues to powerfully impact me.

A New Passion: The Cross

All my life I had to be strong. Now I was making up for the lack of release, and the walls around my heart were tumbling down. These tears, however, were for my Savior and what He went through for me.

Never had love been more real or overwhelming to me. I was being healed, and as I pushed through my memories something inside me knew that I would never be the same. This would be the beginning of a new journey for me, a journey that has unfolded into the discovery of what I had been missing in my spiritual walk. I suddenly wanted to know everything I could about the Cross of Christ, and as soon as I was able to finally compose myself, I rushed to my computer to begin research on it.

I tried to think of messages I'd heard on the Cross, and to my amazement I couldn't think of any. I had occasionally heard reference to it, but rarely if ever a message just on it. Obviously most Christian messages are a result of the work of the Cross, but many stray from the depth of its real meaning and become more self-focused. The true message of dying to self seems to be more a side issue than the main point. A large portion of the body of Christ has become more concerned about what they can get than about sacrificial giving. And even if they do teach on selflessness, without the focus of the Cross it becomes a teaching on how good we can be. Being good is difficult to do; therefore, it produces guilt and condemnation. The Cross must be at the core of our beliefs in order to truly change our desires from self-orientation to God. I know that many have taught and written on it, but in my experience, few centralize its message as the heart of the Gospel.

My search for information on the Cross became an obsession for me, but little did I know how much God was setting me up. Later that week through a series of circumstances and commitments I had made, I viewed the movie several more times, then attended an encounter weekend. The weekend was held by a church of dear friends of mine, Pastors Paul and Elaine Yuke. I had booked to attend weeks earlier and the timing couldn't have been more perfect! I had no idea what this weekend was about, but as it turned out it, its primary focus was on the Cross.

As my pursuit for revelation of the Cross grew with great intensity, I purchased and read every book I could find on the subject and diligently devoured the Word. My prayer life began to become a continual glorious time in the presence of God as I reveled in the realities of what He accomplished on the Cross, weeping with a gratitude that is now deeply rooted inside me. Often when I see a cross, my heart beats with the knowledge of how much I'm loved.

After more than a year since this journey began, my spiritual life has grown in leaps and bounds. The desire to pray and read the Word has changed from being an effort to my favorite thing to do. I desire to be in His presence more than anything else, and I am amazed with the love, joy, and peace that the Word promises. My favorite scripture became something that the apostle Paul said in Galatians:

> *As for me, God forbid that I should boast about anything except the cross of our Lord Jesus Christ. Because of that cross, my interest in this world died long ago, and the world's interest in me is also long dead* (Galatians 6:14).

This scripture has now become my reality!

Over the years as a minister, my gift in the body of Christ has been teaching. Several months after I began pursuing all I could learn on the Cross, I knew for the first time exactly what I am called to teach. As I shared this with my husband, he agreed. He had seen incredible changes in me, in my attitude, and in my love walk, and it had dramatically improved our relationship. Naturally my experience began to impact positive change in him as well, and we went from having a comfortable marriage to a passionate one. We rarely argue anymore, and through what we have learned about the Cross, we both easily die to our self-will, which used to cause strife between us. The more I saw the Cross as the most important thing in my life, the more I fell in love with Jesus. We have both learned to center our marriage around its work and allow the Holy Spirit to show us how to die daily to live. The more I love Jesus, the more I love my husband and others, and the more love I feel.

The more I love Jesus, the more I love my husband and others, and the more love I feel.

The Cross is now my passion. Jesus' suffering, death, and resurrection are everything you and I need. As you discover the eternal messages that the Cross speaks, you can live a victorious Christian life instead of the defeated life that so many settle for. I know, for it has changed my life, the life of our church, and the lives of many others whom I have had the opportunity to share with or who have heard it elsewhere. Never have I discovered a message more powerful.

It is possible to live every day and take every circumstance you find yourself in and examine them in the light of the Cross. It is then that you can deal with them effectively to produce the power of God to overcome the works of the flesh. The Cross demonstrates perfectly the Spirit of Christ and His nature of dying to self, as Jesus talked about in the gospel of Matthew:

> *Then Jesus said to the disciples, "If any of you wants to be my follower, you must put aside your selfish ambition, shoulder your cross, and follow me. If you try to keep your life for yourself, you will lose it. But if you give up your life for me, you will find true life"* (Matthew 16:24-25).

The Cross empowers us, shows us how to let go of our life, and gives us the desire to do so. There is no other place where that can truly happen. The

Cross has many messages to us as believers, each one empowering us in a specific area of our life. It is my desire to share some of its life-changing truths with you.

The Cross truly is the wisdom of God, the light and glory of God, and the way to God, as the Bible says. It is the tree of life and the place of victory. It is the central message of the Word, and it teaches us by example all we need to know to succeed in life. Knowing it is the greatest thing that has ever happened to me. There are still days when the demands and busyness of life overpower my awareness of it, and I begin to feel more like I used to. However, with the knowledge that has now become a part of me, it doesn't take long for me to run to the Cross, get what I need, and experience again joy unspeakable and full of glory. It is amazing that I can praise Him all day long in everything; it has become my anchor, my rock, my refuge, and my hope. The following chapters will unfold the truths I have learned about the Cross of Jesus Christ and explain how to make them a daily part of your life.

> *Knowing the Cross is the greatest thing that has ever happened to me.*

I have come to realize that the revelation of the Cross can't be fully understood simply through teaching; it must be caught by the spirit. Those who seek and hunger for it will find it, and if you ask God for it with a sincere heart, He will answer. My desire for you is that you would experience the fullness of God's love daily and ask Him for it. If that is your desire, pray this prayer for the Holy Spirit to open your eyes to catch the revelation of the Cross.

Dear heavenly Father, I realize that You love me and have so much more for me. I surrender myself entirely to You, and I pray that You will help me see and understand the magnitude of what Jesus did for me throughout His suffering, crucifixion, and resurrection. I pray that the message of the Cross will change me from the inside out and that I will never be the same. Overwhelm me with the realization of how much You love me and how far You went to win my heart. May Your Cross change my perception of life itself and may I truly love You with my whole heart because of it. In Jesus' name, amen.

Chapter Two

What Happened to the Cross?

For I decided to concentrate only on Jesus Christ and his death on the cross (1 Corinthians 2:2).

To concentrate only on Jesus and His death on the cross is the essence of God's power. Every step of Jesus' passion contains messages of what He conquered for us and how we can overcome the sin that He so thoroughly paid to destroy in us. He planned every part of the Cross with purpose and detail, covering every aspect of human suffering and our fallen nature. That is what this message is about.

Never has there been a more important message than the one of the Cross. I have come to realize that much of the church lacks power because believers are limited in their understanding of it. So many believers are seeking the supernatural hand of God while ignoring or minimizing its source. (One point I want to make very clear is that when I say "the Cross," I am referring to the suffering, death, and resurrection of Jesus Christ. It all goes together and cannot be separated without losing its true meaning.) My experience has been that many believers have strayed from the foundation of their faith. Why? Read on.

Not long ago my husband and I were ministering in Italy when someone confronted us following a service. I couldn't believe what I was hearing. I stared in shock at the middle-aged man standing in front of me. As I absorbed the words that my interpreter had just said on this gentleman's behalf, I was amazed at how far off we can get as Christians. "It is idol worship to have a cross in church," he announced to me. "Here the cross is viewed as a good luck charm, and it is wrong to worship it in any form."

My husband Rick and I had just finished a message on the importance of the Cross and were passionate about how it had to be the center of our lives as believers. I realized that this man had come out of a religion of one form and, because of its abuses, had taken on another. My heart wept as I realized how far religion has made God's greatest work common and meaningless. Yes, it was true that crucifixes were everywhere in this historical land where Christianity had many roots. Rick and I had seen them wherever we went as we traveled from northern Italy down to Sicily. They adorned doorways, were displayed over cash registers, hung in windows, and adorned people's necks. Many actually believed that the piece of wood, metal, or plastic itself would ward off evil or somehow sanctify what they were doing. The Cross had become a superstitious icon, and few really understood its true meaning.

*The Cross is the very heart of every aspect of **how** to live the Christian life.*

I smiled at this sincere man and shared with him that just because some take it for granted, we as believers do not have to throw it out or minimize its importance. In fact, we have a responsibility to declare its true message.

As I continued to converse with this gentleman, I thought back to one year earlier and how I had come to have the love and honor I now held for the work of the Cross. I treasured above all else how it had become a daily part of my life and deeply regretted how for 33 years as a believer I had taken it for granted.

I had thought, like many others, that the Cross was where we go to get saved and because Jesus was no longer there, we moved on to walk out our faith. I never realized how necessary it was for it to become a constant and integral part of my life. It is in understanding its power that we can find the ability to be all God called us to be. Many only see the salvation part of it and miss tapping into its ageless and rich wisdom that enable us to live the life we are called to.

The Foundation of Our Faith

We will learn how to take our relationship with God, family relationships, job, ministry, and all life's experiences and process them through the Cross to discover God's heart and will for us.

First, though, it is imperative that we embrace the work of the Cross as the literal foundation of our faith; we must recognize that everything we do should begin and end with it. This means that whatever we go through or decide to do must pass through the Cross to produce its life-giving power. By that I mean we must look at our daily circumstances and learn how to relate them to what Christ accomplished on the Cross. We will discuss how to do that as we go through each step of Jesus' passion. For now I want to establish a foundation on the importance of the Cross in our lives.

In 1 Corinthians we read that the Cross is *"the very power of God,"* a power we desperately need:

> *I know very well how foolish the message of the cross sounds to those who are on the road to destruction. But we who are being saved recognize this message as the very power of God* (1 Corinthians 1:18).

From Genesis to Revelation, the entire Word of God has a common thread. It foretells the coming of the sacrifice on the Cross in the Old Covenant and testifies of its work in the New. Everything God said and did in relation to man revolves around this message and the power it contains. I don't know about you, but I need all the power I can get, and God clearly shows us the source of His!

I have now learned how to stay plugged in to the flow of His power and truly overcome even in the toughest times, and it is more wonderful than I can ever describe!

The Cross is *the message of the Gospel* that the apostle Paul preached—and the message that he claimed to be *the very power and wisdom of God,* as we read here in 1 Corinthians:

> *So when we preach that Christ was crucified, the Jews are offended, and the Gentiles say it's all nonsense. But to those called by God to salvation, both Jews and Gentiles, Christ is the mighty power of God and the wonderful wisdom of God* (1 Corinthians 1:23-24).

So not only is the Cross God's power, but it also is His wisdom. Wisdom is the ability to judge and discern what is true, right, and lasting; it also means having insight and good judgment.[1] So in other words, the Cross will give us the right insight and judgment for the circumstances in our lives once we know how to relate its message to them.

Paul also declared that the Cross was the message that he would concentrate on, as we read on into chapter 2 of 1 Corinthians:

For I decided to concentrate only on Jesus Christ and his death on the cross (1 Corinthians 2:2).

That word *concentrate* means to converge toward and to meet into a common center; it also means to fix and direct one's thoughts, powers, efforts, and attention to one thing.[2] This is the key to tapping into the power of the Cross. In other words, we must take every area of our life and make the Cross our perspective of how we choose to live that part of our life.

That one thing the apostle Paul referred to in this verse, the one thing he concentrated on, was Jesus Christ and His death on the Cross!

What we do with the Cross on a daily basis will determine the victory we will experience each day! It must be our focus, the point where we concentrate and base all we believe!

The Cross Above All

There are many awesome teachings in the body of Christ, and many believers continually search for the newest and latest revelation. I do believe that God does operate in dispensations or time periods and releases truth and revelation to the body as He sees fit, but like the apostle Paul, we must concentrate on the main message of the Cross. Unfortunately, it is not uncommon for the church to take truths and make idols of them, separating them from their foundation. Whether it is a message on the baptism of the Holy Spirit, healing, faith, deliverance, or God's blessings, when separated from the foundational message of the Cross, any teaching can become something that feeds the ego of man to look down upon those who don't see things quite the same. Instead of building the body, we allow our revelations to become sources of division. The power of the Cross supersedes every truth with God's love when we anchor each truth to it. That means that the main messages the Cross teaches must be the higher or more important realities of any other truth we adhere to.[3] It must be the common ground to all truth and show us the way to walk in God's love and humility, especially when we gain spiritual insight others

12

have not yet seen. When spiritual truths are isolated from the message of the Cross, they become religious idols that produce death instead of life.[4]

For the man in Italy who confronted us after our message, his experience was that the Cross had become a meaningless charm. It seems that though many know its true meaning, some only sorrow over the death of Christ and never seem to really understand the resurrection side of it. That is one way the Cross loses its power in our lives. When we live out of dead, religious rituals and never experience the life of the Spirit that was given at the Cross, we miss the purpose of His life being imparted to us.

> *It is because of the Cross that everything He has belongs to us—and the more we understand it, the more we are able to access it.*

We now have a direct line to Him, and He is always with us! We all have been made righteous and holy because of what Jesus did on the Cross. Without that revelation, we will resort to other ways to gain God's favor, thus diminishing and devaluing His work by relying on superstitious means or the futility of the law to try and gain salvation and pro-

tection from evil. It is only the blood of Jesus that gives us the right to approach Him and by it He has made us to be His very own children.

> *And because you Gentiles have become his children, God has sent the Spirit of his Son into your hearts, and now you can call God your dear Father. Now you are no longer a slave but God's own child. And since you are his child, everything he has belongs to you* (Galatians 4:6-7).

It is an incredible blessing to know that everything He has belongs to us— and just think of what He has! The Bible tells us that all power and authority belong to Him, and it reveals to us that the riches in heaven, the ability to rule, and the supernatural things that Jesus did are all a part of what He has. We now have access to a power and ability that we cannot even fathom with our minds.

Just as there are Christians who get stuck on the suffering side of the Cross, there are others who believe they've been there, done that, and now they only want to enjoy the benefits of resurrection life. They would rather ignore the messages of suffering and death that are necessary to obtain resurrection life. I grieved at how our church, like many others, had neglected its importance. For example, for years we didn't have a cross in our sanctuary because it just wasn't a priority. We celebrated Communion once or twice a month more out of ritual than heartfelt worship. That has now all changed; the Cross is now honored in every service, and every message we deliver makes reference to it.

I was shocked to learn that some churches in North America won't have a cross in their sanctuary because they find it offensive. Like the Italian gentleman, some won't know it because of the abuse of its meaning. A cross, wherever displayed, is just a symbol of what it represents. When you truly know its message, you will honor it for what it stands for.

There are many awesome truths that can only be seen through meditating on the work of the Cross regularly, as we will continue to learn. I am not implying that all believers are missing it in this area, but countless numbers are, and they live defeated as a result. Some are stuck on one side of the Cross while many are stuck on the other; each failing to realize that it is a package deal. In other words, the Cross without the resurrection is just a sad story of a good man who died a cruel death. At the same time, the resurrection couldn't have happened without the Cross. The resurrection of Jesus Christ verifies that it was not just a man who died there, but God Himself, and it proved the enormity of His power! We cannot separate any part of it. It is essential that we stay focused on all aspects of the Cross and keep it at the heart of all we believe in every day. Why? Because *the Cross represents the core or essence of all that exists.* Without it there would be no life or light. The Cross is the beginning and end of all things; it determines what will live for eternity and what will be destroyed by the wrath of God.

The Power of the Cross

As we continue, I will be sharing some incredible truths about the Cross that will empower you in ways that will change you forever, just as it has done for me. We will be talking in depth about its two sides, one of wrath and one of love; injustice and justice; life and death; and judgment and mercy. We will discover it as the source of our life and the death of our flesh. It is where the light and darkness are separated; it is where we see our corruption and sin yet find complete mercy and grace at the same time. The stories I will share in this book of what it has done to change lives are amazing. Some you can relate to and some will cause you to weep, yet each one will illustrate an aspect of the Cross and its power to change lives.

I could see that this precious man in Italy sincerely wanted to understand, and I watched how the life in my words opened his heart and he began to see the power of the Cross. As the light went on for him, he smiled widely as he thanked me for sharing with him. He had realized his deception was a result of fear of doing the wrong thing, and, like so many, he had "thrown the baby out with the bath water."

When we look at the Cross, we can see the true character and nature of God and how He really feels about us!

When we lack in our understanding of the Cross, we will constantly struggle and fail to see that it is the key to our life. When I think of the Cross now, my heart beats with excitement and warmth. The love of God that it shows has become so real and obvious to me as I purpose to center everything in my life on the Cross. Rarely a day goes by that I do not shed tears of overwhelming gratitude for the Cross. In my quiet times with God I bask in its realities and experience incredible joy and sense His glory, sometimes so much so that I can hardly stand it! It has become so real to me that I am just in awe of my God. Everything the Word says about Him, He has proved to me.

One of the main reasons we miss out on this awesome experience and miss this message is that we judge God based on our circumstances. We accuse Him for what is going on in the world instead of judging Him by what He did on the Cross. He gets blamed for things we do not understand, and as a result we question His character. As I understood the Cross, I grieved when I realized how often my God, who is so awesome, could be treated with so much disrespect and accusation by our misdirected anger. When I thought of how often I broke His heart, mine melted with more love and appreciation for Him.

The devil will always try to minimize the importance of the Cross. As God was revealing more of it to me, I was attacked with thoughts in my mind that said I was taking it too far—especially when I realized few others seemed to feel as strongly about it as I did. But I couldn't deny the fruit of love, peace, joy, and the presence of God that was so real to me. I have never felt more confident, happier, or satisfied. Seven months after my life became centered on these truths, I found a book that confirmed I wasn't the only one having this incredible experience. C.J. Mahaney's book, *The Cross Centered Life*, confirmed what I had learned. He makes a statement in the book that I love, which emphasizes what I am sharing. He says, "If there's anything in life that we should be passionate about, it's the gospel. And I don't mean passionate only about sharing it with others, I mean passionate in thinking about it, dwelling on it, rejoicing in it, allowing it to color the way we look at the world. Only one thing can be of first importance to each of us. And only the gospel can be."[5] To me his book was a breath of fresh air. After reading it, I knew I was on track!

There is absolutely nothing more important than the Cross, as you can read here in 1 Corinthians:

I passed on to you what was most important and what had also been passed on to me—that Christ died for our sins, just as the Scriptures said (1 Corinthians 15:3).

No other revelation can supersede it. When something is *"most important,"* it takes priority over other things. When we believe in our hearts that the Cross is the most important thing, then and only then will we truly change from the inside out, for it puts everything else into proper perspective.

The body of Christ often drifts from this most important message and allows other messages to take its place, which only leads to futility, discouragement, and failure.

There are countless books and sermons, with multiple steps and formulas, about how to gain victory in your life, but only those that are centered on the Cross really work. As a pastor it seems to me that the people who get the most counseling rarely get free. I am not knocking counseling; it has its place, but not above or in place of the Cross.

We all look at life through filters, and these filters color how we see things. This is called our perspective on life. As we filter everything through the Cross, our perspective will change and line up with God's. *The Cross has the power to change how we see everything, and it is the way we see things that produces the results we will have. There is nothing we can go through in life that cannot be shaped by its perspective!*

The Cross was meant to be the source of life for every part of you, and as you see it you will cease from your works and learn to rely on its power. I have discovered that life can never be better or simpler as a believer than when I make the Cross my priority!

We must realize that it alone has the power to define who we are, what motivates what we do, and who we will become.

The Cross is the single most important, incredible, powerful, amazing event that has ever occurred on earth!

Chapter Three

The Cross and the Wrath of God[6]

For God sent Jesus to take the punishment for our sins and to satisfy God's anger against us. We are made right with God when we believe that Jesus shed his blood, sacrificing his life for us. God was being entirely fair and just when he did not punish those who sinned in former times (Romans 3:25).

The first purpose of the Cross was for Jesus to take our punishment and satisfy God's wrath against us.

The wrath of God is greatly misunderstood in the body of Christ. Nevertheless, it is extremely important in relation to the work of the Cross. We must understand God's wrath as a necessary part of His character to fully "get" and appreciate the true revelation of God's love for us and why it is necessary for the survival of all things. *The Cross is the ultimate expression of God's character, revealing both His love and wrath!*

The Father's absolute hatred of sin and His need to see justice are evidence of His goodness! How? We can read in Isaiah this prophetic word about Christ and how He would reveal justice to the nations. The Cross is the place where wrongs are made right.

Look at my servant, whom I strengthen. He is my chosen one, and I am pleased with him. I have put my Spirit upon him. He will reveal justice to the nations. He will be gentle—he will not shout or raise his voice in public. He will not crush those who are weak or quench the smallest hope. He will bring full justice to all who have been wronged. He will not stop until truth and righteousness prevail throughout the earth. Even distant lands beyond the sea will wait for his instruction (Isaiah 42:1-4).

This means that the purpose of the Cross was to bring God's justice because justice and the goodness of God go together.

If God were not just, then He would not be righteous. But because God is just and righteous, He has zero tolerance of sin. Unlike us, He cannot allow any sin to abound. He sees sin like we see cancer. As soon as someone is diagnosed with cancer, that person will do everything possible to get rid of it, even if that means cutting off a limb or removing part of an organ. The person will poison his or her body with chemotherapy or radiation and will take whatever chemicals or drugs needed to eliminate it. Why? No one can afford to allow even one cancer cell to wander through the body, only to return with a vengeance. Sin is like that. Every seed of sin is like a cancer cell that has the potential to multiply and kill us if we allow it to grow in us. It must be dealt with by every means available. God desires to do the same thing. God, who is pure, sees sin for the spiritual cancer and path to death that it really is, and He hates it because He loves us and loves righteousness.

Unlike us, God cannot and will not tolerate sin. If He left sin alone, He would cease to be just and there would be no righteousness. He must judge and punish sin or He would not be a just God.

I love what William P. Farley says in his book *Outrageous Mercy*: "God's justice is inflexible. It is mandatory. Were He ever to relax His standards, He would cease to be God and the universe would implode."[7] That means it would collapse inwardly and violently.[8] Everything would self-destruct.

Knowing the character of God has everything to do with understanding His wrath and judgment. Understanding Him then changes how we see Him—and that changes everything!

The Cross—Revelation of God's Character

What God is most concerned about is the destruction of the sin nature in us. In my 34 years as a Christian, I have come to realize that God is about the development of my character. However, to develop my character, I must understand His. Character is the distinct features or attributes that make up a person's moral or ethical strength.[9] Sin is its enemy. The work of the Cross is all about the character of God and reveals what He is really like so we can be like Him.

Many Christians have misperceptions about what God is like and find it difficult to grasp beyond head knowledge just how much He really does love them. This is usually a result of focusing only on the love message of the Cross and not fully understanding the wrath of God that was satisfied there. The truth is, before you can fully grasp His love for you, you must first understand His wrath and judgment.

A pastor friend of mine came to see my husband Rick and I about six months after I had begun my pursuit of the Cross. He and his family had dropped in on their way to a family vacation they had planned. During their visit, I zealously shared what I had been learning on the Cross and how radically it had transformed my life. I shared everything I had done to get the awesome revelation I was now experiencing. They listened intently and then left to continue their trip.

> *Understanding Him changes how we see Him—and that changes everything!*

Just over a month later I ran into this pastor at a convention as he rushed up to me and said that he needed to talk to me. He quickly unfolded his story of how that family vacation was something he had planned to do before he committed suicide. He shared that when they had dropped in on us, he had already written the suicide note and was planning on carrying out the act on return from the trip. The devil had somehow deceived him into believing that he was created for the wrath of God, and he was being tormented by this lie. When he returned home, he decided to do what I did to gain the revelation of the Cross before he carried out his plan. Upon doing so, God delivered him from the tormenting spirit that had somehow attached itself to him. He was now experiencing what I was and had come to the place of revival in his heart. It was now impacting his life, his family, and his church!

You may wonder how a pastor can contemplate suicide, but when the church strays from the foundation of the Cross, the enemy has the power to deceive us in many ways. It is only the power of the Cross, which begins with understanding the wrath of God, that can deliver us and set us free—and that power is at work every day if we seek it.

It is important to see how much God's wrath relates to His love, but trust me, without comprehension of it we will have a watered-down Gospel and will continually vacillate in our faith and security of His unending love. Failure to understand His wrath can result in believing that we are still subject to it, or we will go to the other extreme and take His love for granted, thus minimizing its power to change us. After all, when I realize that I deserve punishment but that someone took it for me, I will appreciate that person's love for me much more.

Several years ago I did an intense study on God's character because my faith was being shaken by thoughts of Him that were not accurate. There were times when I was angry that He did not act when or how I thought He should, and I blamed Him for things I did not understand. Because of my struggle with low self-esteem and my false concepts of God, I was unable to trust in His love. Finally, out of frustration, I made a decision that I was going to *choose* to believe by faith that He was who the Word said He was. It was incredibly liberating as I meditated on the truths that described His nature and began to confess them out loud daily until they became a part of my belief system. Such truths that God is good, merciful, kind, love, pure, holy, and faithful became a part of my worship to Him, but attributes such as "God is a consuming fire" and "jealous" seemed contradictory. I had to rationalize that if He loved me and was all the good and perfect things that the Word says, then there had to be justification for the other.

> *Justice is standing for what is right; therefore, it is righteousness.*

I learned to appreciate the wrath of God and His need for justice. Today I am continually amazed at how many professing Christians know little about His nature. They quickly judge and blame Him for things that are difficult to understand, and often they harden their hearts against Him, assuming that He's not fair.

In learning about His character I realized that there was one characteristic of God that is absolutely mandatory, and that is *He is just*. To be just is to be righteous. "What is justice?" you might ask. According to the dictionary, it is the quality of being right and fair, it is moral rightness, and it is the act of determining rights and assigning rewards or punishments.[10] Justice deferred is justice denied. When justice isn't carried out, then an injustice is done. Justice is standing for what is right; therefore, it is righteousness.

God rules with justice because He is a righteous God!

We can read about this in the psalms as King David prophesies of the coming Christ:

Your throne, O God, endures forever and ever. Your royal power is expressed in justice. You love what is right and hate what is wrong. Therefore God, your God, has anointed you, pouring out the oil of joy on you more than on anyone else (Psalm 45:6-7).

Notice that His royal power is expressed in justice. That means it is through His justice that His power is revealed.

The Truth About Justice

It is impossible for evil people to understand justice, and unfortunately even many believers today don't comprehend it. As a result, they do not even believe in hell. Because of their lack of understanding of justice, they fail to see the true Gospel, which reveals to us that without His justice God would be neither just nor righteous. Without His justice we would be destined for destruction and life would cease to exist. Sadly, human pride has a habit of rationalizing sin. Because we are sinful in our nature, we conclude that real justice is unreasonable and that hell is not fair, making the wrath of God a bad thing. Such lack of the fear of God shows up everywhere in our society, relegating absolutes to a thing of the past. When man does not fear God there automatically comes a decline of justice in society, which in turn leads to the corruption of the judicial system. This is no surprise to God; He describes it here in Ecclesiastes:

I also noticed that throughout the world there is evil in the courtroom. Yes, even the courts of law are corrupt! (Ecclesiastes 3:16)

The Bible also tells us that what is evil will be called good and what is good will be called evil because of the sin of man's hearts.

Destruction is certain for those who say that evil is good and good is evil; that dark is light and light is dark; that bitter is sweet and sweet is bitter (Isaiah 5:20).

We live in a day when, if we stand for righteousness, we are classified as bigots by many. "Close-minded," "judgmental," and "intolerant" are common accusations heard by Christians who stand up for morality in our land. Absolute right and wrong has become a thing of the past.

One of the first and most important facts about the Cross is that it is the place where God poured out His wrath and judgment to bring about justice on our behalf!

Many Christians make the mistake of viewing God in their own image of who they want Him to be rather than discovering who He is and what He is like.

Without the reality of a real hell, the Cross means little.

Because He has aspects that we find difficult to wrap our heads around, we determine who we think He is and what He will do based on what our value system is. For example, the concept of hell is very difficult for many believers to accept, along with many of the absolutes of the Bible. We often find these things to be viewed as "narrow-minded" and "politically incorrect," and question how a God of love can send anyone to hell. We rationalize that if He has wrath, then He doesn't love, but the truth is *He has wrath because He loves!*

We view wrath as a bad thing because man's wrath often is. However, with God, because of His righteous nature, it is a good thing and is completely motivated by His love for man. We can read here in the epistle of James that God's wrath and man's wrath have a different purpose.

For the wrath of man worketh not the righteousness of God (James 1:20 KJV).

This means God's wrath works righteousness.

Until we understand the nature of Christ on the Cross, we will always be confused about the truth of His wrath and love. Because God is just by His nature, He must destroy sin, and He loves us so passionately that He put our sin on Himself and then poured out His wrath in order to save us. *The Cross takes our sin and is consumed by God's wrath while at the same time it marries us to Him and consumes us with His love.* That is why the Cross is the end and the beginning of our life. Without the reality of a real hell, the Cross means little because there would not be anything to be redeemed from.

God's Wrath Shows His Love

Without this understanding, talking about God's wrath sounds negative. When I read the Old Testament before I understood God's wrath, some scripture passages scared me and made me question the character of God. Until we understand the need for the law and justice of the Old Testament, these passages describing His wrath do not seem to correspond with the loving God of the New Testament. For example, in Psalm 90 we can read this verse that talks about the power of His anger and wrath:

Who can comprehend the power of your anger? Your wrath is as awesome as the fear you deserve (Psalm 90:11).

This says that His wrath is awesome, which means to be in dread and respect of.[11] It also says that to fear Him is something *He deserves from us.* That means He is worthy of being feared. This type of fear is a reverential respect, indicating that we don't treat Him lightly. Can you imagine how God must feel when man frequently forgets who He is and lifts himself up as better than Him? We can read how He feels about that here in Isaiah:

Destruction is certain for those who argue with their Creator. Does a clay pot ever argue with its maker? Does the clay dispute with the one who shapes it, saying, "Stop, you are doing it wrong!" Does the pot exclaim, "How clumsy can you be!" How terrible it would be if a newborn baby said to its father and mother, "Why was I born? Why did you make me this way?" This is what the LORD, the Creator and Holy One of Israel, says: "Do you question what I do? Do you give me orders about the work of my hands? I am the one who made the earth and created people to live on it. With my hands I stretched out the heavens. All the millions of stars are at my command" (Isaiah 45:9-12).

God created us, and everything we have is because of Him. In reality, we owe Him our lives. What must He think when we treat Him like He is nothing to us? If you have ever had a child you love rebel against you and break your heart by separating from you in anger and defiance, you will have a glimpse of what we put God through. God has every right to feel anger against the atrocities of man that have trashed everything He stands for.

Nahum says that God is filled with vengeance and wrath when we live to oppose Him.

The LORD is a jealous God, filled with vengeance and wrath. He takes revenge on all who oppose him and furiously destroys his enemies! (Nahum 1:2)

To furiously destroy your enemies seems very contradictory to loving them as the New Testament teaches, but John's gospel explains that outside of Christ, His wrath still remains.

And all who believe in God's Son have eternal life. Those who don't obey the Son will never experience eternal life, but the wrath of God remains upon them (John 3:36).

This means that the wrath of God still exists, but the Cross is what protects us from it. That is why it is so important that we understand it. All of our sin has already been punished on the Cross as we acknowledge and surrender it there.

> *The fact is, the essence of the Good News is the Cross!*

When we ignore a very real part of God, such as His wrath, we are minimizing who He is and undermining His character. Make no mistake, it is because of His love for us that God's wrath is real. How? It is not against us but against the sin that keeps us in bondage. Jesus came to set us free, and, until we know the reality of His wrath, we will miss the point of the Cross.

The Word also tells us that God is rich in mercy and loves us very much (Ephesians 2:4). His love and mercy are extended to all mankind through Jesus Christ. So how do we reconcile these characteristics of God's wrath and love that appear to contradict themselves?

We can see in Romans that the first purpose of the Cross was to satisfy God's anger against us. When we believe that Jesus took the punishment for our sins, we do not have to fear His wrath any longer!

For God sent Jesus to take the punishment for our sins and to satisfy God's anger against us. We are made right with God when we believe that Jesus shed his blood, sacrificing his life for us. God was being entirely fair and just when he did not punish those who sinned in former times (Romans 3:25).

Jesus was sent to satisfy God's wrath and bring justice to mankind! Could you imagine all of God's incredible wrath being poured out on His own Son? Jesus loved us enough to take our place and suffer everything we deserved so we could be spared from sure death and hell! We can read here in Matthew how it was prophesied that He will proclaim justice to the nations and *bring full justice with His final victory!* The whole purpose of the Cross was to *spare us from His wrath.*

Look at my Servant, whom I have chosen. He is my Beloved, and I am very pleased with him. I will put my Spirit upon him, and he will proclaim justice to the nations. He will not fight or shout; he will not raise his voice in public. He will not crush those who are weak, or quench the smallest hope, until he brings full justice with his final victory. And his name will be the hope of all the world (Matthew 12:18-21).

The sin that is put on the Cross has already been destroyed by God's wrath! The Cross was His final victory and His work of justice. It is our hope and that of the world, that we would know our sins were paid for and we are now justified.

Let's take a moment and contemplate the incredible magnitude and faithfulness of God. Think about it. Suppose someone you love deeply "stabs" you in the back by defaming your name and accusing you of things you did not do. You bless that loved one, but the person defiantly turns his or her back on you, hurting and killing others whom you love dearly, ignoring your pleas for love and mercy. You send others to warn that individual, but he or she continues to destroy all that you have accomplished until finally you send your only son to reason with him or her. Only this defiant loved one tortures and kills your only son. How angry would you feel? Would you be willing to take all your anger out on yourself and let the other go free, giving him or her all you had? That scenario is mind-boggling to me, and yet that is exactly what God did for us, only more! Why people would reject His offer is amazing to me. You may say that you didn't commit any crime that was that bad, but we will determine that in the next chapter!

When we understand the work of the Cross, we can really understand and know every part of God's character. Until we do, we will always vacillate in our relationship with Him and will allow circumstances to dictate to us what He is like.

The Cross is the place where God implemented His divine judgment and justified us. His wrath and judgment were poured out, and a justification was accomplished that would not compromise His good and holy character while satisfying the necessity of justice. God's wrath is to be taken seriously, and until we fully appreciate what we have been saved from, it is difficult to really understand the magnitude of what God has done for us on the Cross.

Chapter Four

The Cross Removes the Desire to Sin

Those who belong to Christ Jesus have nailed the passions and desires of their sinful nature to his cross and crucified them there (Galatians 5:24).

One of the most important aspects of the Cross is how it reveals the sinful condition of our heart by showing us what a perfect heart is in the person of Jesus Christ. When Jesus willingly took on our sin and the punishment for it, He demonstrated to us pure unselfishness and love. He set the example of how we are supposed to be. When we consider Him on the Cross, His holiness is a light that shines into our heart, exposing the sin in us. But it happens with such love that we *lose our desire to sin* when we see it.

Jesus is God in the flesh. The book of Hebrews tells us that He represents God exactly; therefore, He revealed the purity of God Himself when He went through His passion.

The Son reflects God's own glory, and everything about him represents God exactly. He sustains the universe by the mighty power of his command. After he died to cleanse us from the stain of sin, he sat down in the place of honor at the right hand of the majestic God of heaven (Hebrews 1:3).

To see Christ is to see God, and the purpose of His work on the Cross was to cleanse us from the stain of sin. In other words, He freed you from being spoiled or tarnished by sin. It is like the laundry commercial when they hold a white shirt up that appears clean until another much whiter and brighter shirt is held up next to it. The first shirt then appears dingy and gray in comparison. The purity of the Christ on the Cross reveals how impure we are when we compare ourselves with Him.

Now, if I create something for a purpose, then to accomplish the purpose intended I must apply or use what was created for it. When I do my laundry, bleach has been produced for the removal of stains and brightening of my clothes. If I want those results, I must apply the bleach as instructed. If I don't apply it, my clothes will continue to be dull and stained. In the same way, the purpose of the Cross was to remove the stain of sin from us, but in order to enjoy that result we must apply the Cross to the sin. However, like anything else in life, you cannot fix what you don't know is broken.

The glory of Christ on the Cross sheds light on our heart and reveals things that cannot be seen when compared with anything else.

This brings us to the biggest problem that I have observed that hinders this process: Most people do not think they are that bad. When we believe we are pretty good on our own merit, then we will not see the need or importance of applying the Cross to our sin. In fact, we will tend to justify and excuse it. So the first step is recognizing that we desperately need to be cleansed.

I remember having company one day, and I thought my house was clean. As I was preparing for my guests' arrival, I decided to open some window blinds. I was horrified as the light flooded in and I saw dust and dirt that was hidden while the blinds were down. The light revealed what was there; I couldn't see it in the dark, but it was there.

The glory of Christ on the Cross, which is the ultimate manifestation of His true nature, sheds light on our heart and reveals things that cannot be seen when compared with anything else. If I want to see where the dirt is in my house, I have to open the blinds to see what is really hidden. Similarly, I must see the light of the Cross to reveal what's in my heart.

Sin Deserves Judgment

In order for the light of the Cross to perfect us, we need to first ask ourselves, "Do I really believe that I am deserving of God's wrath and judgment?" Most people will answer no. However, we will look at what the Word says about the hearts of men and how we compare with God. The book of Romans says that *all man* has sinned—and that means you and me.

> *When Adam sinned, sin entered the entire human race. Adam's sin brought death, so death spread to everyone, for everyone sinned* (Romans 5:12).

First let us define sin. Sin is described as the deliberate disobedience to the known will of God.[12] It is any violation of the laws of God, and I have heard some call it "missing the mark of what should be." Sin is not neutral or dormant; it is like a seed that grows and takes over wherever it resides, just as a cancer cell multiplies.

The book of Ephesians explains that we were born with an evil nature and were under God's wrath as a result. That evil nature is evident in our selfishness, which manifests even when we are young children. Without intervention children would destroy themselves and others, as many frazzled parents have discovered.

> *All of us used to live that way, following the passions and desires of our evil nature. We were born with an evil nature, and we were under God's anger just like everyone else* (Ephesians 2:3).

Most unbelievers will tell you that they think they are good enough to go to heaven. I used to think the same way. I remember back in the 1960's, before I became a Christian, going into my closet and praying. I professed to be an atheist at the time, but I was going through a difficult period in my life so I decided to pray. I rationalized that I would go to heaven if I died because I was a pretty good person. After all, I hadn't hurt anyone; I hadn't killed someone. But I was smoking pot every day, living common law, swearing like a trooper, shoplifting, and partying hard. I never attended church, gave much to others, or cared about God. My rationale was based on comparing myself with those I considered worse than I was—a common error of self-righteousness.

It is our human pride that has trouble with the concept of our deserving punishment and the need to admit the true depth of the sin nature in us. That is why so many are offended by the Cross and refuse its message. Let's take a realistic look at this based on the current laws of our land. In our society in North America, you only have to murder one person to be a murderer. You only have to steal once to be a thief. You only commit adultery once to be an adulterer. Maybe you've never committed murder or adultery or stolen anything, but you thought about doing it. Jesus addresses how even thinking of it is a sin in the gospel of Matthew:

> *But I say, anyone who even looks at a woman with lust in his eye has already committed adultery with her in his heart* (Matthew 5:28).

> *You have heard that the law of Moses says, "Do not murder. If you commit murder, you are subject to judgment." But I say, if you are angry with someone, you are subject to judgment! If you call someone an idiot, you are in danger of being brought before the high council. And if you curse someone, you are in danger of the fires of hell* (Matthew 5:21-22).

Why are we guilty for just thinking it? It is our *desire* to sin that condemns us.

What we desire in our heart reveals the nature of our heart, and if our desire is to do evil, then that is proof that we have an evil nature. Often it is only the consequences of sin that keep us from doing what we really want to do. If we are honest, we all have at one time or another wanted to do something evil but didn't because of the price we would pay.

Years ago I was very jealous of a girl because she seemed to be so much more blessed than I was. For days I actually wished she were dead because I felt threatened. My low self-esteem resented her as I compared myself to her. The desire to kill was there, and even though I would never do it, I wanted to.

Just think for a moment of what you wanted to do to someone whom you were envious of. When someone has what we want, it is the evil nature in us that desires to hurt that person. I had to wrestle with that evil desire against that girl and recognize it as sin. I'm sure you've been there.

After years of pastoring, I can tell you that innumerable people in the church live with hatred, jealousy, and ill wishes toward others just because of their hurt pride. Some wish they could leave their spouse, some covet the blessings of others, and some speak negatively of someone they are jealous of. The list goes on as our selfish ambitions and wrong desires multiply the sin in us. Can you and I be honest and willing to allow the Cross to expose evil motives in us? This verse in Proverbs tells us that our heart reflects who we are.

As a face is reflected in water, so the heart reflects the person (Proverbs 27:19).

What we desire in our heart reveals who we are!

No Excuses

I have learned that compared with God's standard, we all are guilty of just about everything. We all are liars, adulterers, thieves, and murderers, and we are proud and selfish. The tendency of man is to think of himself as better than he is and to justify his behavior. Before I understood the full meaning of the Cross, I used to often minimize or justify my sin. That means I believed that what I did wrong was not that bad and that I had good reason to do it. Just as we minimize our sins, we maximize the sins of others. Worse than that, we think God is not as good as He is because we blame Him for all that is wrong in the world.

Years ago I did a Bible study in a prison. Upon getting to know some of the convicts, I discovered that they all think they are justified in their crimes and blamed God, citing that He wasn't there for them when they needed Him.

Justice says there is no excuse for sin, and in a good court of law excuses do not hold up. If you murder someone, you're guilty. The bank robber will say he (or she) needed the money, the murderer will say he wasn't treated fairly or his father neglected him, the pedophile will say he was molested so he can't help himself, the abusive husband will say his wife upsets him and that she made him do it. Man will always find an excuse to sin. And as long as we believe that we are justified in sinning, we will continue to sin. This is where the blame game comes in.

We often think our sin is someone else's fault. Everybody thinks that he or she has rights because of his or her lot in life. "My wife doesn't understand me; therefore, I can leave her"; "my husband is selfish; therefore, I can neglect and dishonor him"; "she hurt me, so I'll hurt her."

I once read about an abusive man who, as he beat his wife, shouted these words, "Look at what you are making me do!" over and over again. He thought that her actions justified his wrongdoing. When we blame someone else to justify our wrong behavior, we are allowing the person we blame to have authority over our ability to choose. Therefore we are giving that person the control of our life because what he or she did directed our choice.

The list of such excuses can go on forever, and we will never run out of people to blame for our sins. However, as we continue to blame, we give away our power. You see, God has given us freedom of choice, empowering us with authority over our own will.

The Cross takes away our excuses.

I have discovered that one of the most awesome things about the Cross is that it sheds light on the deception of my excuses. It does this when I see the character of Christ on the Cross as He refused all excuses to sin, even when He had every justifiable reason to rebel against God and condemn us all.

The Cross takes away our excuses because, when we look at Jesus, we see that He had every excuse to lash out and blame others, but didn't.

Imagine what Jesus must have been thinking while on the Cross. He was every bit a man like we are and He had every emotion and feeling that we do. He must have wanted to shout back and call them liars, fighting with every fiber of His being to endure their contradiction and keep from throwing back what they were inflicting on Him. He may have fought the emotions of hatred and retaliation, and the temptation to use His power to wipe them all out. He must have cast down the excuses that bombarded His mind to call on God to deliver Him. He seemingly had every right to do these things because of the injustice and undeserved treatment He was being subjected to, yet He did not. He chose to give His life for you and me because, instead of thinking of excuses and blaming us, He thought of how much He loved us and wanted a relationship with us. He thought of how much He could show us His love and lavishly pour out the riches of His blessings on us. He thought of how we would one day be purified and living with Him because of what He was doing. He thought of how much He loved His Father and how glorious it was to be with Him and how much He wanted to please Him in all He did. If He saw no excuse as reasonable, then how can I?

The key that kept Him was that He lived to obey His heavenly Father. John 15:10 says,

When you obey me, you remain in my love, just as I obey my Father and remain in his love.

Remaining in His love is remaining in the truth of the Cross.

If we look at Jesus and the Cross and absorb His message of doing the right thing regardless of what others do to us, we are left without the excuse to sin. *Without an excuse to sin, it is easier to recognize sin and cease from it.* That is why it is so important for us to evaluate the motives of our heart by comparing them with the motives of the heart of Jesus. This is what looking at the Cross is all about! Jesus Himself said that we now have no excuse for sin!

> *The Cross is our standard of true justice and righteousness.*

They would not be guilty if I had not come and spoken to them. But now they have no excuse for their sin (John 15:22).

Once we see that the Cross deals with our excuses to sin and helps us take the responsibility for them rather than blame others, then we can actually begin to see the sin lurking in us.

Most of us, however, compare ourselves with others, feeling either better or worse than them rather than comparing ourselves with Jesus Christ and His standard.

As we raised our six children, we found that in their teen years they occasionally wanted to go to shows or parties that we felt uncomfortable with. When we denied them their way we heard comments such as "Well, so-and-so can go. And they go to the church and their parents will let them. Why can't we go? You're not fair; everyone else is doing it!" If you have teens I'm sure these words ring a familiar bell.

The Cross Is Our Standard

Our human nature determines standards for right and wrong based on what others do. We can see how the moral standard of our nation has declined over the past 50 years by that concept. Television in the 1950's wouldn't even allow a married woman to show herself pregnant, or a married couple to be seen in a bed together fully clothed. Now anything goes, for when sin is tolerated, it takes over like cancer.

Whenever you set a standard, everything relating to it must be measured by it. The Cross is the measuring stick for whether or not there is sin in our heart. Only it can reveal the truth by the Spirit of Christ who died on it. His life reflects true righteousness and reveals our motives. As we look at the Cross, we see the truest purity, justice, and righteousness that ever existed. The glory of God is revealed through its perfect work.

> *God wanted to capture my heart and deliver me from the judgment I deserved.*

When I look at what He has done for me, the total obedience, love, humility, unselfishness, commitment, purity, and patience He displayed is my standard, and I cannot compare.

It is futile to try and be good enough by comparing ourselves with others; there will always be someone more or less spiritual than we are. This leaves us either with a feeling of pride or inferiority, both of which reinforce a negative identity in us. It is much easier to simply realize that we will *never* be good enough for God and rest in His power to sanctify us. It is only our pride that thinks that somehow we have something to do with our righteousness.

The more I gaze on Him, the more I see the evil in me and the more I see His love for me. As I see His love, I see the righteousness that He had made me!

It is His Spirit, the Holy Spirit that is the nature of Christ, who made Him perfect and led Him to the Cross. He has now given us that same Spirit because of the Cross. That Spirit is His own nature, and John told us what His Spirit will do in us.

And when he comes, he will convince the world of its sin, and of God's righteousness, and of the coming judgment (John 16:8).

The Spirit convinces the world of its sin, of God's righteousness, and of the judgment to come. This is exactly what the Cross does.

God knew that punishment alone could not deal with the *nature* of sin. Something greater had to transpire, but because of the need for justice, God had a problem. He had to change the desire of our heart and deal with our sin without destroying us.

Jesus completely identified with me as a human and took all my sin and punishment on Himself in the hope of winning my heart. He knew that if He won my heart, my desire would change from sin to Him.

All of our sin was nailed to the Cross, as it says in this verse in Galatians:

Those who belong to Christ Jesus have nailed the passions and desires of their sinful nature to his cross and crucified them there (Galatians 5:24).

A Change of Heart

Notice that Galatians 5:24 says the *"passions and desires"* of our sinful nature was crucified on the Cross. That means the Cross has the ability to take away our desire to sin. Therefore, if we still have the desire, we are not fully seeing or understanding the work of the Cross. Until I come to the full realization of my sinfulness, recognize the depth of my pride and selfishness, and see that I was condemned, I will never fully appreciate or understand the fullness of God's love. *It is His love that has the power to change the desires of my heart so that I no longer want to sin.* Consequences do not change the desire in your heart; they only control them.

Many criminals spend their days in prison, planning their next crime. Their punishment does little to change desire. It can curb sin, but God is looking for more than that. He seeks those who hunger and thirst for righteousness.

The work of the Cross has the power to change our desires because it actually gives us a new heart. We can read the prophecy about this promise in Ezekiel.

And I will give you a new heart with new and right desires, and I will put a new spirit in you. I will take out your stony heart of sin and give you a new, obedient heart (Ezekiel 36:26).

The more we are aware that our old sinful nature was crucified and that we have been given a new perfect heart by receiving the nature of Christ, the more we will desire to love and obey Him.

Some may say this is sin-consciousness, and it can be if you are not looking at the Cross, for it is the Cross that changes it into love-consciousness.

The following verse in Luke shows us through the testimony of a forgiven prostitute that when we see our sinful state, we recognize how much we are loved.

Wherefore I say unto thee, Her sins, which are many, are forgiven; for she loved much: but to whom little is forgiven, the same loveth little (Luke 7:47 KJV).

This verse does not refer so much to the fact that others weren't great sinners, but that when we are aware of the sin in us, we will see how much He loves us and love Him more for it. That is why it is so important to know that we deserved His wrath and judgment!

> *It is the Cross that changes sin-consciousness into love-consciousness.*

If we don't believe we deserved wrath and judgment, then the Cross is no big deal. When we realize that all the wrath of God that we deserved was absorbed into Christ on the Cross and that He took every sin and bore the full punishment for everything we have ever done or will do, then we are overwhelmed with His love!

We can read about this in an awesome prophecy predicting the amazing work of the Cross:

He has not punished us for all our sins, nor does he deal with us as we deserve. For his unfailing love toward those who fear him is as great as the height of the heavens above the earth. He has removed our rebellious acts as far away from us as the east is from the west (Psalm 103:10-12).

We also must recognize that the Cross is the tree of life. When we partake of it, it saves us from death and gives us eternal life.

A type of the Cross is revealed in the Word of God when the Israelites were wandering in the desert and angered God. Poisonous snakes were sent, and many died. To remedy the problem, those bitten by the snakes had to look at a bronze snake on a pole to save themselves from certain death. The serpent on the pole represented our sin that was nailed on the Cross. We can read about this prophetic analogy of the Cross in the book of Numbers:

So the LORD sent poisonous snakes among them, and many of them were bitten and died. Then the people came to Moses and cried out, "We have sinned by speaking against the LORD and against you. Pray that the LORD will take away the snakes." So Moses prayed for the people. Then the LORD told him, "Make a replica of a poisonous snake and attach it to the top of a pole. Those who are bitten will live if they simply look at it!" So Moses made a snake out of bronze and attached it to the top of a pole. Whenever those who were bitten looked at the bronze snake, they recovered! (Numbers 21:6-9)

Jesus explained its meaning in the book of John, referring it to His death on the Cross.

For only I, the Son of Man, have come to earth and will return to heaven again. And as Moses lifted up the bronze snake on a pole in the wilderness, so I, the Son of Man, must be lifted up on a pole, so that everyone who believes in me will have eternal life. For God so loved the world that he gave his only Son, so that everyone who believes in him will not perish but have eternal life (John 3:13-16).

What does this means to us? Simply that when we are bitten by sin and poisoned from it, God has provided a remedy that is always there for us. When we keep our eyes on the Cross and see that our sin was permanently dealt with, we will experience life. If we don't keep our eyes on the Cross, we will produce death as the enemy bombards us with relentless guilt and condemnation and deceives us into attempts to earn right standing with God.

Colossians tells us that He canceled the record of the charges against us and destroyed it on the Cross. That means it no longer exists! It is imperative that we realize there are no longer any charges against us for anything we have done against God. Now that is a merciful God!

He canceled the record that contained the charges against us. He took it and destroyed it by nailing it to Christ's cross (Colossians 2:14).

If we ever walk around feeling condemned, we do not understand what He has done. His act of love didn't just reveal my sin; it removed that sin and justified me so that I am completely righteous like He is. It is not because of what I have done or ever could do, but because of what He has done. This may sound very foundational to some, but my experience and that of most Christians is that God's love for them is questioned all the time. Legalism, which is trusting in how good we are in order to gain salvation, is rampant in the church. So many Christians walk around with the weight of their sin and guilt, lacking love, joy, and peace because of it. They are performance-based, constantly trying to prove themselves to be something when the Cross says they are something! Ephesians tells us that there is nothing we can do to save ourselves:

Only when we recognize that we are made right with God by the work of the Cross alone can we cease from trying to "get" saved and simply focus on doing good works.

God saved you by his special favor when you believed. And you can't take credit for this; it is a gift from God. Salvation is not a reward for the good things we have done, so none of us can boast about it. For we are God's masterpiece. He has created us anew in Christ Jesus, so that we can do the good things he planned for us long ago (Ephesians 2:8-10).

Positionally speaking, we cannot get more right with God than by what He did for us. It is a gift and cannot be earned. In fact, the Bible says all of our works are like filth compared to what He did for us. Somehow, though, our pride seems to continually get caught up in the "works for salvation" mode. If salvation is based on anything that we do, than what He did was not necessary. And when we consider our works as acceptance with God, we exalt ourselves and negate the work of the Cross. That is why God hates self-righteousness so much. It is only when we recognize that we are made right with God by the work of the Cross alone that we can cease from trying to "get" saved and simply focus on doing good works—motivated by the knowledge that we are already righteous.

Jesus' death and resurrection secured our righteousness so completely that it is now who we are. Your old man—your sin nature—is dead; it was crucified with Christ, and your new man is now the real you. Stop focusing on the dead man and focus on the new man. God is making us holy. It is a process that by faith is already completely done. If God says it is done, it is done!

To see ourselves differently than righteousness undeserved is to undermine Jesus' work on the Cross. In other words, when I see myself as righteous in my own right, I make the sacrifice for my sins useless and I am sinning. But when I see myself righteous because of what He did for me, I put the hope of my future in the Cross and recognize its value.

God had to justify me and did so by paying the price Himself. To meditate every day on the Cross is to know and appreciate His amazing love and grace and to desire to do what's right.

There can be no greater love, and if that doesn't capture your heart, something else has.

Chapter Five

From Heaven to the Cross

Though he was God, he did not demand and cling to his rights as God.
He made himself nothing; he took the humble position of a slave and
appeared in human form. And in human form he obediently humbled
himself even further by dying a criminal's death on a cross. Because of this,
God raised him up to the heights of heaven and gave him a name that is
above every other name (Philippians 2:6-9).

Knowing who Jesus is, where He came from, and what authority He has is necessary to have a proper perspective of how far He went to redeem us. For example, if a neighboring family on your street dropped by and told you that they were giving you everything they owned, that would be great news. But if Bill Gates, Oprah Winfrey, or Queen Elizabeth dropped by and told you that they were giving you everything they owned, that would be a whole lot better news!

Who Jesus is, where He came from, and the authority He has is far beyond that of anyone else in this world. He left all the riches of heaven and came down to earth to our level and gave us everything He had, to win our heart!

In my early years as a Christian, God's love was very real to me, and I was passionate about Him. However, over time, when difficulties began flooding my life, I began to question His love. As a result, my love for Him diminished. I did not realize that I was doing what many other Christians do, and that is measuring God's love for me by the circumstances that I find myself in. My difficulties and how people treat me have nothing to do with how much He loves me. Because I fell for the lie that His love is determined by what I am going through, I allowed my old fears and insecurities to rob me of what He had suffered and died to give me.

Just as we must understand the wrath and judgment of God to appreciate what we were spared from, so we also must realize God's immense love for us.

We need to understand just how far God went to win us.

To win something indicates that you have to do something to attain it. God did not want to "take" our heart. He could have, but that would mean we would be forced to love and serve Him. That would not be real love but slavery; we would be nothing more than robots. God loves us enough to allow us to make our own choices. He created us and gave us a free will, even though it would be costly to Him. His desire was to win our heart, not take it forcefully; therefore, He came up with a secret plan. The book of Ephesians says,

God's secret plan has now been revealed to us; it is a plan centered on Christ, designed long ago according to his good pleasure (Ephesians 1:9).

To appreciate this plan, we must fully understand who Jesus Christ is and know exactly what He did for us. Most of us know He laid down His life for us, and that in itself is amazing. However, the depth of that sacrifice, that He did much more than just die for us, is rarely understood. First we must consider who He is and what He gave up in order to accomplish this incredible plan.

Who Jesus Is

Just who is Jesus? Many scriptures describe Him in God's Word, and they show us just how incredibly awesome He is! The Word says that everything in the heavens and on the earth belong to Him. He rules over all things; riches and honor come from Him alone; and all power and might are in His hands. He is the King, robed in majesty and armed with strength. His throne has been established from before time, and He is from the everlasting past. He is mightier than the roaring oceans, and His decrees cannot be changed. He has placed the earth on its foundation so it will never be moved, and He has made all that is in it. Without Him there would be nothing!

He is the cornerstone, the judge of the living and the dead, the great Shepherd, and the King of kings and Lord of lords. His eyes are like flames of fire, and on His head are many crowns. He is the Word of God and the bright and Morning Star. He is the righteous One and the Author of life itself.

The government rests on His shoulders. He is called Wonderful, Counselor, Mighty God, everlasting Father, and the Prince of Peace. He is the Anointed One and the Son of man, and His face is as bright as the sun in all its brilliance. He is the first and the last. He holds the keys of death, hell, and the grave, and everything exists through Him and by Him and was made for Him. He holds all things together, and He is the light in the darkness that cannot be extinguished. He is God in the flesh, full of unfailing love and faithfulness as the glorious Son of the Father. And if you have seen Him, you have seen the Father.

All of the above are just some of what describes Jesus Christ. The Bible says in the gospel of John that all these things were written so we would know who Jesus Christ is:

But these are written so that you may believe that Jesus is the Messiah, the Son of God, and that by believing in him you will have life (John 20:31).

I cannot emphasize enough how important it is to understand who He is in order to appreciate the magnitude of what He did.

What Jesus Did

Look closely at these scriptures in 2 Corinthians. They tell us that we can know how full of love and kindness Jesus was because of His willingness to leave all His riches to come to earth. This is no small thing; what He had surpasses all the wealth earth has to offer, and He chose to come with nothing.

You know how full of love and kindness our Lord Jesus Christ was. Though he was very rich, yet for your sakes he became poor, so that by his poverty he could make you rich (2 Corinthians 8:9).

In Philippians it says that He gave up His rights and made Himself nothing, took the position of a slave, and humbled Himself to a criminal's death. Can you imagine going from the top place of authority of all that exists to the lowest place? It would be worse than the most powerful man on earth being put on death row to pay for the crimes of his subjects.

Though he was God, he did not demand and cling to his rights as God. He made himself nothing; he took the humble position of a slave and appeared in human form. And in human form he obediently humbled himself even further by dying a criminal's death on a cross (Philippians 2:6-8).

He loved us so much that although He is our Creator, our God and Master of the universe, He did not cling to His rights as God but chose to leave it all to win our heart.

We often think our good deeds are a big deal, but nothing can compare with His leaving all the majesty, glory, and power of His kingdom to come to earth as an infant. That alone must have been humiliating—He was our Creator! Imagine God becoming a baby and allowing His creation to take care of Him in a helpless state. He loved us enough to subject Himself to man as a vulnerable infant, having to grow and mature as a normal human being. He chose to come to earth at a primitive time, when feet, camels, and donkeys were the transportation of the day. There were no TVs, computers, phones, microwaves, or other common luxuries we have available today. (Though I'm sure our modern technology is primitive compared to what exists in heaven.) To do all that for us was a major sacrifice, more than we will ever really know or comprehend.

He did not cling to His rights as God, but chose to leave it all to win our heart.

Occasionally, I hear a story of a prince or king who gives up his throne for the woman he loves, but Jesus gave up everything good and perfect and subjected Himself to a cursed world for those whom He loved.

It is an amazing thing when people give up their lives for someone, and there are few to be found. I recently met and interviewed a young American girl, Carrie McDonnell, who along with her new husband David, went to Iraq at the beginning of 2004 to do mission work. They chose to go in spite of the danger to their lives because of their love for Christ and their desire to win the Moslem people. Just a few months into their assignment in the city of Mosul, they were surrounded by insurgents shooting relentlessly into their vehicle with machine guns. Her husband, along with three other missionaries, was shot to death. This beautiful young newlywed was hit by 22 bullets, but with the help of her critically injured husband was brought to a hospital where she received the care she needed to survive. Her husband succumbed to his injuries a few hours later, and she was left a widowed newlywed, with lifelong scars for the cause of Christ.[13]

Carrie gave more than I ever have, and it was the Spirit of Christ in her that enabled her to take the risk to reach the lost for Him. As amazing and selfless as that is, it pales in comparison to what Jesus gave up for us, and I'm sure Carrie would be quick to agree. Jesus humbled Himself to the utmost, stripping Himself of all that one could desire and willingly submitted to ridicule and humiliation in the vilest form and die the shameful death of a criminal.

> *He loved us enough to die a slow torturous death instead of a quick, easy one.*

Under the old Levitical law, when an animal was sacrificed for the sins of the people, the priests would take the animal, place it on top of the altar, and cut its throat with a knife. It was a quick, easy death, without much suffering on the animal's part. Jesus could have died this way and still have accomplished our redemption as the sacrificial lamb, but that is not the way He chose to die. He chose a long, drawn-out, torturous, humiliating way to be sacrificed. We will cover later His incredible reasons for this, as everything He did had a purpose and was motivated by His great love for us.

Jesus Came By Abraham's Faith

God loved us enough to respect the will of man for our redemption plan. Even making the choice to die for us was not forced or done without the faith of man first. God is always moved by the faith of men, and He did not force His plan of salvation on us. Instead He tested a man to see if He had an open door to implement it.

God subjects Himself to His own laws and does what is right. He refused to act without the legal right to be our atonement, and that is where Abraham came in. Abraham chose the way of the Cross by what he believed, giving it a legal entry to redeem mankind, for *God always works through a man for all He does for man.*

In the book of Galatians it is recorded that Abraham had two sons, one from the promise and of God and one from man's way of doing things:

The Scriptures say that Abraham had two sons, one from his slave-wife and one from his freeborn wife. The son of the slave-wife was born in a human attempt to bring about the fulfillment of God's promise. But the son of the freeborn wife was born as God's own fulfillment of his promise. Now these two women serve as an illustration of God's two covenants. Hagar, the slave-wife, represents Mount Sinai where people first became enslaved to the law (Galatians 4:22-24).

His son from the promise was Isaac. We also know that Isaac was born supernaturally since Sarah was barren and they conceived him in their old age when it was physically impossible. The book of Romans talks about the faith Abraham had to have to believe for this miracle:

And Abraham's faith did not weaken, even though he knew that he was too old to be a father at the age of one hundred and that Sarah, his wife, had never been able to have children. Abraham never wavered in believing God's promise. In fact, his faith grew stronger, and in this he brought glory to God. He was absolutely convinced that God was able to do anything he promised. And **because of Abraham's faith***, God declared him to be righteous* (Romans 4:19-22, emphasis added).

It involved having faith in specific things to be declared righteous, and Abraham had the right faith for the right things.

So Isaac was the son of promise, had a supernatural birth, and came by faith.

You can read in Genesis 22:1-14 the account of God asking Abraham to sacrifice his *only son* Isaac as a burnt offering to the Lord, and how Abraham willingly set out trusting that God would raise his son from the dead if he obeyed. The book of Hebrews describes how Abraham's faith was willing to trust God enough to sacrifice his son because he knew He was able to raise him up.

It was by faith that Abraham offered Isaac as a sacrifice when God was testing him. Abraham, who had received God's promises, was ready to sacrifice his only son, Isaac, though God had promised him, "Isaac is the son through whom your descendants will be counted." Abraham assumed that if Isaac died, **God was able to bring him back to life again.** *And in a sense,*

Abraham did receive his son back from the dead (Hebrews 11:17-19, emphasis added).

Let's look at the specific things Abraham believed that made him righteous in God's eyes.

First, he believed for a promised son, and he believed in a supernatural birth. He had faith to sacrifice his only son, and for three days he believed his son dead. (It took him three days to climb Mount Moriah.) He believed God would provide a sacrificial lamb and that God would raise his son from the dead.[14]

Everything in the Old Covenant points to the Cross.

These are all the things we have to believe to be saved!

All that Abraham believed represents the work of Christ, His sacrifice on the Cross, and

His resurrection. Abraham gave Jesus the legal right to come and die for us because his faith activated the work of the Cross before it happened! Jesus told us that Abraham saw it and believed it, as we can read in the gospel of John:

Your ancestor Abraham rejoiced as he looked forward to my coming. He saw it and was glad (John 8:56).

Before I understood this, I used to wonder why God would ask Abraham to sacrifice his son, since that appeared to be a contradiction of His nature. Now it makes complete sense. *God had the Cross on His mind when Abraham was tested!* It amazes me to know each step of our salvation by the work of the Cross was planned from the beginning of time!

God is able to make you strong, just as the Good News says. It is the message about Jesus Christ and his plan for you Gentiles, a plan kept secret from the beginning of time (Romans 16:25).

Everything God did in the Old Covenant was to establish His righteousness and justice and point to the Cross. Nothing is more important.

All the prophets, priesthood, and sacrifices in the Old Covenant pointed to the Cross. It is the core message of the Bible and cannot be removed from any part of it. *The Cross is God's message to man.*

49

Jesus on Earth

Jesus always knew who He was, where He came from, and why He was here. During His entire ministry on earth, He continually referred to the fact that He would be crucified, die, and rise again.

Then Jesus began to tell them that he, the Son of Man, would suffer many terrible things and be rejected by the leaders, the leading priests, and the teachers of religious law. He would be killed, and three days later he would rise again (Mark 8:31).

This knowledge was always weighing down on Him throughout His earthly life, and it grew increasingly more difficult for Him as the time grew closer. Obviously that knowledge climaxed as He wrestled in prayer the night of His arrest in the Garden of Gethsemane.

> *Jesus loved us enough to be in complete obedience to the Father so we would glorify God with Him.*

Jesus did what He did because of His love for the Father and His desire to glorify Him. He knew that if He glorified Him, that He too would be glorified—and so would we. For Jesus the first purpose of the Cross was to glorify His Father. To do the Father's will is what He lived and died for. He also purposed to strip Himself of all the glory and majesty He had to become a man and destroy the works of the devil as a man. He took on Himself all our sins and destroyed the power of sin over us so we could be like Him. His desire was for us to possess the Spirit that was in Him so we too would please the Father. He loved us enough to adopt us as children of God.

His purpose was not just to demonstrate His love for us, but also to take our sin and its punishment and make us the legal children of God. He wasn't just looking for friends, but family. To be someone's child is to be in the center of his or her heart as a part of that individual. If we are good parents, our children will be the most precious things we have, and we will go to the ends of the earth for them. Jesus wanted to become just like us and experience everything that we go through as human beings so He could relate to us completely and destroy the devil's power over us. Hebrews says,

Because God's children are human beings—made of flesh and blood—Jesus also became flesh and blood by being born in human form. For only as a human being could he die, and only by dying could he break the power of the Devil, who had the power of death (Hebrews 2:14).

He came to serve us by making a way for us to become the legal children of God and present us to God. As a true child of God, I will act like my Father—just as young children imitate their parents. As His children, we are heirs to all that Christ purchased for us. Now that is a good deal! He fought the battle, took the rap, and then gave us the goods. Because of His love, we have been made His children, made in the image and likeness of Him. We don't have to become something; we already are something. We are God's kids!

Like any good parent, His desire for us is to develop His character in us. As we grow in character, we will inherit the promises that belong to us as the legal heirs of God. With authority must come responsibility, and to be responsible involves character. *The Cross reveals the true nature of our Father.* Jesus said in the gospel of John that to see Him is to see the Father:

Jesus replied, "Philip, don't you even yet know who I am, even after all the time I have been with you? Anyone who has seen me has seen the Father! So why are you asking to see him?" (John 14:9)

Christ has set the example for the children of God through His death on the Cross and has won us back to His household. He showed us what He is like so we could be full of His glory by imitating Him.

As was mentioned earlier, the Cross was one of the cruelest ways to die in history, yet that is the death He chose. I have often pondered on why a cross? Aside from His desire to die a degrading, painful, and humiliating execution, there are many reasons for why this was His plan. The Cross has two beams similar to that of a plus sign, and it is there that He adds God to man, reconciling us back to the place that we were created for. The vertical beam reaches from earth to heaven, representing God coming down to us and scooping us up to Him, and the horizontal beam reaches across the earth to embrace all who would receive it.

We know that all of time begins and ends at the Cross. It is 2005 A.D. as I write this book; the A.D. signifies that it is after the death of Christ. Just as time flows from it, so does the history of God and man. But beyond all of that, He chose the Cross as His means to die to identify with the worst of our pain. Jesus went from the highest place to the lowest so no one could be left out. And He did it out of a love so immense that He would stop at nothing to win us. When that becomes the anchor of our soul, we will be possessed by His love and overcome evil. His Cross decrees that we were condemned, but now we are set free!

Chapter Six

Enemies of the Cross

But if you are willing to listen, I say, love your enemies. Do good to those who hate you (Luke 6:27).

Whether we realize it or not, we all were enemies of the Cross. We were hostile to the Cross when we opposed righteousness by our sinful nature. The purpose of the Cross is to make peace—us with our enemies, God with us, and us with others.

We have three enemies we need to be aware of. First is Satan, who has been stripped of his power and can hurt us only by deception. Second is the enemy of our flesh, which has been crucified on the Cross. Third are our enemies who wish us ill will, whom we are called to love. Jesus dealt with them all on the Cross by conquering the devil, destroying sin's power, and loving those who opposed Him.

Conquering the Flesh

Not only did Jesus die to His flesh on the Cross, but He also loved us enough to die to His flesh *His entire life*. You see, just as Jesus had to have a legal right to come and die for us, He also had to prove He was without sin.

He viewed the works of the flesh as an enemy and refused to give any opportunity for His flesh to defeat Him. In fact, He recognized it as the very thing He came to destroy and deliver us from.

As I began my pursuit of the Cross, I realized that the suffering of Jesus did not just begin the last 12 hours of His life. As a man, He lived every day of His life without sin. He never allowed selfishness to get the better of Him, no matter what He faced.

This means that as thoughts to do evil entered His mind—just like they do with us—He would refuse to dwell on them even for a second. You may find it hard to believe that Jesus would have such thoughts, but if He were to truly understand our weakness, then He would have to know what it is like to want to act selfishly, covet, feel hurt, and desire to sin. The Bible says He was without sin; therefore, He never allowed the thoughts to take root that His flesh would try and plant in His mind.

Jesus' victory over the temptations released His authority to do all the miracles that He performed during His ministry.

When Jesus was tempted in the wilderness, He proved that the motives of His heart were pure and that His only desire was to glorify God. He had made a decision that He would not live to please His flesh in any way.

The gospel of Matthew, chapter 4, records that Jesus went into the wilderness and fasted 40 days and nights to be tempted by the devil. The Holy Spirit actually led Him there for that purpose. In 1 John we can read of the three main areas in which temptation comes.

For all that is in the world, the lust of the flesh, and the lust of the eyes, and the pride of life, is not of the Father, but is of the world (1 John 2:16 KJV).

The first thing Jesus was tempted with was food, and it happened during the most difficult time: near the end of a long fast. When He refused, He gained victory over the lust of the flesh. The second thing He was tempted with was to test God, which is the test of pride that demands God to prove Himself. When the devil tried to talk Jesus into throwing Himself off a cliff, He displayed His complete faithfulness and honor to God. The third test was that of the lust of the eyes. The devil showed Him all the glory of the world and offered it to Him, but with each test Jesus responded with *"it is written"* and stayed completely focused on what His purpose was.

After He passed the tests of temptation and proved Himself selfless and pure, He was given authority over sickness, disease, demons, and the elements.

When we learn the obedience of dying to our flesh, we too will be empowered with a greater release of the supernatural in our lives. It is already available to us, but God will only release it to those who will live to do His will. Otherwise we would use His power to sin and satisfy our flesh, hurting others along the way. The benefits are there, but they are waiting for us to walk in victory by recognizing that the enemy of our flesh has been conquered by Christ.

The work of the Cross is the ultimate demonstration of power over sin. Jesus conquered all power of the flesh when He laid down His life for us. That was His ultimate test.

Let's think about this perfect man who conquered all sin by resisting every temptation throughout His entire life. Jesus never lied, never stole, and never lusted; He looked away every time temptation came. He cast down every thought and lived solely to please His heavenly Father. He had the purest, most unselfish heart, and He knew that the Cross was His destiny. All He did was to glorify the Father. He lived and died in complete obedience because He knew exactly who He was and who His Father was.

> *By conquering the enemies of His flesh, He loved the enemies of His soul.*

Now let's consider what was done to tempt Jesus in the last 12 hours of His life. He had done no wrong, and now His very own creation was judging Him falsely because of the sin in their hearts—their envy, their pride, their hatred and selfishness, etc. Just think of what He could have done to them. If it were us in the flesh, wiping them all out would have been a reasonable response if we had the power to do so. We would act just like our heroes we see in the movies when the bad guys capture the good guys. We relish the tactics that follow as the good guys get their revenge. But not Jesus—He displayed perfect love, self-control, and confidence in who He was because He loved them. He was completely willing to give His all for His tormentors.

What power He had over the flesh and sin! There has never been a greater demonstration of absolute love and commitment to do what is right than the Cross. He didn't threaten, revile, curse, condemn, or use the power that was available to Him to stop what was happening to Him. He only had to speak the word, and every angel in heaven would have come to His defense. Instead, He chose to resist retaliation and absorbed into Himself all the sin that was being done against Him for all time so that His enemies could go free. Jesus conquered the flesh 100 percent—yours and mine.

Colossians tells us that *we* were His enemies, separated from Him by our evil thoughts and desires. It was by His blood on the Cross that we were brought back to God as His friends.

> *For God in all his fullness was pleased to live in Christ, and by him God reconciled everything to himself. He made peace with everything in heaven and on earth by means of his blood on the cross. This includes you who were once so far away from God. You were his enemies, separated from him by your evil thoughts and actions, yet now he has brought you back as his friends. He has done this through his death on the cross in his own human body. As a result, he has brought you into the very presence of God, and you are holy and blameless as you stand before him without a single fault* (Colossians 1:19-22).

His Love in the Midst of Our Sin

The Cross exposes the ugliness of our sin, as it was an outward manifestation of the heart of man toward a loving God who made them.

I remember thinking one day about the Cross and all that Christ went through, and I suddenly realized in my heart that all the pain and sin He bore was what *I* did to Him. I had known that in theory, but the revelation that I continue to hurt Him every time I sin became increasingly real. Everything that was done to Him during His suffering and death is an outward demonstration of what we do to Him in our heart every time we sin. The desertion, mocking, denial, shame, and abuse have been man's response to God since the fall of man. This revelation is incredibly humbling and overwhelming when acknowledged. When I weep with sorrow for how I have treated Him, He does not condemn me but enfolds me in the most incredible love that exists. He loved us enough to ie while we broke His heart.

The ultimate message of the Cross is to love your enemies. That is exactly what Jesus did and said:

> *But I say, love your enemies! Pray for those who persecute you!* (Matthew 5:44)

He meant it and lived it out to the fullest. He didn't just tell us to do something and not do it Himself. He told us to love our enemies, and, in His suffering, showed us how to do it. He chose to love me even though I opposed Him as His enemy.

First John tells us that He was full of love and faithfulness:

So the Word became human and lived here on earth among us. He was full of unfailing love and faithfulness. And we have seen his glory, the glory of the only Son of the Father (John 1:14).

God's glory was revealed in the love of Jesus Christ. He left heaven and came to earth to absorb all that we deserved to prove His love, yet so many question it because they base it on everything but His Cross. The Cross forever speaks of God's love for us.

The Cross is an eternal, never-changing memorial to us. It is always there and forever speaks of God's love for us. When we question His love, we just have to look at the Cross and meditate on what He did. It is a great thing to die for one's friends. But it is an even greater thing to die for one's enemies.

> *The Cross was the ultimate demonstration of His love for His enemies.*

But God showed his great love for us by sending Christ to die for us while we were still sinners (Romans 5:8).

Everything God did in His Word was centered on this plan—to die for His enemies and make peace with them. He did it in the hope that we would accept His peace offering and realize how much it cost Him and how much He loves us.

Failure to focus on the Cross will result in wrong responses to our enemies, for the more we know His love, the more we can love those who oppose us. There is nothing we can do to make Him stop loving us. All the hatred of man at the Cross didn't stop Him from loving us. There is absolutely nothing that can ever separate us from His incredible, unending love.

If anyone was a blatant example of being an enemy of Christ, it was the apostle Paul. His mission before his conversion was to imprison and kill Christians. He did that passionately, firmly believing that Christ was a heretic. Paul called himself the worst of sinners, and yet he discovered the love of Jesus Christ. Then, just as passionately as he was against Christ, he became an advocate for Him. Very few of us have gone as far as Paul and actually killed believers. When he got the revelation of the Cross, nothing was going to move him from the love that he found there. It was that truth that enabled him to go through more difficulties than most of us will ever have to experience. Because he was rooted in the love of the Cross, he was not moved by thoughts questioning God's love for him when things got tough.

The Cross eternally speaks of His love for me, and knowing that love validates who I am!

Paul could have believed the lie that God didn't care about him after he was beaten, shipwrecked, jailed, and stoned a few times. He could have wrestled with the thought that maybe Jesus really was trying to get even with him and didn't love him after all. No matter what Paul went through, he was convinced of God's love because he knew the source of it was found at the Cross.

If you struggle with knowing God's love, your faith is not centered on the Cross but on yourself and your circumstances. I used to struggle in this area because of my self-image, but the Cross changed my image of who I am. Because my father left when I was five years old, knowing the love of a father was a foreign concept for me. This kept me from fully understanding the character of God until I saw it through the Cross. For years as a Christian I wrestled with the fear that God couldn't really love me, and that lie hindered me from becoming the person I could be in Christ.

As a leader I know that the enemy attacks a lot of believers with the same thoughts, but when we understand the Cross we will no longer question His love. In fact, as soon as negative thoughts enter my mind, I immediately think of all He suffered for me and I feel so loved. Low self-esteem cannot stay with that knowledge, and we will grow in confidence and faith as we become more grounded in it.

Everything that Jesus did, as we will continue to explore, He did for us so that we would base our faith on the incredible love that He demonstrated at the Cross. He knows that it is His love that empowers us to change. The Cross has solidified this in me so much so that my love for Him is passionate and my desire to please Him is out of love, not duty. I am absolutely crazy about Him and how far He went to win my heart. When we don't know His love, we will become performance-based, always looking for man's acceptance. When we don't get it we will become hurt and bitter. The only place to stay rooted and grounded in His love is in the Cross.

The Power of His Love

The book of Ephesians tells us it is His love that gives us the power to do His will:

> *And I pray that Christ will be more and more at home in your hearts as you trust in him. May your roots go down deep into the soil of God's marvelous love. And may you have the power to understand, as all God's people should, how wide, how long, how high, and how deep his love really is. May you experience the love of Christ, though it is so great you will never fully understand it. Then you will be filled with the fullness of life and power that comes from God* (Ephesians 3:17-19).

The fullness of His power is to enable us to love those who oppose us, and we can never truly love them until God's love is real in us. If I am performance-based, I will look for love from man and rob myself of knowing God's love. Only His love has the power to get our eyes off ourselves and focused on loving others, regardless of how they love us. This pleases God, as Ephesians says:

> *Live a life filled with love for others, following the example of Christ, who loved you and gave himself as a sacrifice to take away your sins. And God was pleased, because that sacrifice was like sweet perfume to him* (Ephesians 5:2).

The Cross teaches us how to love. The Cross is the example, demonstration, and proof of God's love for us and shows us how we should love our enemies and each other.

> *But I don't need to write to you about the Christian love that should be shown among God's people. For God himself has taught you to love one another* (1 Thessalonians 4:9).

The Cross teaches us how far love will and should go for others, and it strips us of all our excuses to hate. It is only our flesh, our old nature, that wants to hang on to anger, resentment, bitterness, and vengeance. First John says that when we live in God's love, our love grows more perfect!

We know how much God loves us, and we have put our trust in him. God is love, and all who live in love live in God, and God lives in them. And as we live in God, our love grows more perfect. So we will not be afraid on the day of judgment, but we can face him with confidence because we are like Christ here in this world (1 John 4:16-17).

Real love will go as far as the Cross did.

Knowing God's love through the work of the Cross absolutely convinces me that God is out for my best interest. That makes it easy to trust in Him and His plans for me.

Every day as I look at the Cross, measure my love walk by His, and see how much He loved His enemies, I realize that I was one of them. So when I am hurt by someone, I compare my pain with the pain I caused Him and find it easy to forgive, love, and bless the person who did me harm. That does not mean that I let people walk all over me or deny necessary consequences. It does mean that in my heart I can truly love and believe the best for my offenders. I am then able to let go of all ill will, hope and believe for their deliverance, and do what I need to do to help them find it.

Real love will go as far as the Cross did, and if you struggle with faith in God's love, I encourage you to spend time meditating and processing the facts of how far He went to prove it to you.

The key to our love walk is keeping our eyes on how He loved. For example, now every time my husband does something that irritates me (as all spouses will occasionally do), instead of getting angry and resentful like I used to, I have learned to take it to the Cross. I simply have to look at what I put Christ through. Somehow my husband's offense seems so minor that I can easily let it go. I no longer have to give in to my flesh and try and punish my husband like I used to. If the offense is something that I need to confront, then after going to the Cross I can do so with a gentle and restorative attitude. I do the same when others come against me and hurt me in some way.

Obviously there are days when I don't go to the Cross as fast as I should, but it is so real to me now that it doesn't take long to lay offenses down and forgive because I have purposed to center my life on it. This has saved my marriage from countless arguments and made it easy to keep the love flowing. "Taking it to the Cross" is a regular part of my day.

Jesus was able to see past what He was going through and focused on what was most important: pleasing God and winning our heart.

Every day when I look at the Cross and realize that I did not get the wrath and punishment that I deserved, I am overwhelmed with His immense love for me. This continually causes me to be so grateful for what He has done. When I thank Him from my heart for His great act of love, His presence is quick to show up, and with it peace and joy.

It is difficult to be discontented and complain when we keep the Cross before us. If He never did anything else it is enough. But He did so much more! God Himself reached down to touch every part of our life in order to bring us the healing that we need from the damage of sin. He spared nothing to connect with everything that we could ever go through in life. There is no limit to His love for us!

Chapter Seven

The Fear Factor of the Cross

And they came to an olive grove called Gethsemane, and Jesus said, "Sit here while I go and pray." He took Peter, James, and John with him, and he began to be filled with horror and deep distress. He told them, "My soul is crushed with grief to the point of death. Stay here and watch with me" (Mark 14:32-34).

Jesus lived His entire life without fear; nothing caused Him to cower, worry, or lose sleep. Wherever He went and whatever He did, He was in control and confident—up until the night before the last day of His life. When Jesus was in the Garden of Gethsemane He was confronted with the greatest fear known to man, and with great agony He conquered it so you could face yours.

Jesus Conquered Fear

Jesus knew that what He had to go through was beyond what we could ever imagine. Every sin and demon in hell would rise up against Him and destroy His flesh as a man. He knew that He would be stripped of all that He had ever had or known and would be immersed into the pit of hopelessness itself before the glaring eyes of multitudes of enemies rejoicing at His demise. Jesus, as the sacrificial lamb, could have chosen a simpler death like the swift knife that had killed the sacrifices of the law. But not only did He choose to die the slow death of crucifixion, He also purposed to suffer every pain and torment known to man that led up to it.

The greatest and worst of all that He went through was not just the physical suffering or abuse that was done to Him; it was taking on Himself the sins of the world and the full wrath of God. We cannot even begin to comprehend

63

just how horrible that must have been for Him. To fully appreciate what a great sacrifice it was, we must remember that He is God; the perfect, pure, and holy God the Word describes. Sin was His enemy. Jesus was the complete opposite of it; to Him it was the most despicable thing. Just to relate, try to think of your worst nightmare happening to you, and whatever that is, His suffering was far worse. It was the reality of all nightmares combined into one day in time and put on Him.

The greatest and worst of all that He went through was taking on Himself the sins of the world and the full wrath of God.

Now, it is difficult for us to relate to purity since every human being is tainted by sin even very early in life, but a newborn baby is about as pure as a natural man can get. Recently I had the privilege of seeing my grandson, Zander, born, and looking at that precious newborn and seeing him so new, pure, and vulnerable just melted my heart. Surely no one could harm someone so innocent! Now consider all the atrocities that have been done by man—the murders, tortures, rapes, genocides, hatred, corruption, destruction, sexual perversions, and broken promises, along with the guilt, shame, and utter hopelessness that accompany these things. Think of the Rwandan genocide, the Holocaust, September 11th, 2001, suicide bombers, and every other terror that is known to man, and picture all that being done to an innocent baby.

Even though Jesus Christ was not a baby on the day He hung on the Cross, He was even purer than a newborn in His heart. He was totally trusting and dependant on His Father in heaven. The only difference between Him and a newborn was that He was a man and had complete knowledge and understanding of what was being done to Him, and He chose to go through it out of obedience to His Father.

This was not something that He wanted to do. Everything in Him was totally repulsed by sin. Taking on all the sin of the world was the worst thing that could happen to Him.

It was His ultimate fear coming to pass, and He knew the horror and consequences of it. The scripture passage quoted at the beginning of this chapter shows how, just before His passion was to begin, the very thought of it was agonizing to Him. The Word says He was *"filled with horror and deep distress."*

To be in horror means to have intense abhorrence or a feeling of repugnance and fear toward something.[15] It was absolutely His worst nightmare, and He had overwhelming anxiety over it to the point of feeling crushed to death. Let's read those verses again:

> *And they came to an olive grove called Gethsemane, and Jesus said, "Sit here while I go and pray." He took Peter, James, and John with him, and he began to be filled with horror and deep distress. He told them, "My soul is crushed with grief to the point of death. Stay here and watch with me"* (Mark 14:32-34).

Could you imagine what He was thinking when He knew the magnitude of what He faced? Every ounce of His being must have shuddered and recoiled in terror as the nightmare of violence, perversion, addiction, and abuse paraded mockingly before Him.

It was freeing you that kept Him going.

In spite of the absolute torment that He was going through, His purity and holiness won over the temptation of His flesh. He embraced it with complete and deliberate authority, knowing fully what He faced. He had the power to stop what lay

before Him, but it was His desire to do the Father's will, and He did it because you were in His heart. It was freeing you that kept Him going. He knew that your destiny was held in the balance by His willingness to face the greatest fear of all. The gospel of John says that He chose to die for you and I; it was a voluntary act of His will. This means that the fear He faced, He was determined to conquer.

> *No one can take my life from me. I lay down my life voluntarily. For I have the right to lay it down when I want to and also the power to take it again. For my Father has given me this command* (John 10:18).

In the television show called "Fear Factor," contestants compete with one another for a monetary prize by facing their fears. To win they may have to lie in a clear box filled with snakes, poisonous spiders, or something else just as repulsive. They may be forced to eat some of the grossest things, like cockroaches or monkey brains. The whole idea of the show is to do what you fear the most. Even though these people are facing fears, on "Fear Factor" they are relatively safe as precautions are taken to keep them from serious harm. Usually being grossed or freaked out is the extent of their fear.

Some fears that we face are imaginary while others are real. There are healthy fears that keep us from doing something harmful, and there are unhealthy fears that limit us and keep us from enjoying life to the fullest.

One such fear for me was that of riding a motorcycle. As a teenager I watched in horror as two friends of mine got in a motorcycle accident and were critically injured. Two weeks later I witnessed another motorcycle accident where a young man was killed. Then less than a year later I was riding a bus when a motorcycle slid and went under the wheels of the bus I was on. My heart pounded in panic and I felt sick to my stomach as I heard it crunching under me. Fortunately the man riding on it had fallen off just in time and was not harmed. Over the next few years I had several other friends in motorcycle accidents: one lost an arm and another was left as a quadriplegic. Needless to say, I had developed a fear of them and for most of my life I would not get on one. Because I am determined to conquer my fears, I have since ridden one, and I would do so again.

> *Jesus would feel and know every agonizing part of hell on earth.*

Because Jesus wanted to feel what you feel when you are afraid, He experienced a fear far surpassing any fear you or I could ever face, and it was not imaginary. It was real, and there were no safety precautions to protect Him. He would bear the full sin of the world—the thing He despised the most—and be tortured and killed because of it.

If there ever was a pit of utter hopelessness, horror, demonic nightmares, loneliness, bondage, and fear known to man, taking on the evil of the entire world was it. What was He thinking when He knew that every perversion known to man would soon overtake Him? He must have wept for those who cannot stop the sexual sins that are ripping apart their families, and He ached for the drug addicts who riddle the bodies He created with chemicals that degrade and destroy them. He grieved at the corruption of a heart filled with greed and the aftermath of murders and rapes. He was moved to act by the heartfelt cries that screamed out in the night that no one else could hear.

He was in utter agony just thinking about the filth that He had to immerse Himself in. For all of eternity He had despised it, He had poured out His wrath on it, and everything He planned was to overcome it for us.

For he hath made him to be sin for us, who knew no sin; that we might be made the righteousness of God in him (2 Corinthians 5:21 KJV).

It is difficult to understand how He took on our sin, but He did, and He felt the effects of it when He drank the cup. He sweat great drops of blood, for this fear stressed Him beyond the natural capacity of His body. Drinking the cup of God's wrath poured out against sin was the ultimate horror. He knew that every part of His flesh would be mutilated beyond recognition, and the shame and humiliation He would be forced to endure was degrading to the uttermost. He would be spared no dignity and be left exposed and vulnerable to the worst of man. The hatred against Him would be relentless, and the thought of it drove Him for the first time in His life to beg God for another way. We can read an account of His heartfelt plea here in the gospel of Luke:

"Father, if you are willing, please take this cup of suffering away from me. Yet I want your will, not mine." Then an angel from heaven appeared and strengthened him. He prayed more fervently, and he was in such agony of spirit that his sweat fell to the ground like great drops of blood (Luke 22:42-44).

He feared the horrors of sin and the wrath of God, yet He knew that He had to take all of it. Everything that was intended for us was now His to bear. He was now the object of satisfying all of God's wrath, and He would be spared from nothing.

He Conquered Fear So We Could Too

Everything Jesus did, from start to finish, He did with us on His mind and on His heart. What was He thinking? His heart must have wept with the desire to release the chains that encumber His creation, and following His love for us He was compelled to finish what He came to do, regardless of the cost to Him.

"They are worth it!" must have crossed His mind as His nightmare glared mercilessly in His face.

When He was wrestling with God to change His mind, He saw you and all the times you've wrestled with God in your life. He heard your pleas for God to change His mind when you faced your fiery trials and saw how often you wanted to run from Him when He tried to deliver you from your wrongful deeds! He saw your hardened heart when you were faced with forgiving someone who devastated you. He felt your struggle when God told you to let go of something you desperately wanted to control. He heard your cries when He told you to stay with your spouse whom you no longer loved or to submit to an unkind authority. Everything in Him wanted to connect with you completely in your temptation to turn from God and follow your own will. I too have wrestled numerous times when God has asked me to do things that caused me to want to backslide because of my fear or pride.

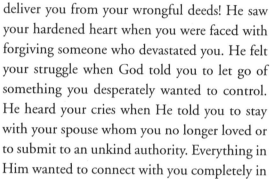

Meditating on the Cross daily is the key to having the desire to obey.

One such time was when a woman in our church deeply hurt me by slandering me behind my back. As a result, I said some things about her in response to what she'd shared against me. The individual I told ran back to this woman and relayed what I had said without informing her that it was in response to her judgment against me. I hope you get the picture. When I heard that she had been hurt by my comments, even though they were shared out of context, God told me to go to her and ask forgiveness.

Still feeling the sting of her words, I did not want to obey. I felt she owed me an apology. Yet the Holy Spirit showed me that I was not responsible for her actions, but mine. It took a lot of pride swallowing to obey, but when I did I was filled with peace and could sincerely love her.

Now that I have learned to center everything on the Cross, when I am asked to do something I don't want to do, my mind races to Jesus in the Garden sweating His blood. When I see the horror of what He was wrestling with, it completely changes my perspective. It is then I am in awe of how far He went to obey God on my behalf, and I am strengthened because my battles seem easier because of it.

Because He overcame, He enables us to overcome the fears we have when we draw our strength from Him as our example and call on His Spirit to help us.

It is important to know He faced His greatest fear so we could face ours! He wrestled with God on our behalf, and He understands what if feels like to want to seek an easy way out. We serve a God who knows what we go through and connects with us so He can truly say, "I know your fear; I've been there, and I know the agony of facing your worst nightmare."

Your fears will limit you, and it is important to be aware of what they are in order to find deliverance at the Cross. You may need to ask the Holy Spirit to show you and make a list. Consider the fears Jesus faced on the night of His betrayal. See that yours too were His, and know that He took them all.

One of my big fears was that of rejection. For years it motivated me to try and please people whom I could never satisfy. He showed me that I had to face the memories of inferiority from my childhood—memories that would stop me in my tracks—along with my fear of failure and surrender it all to the Cross. This is a necessary step to removing the negative limitations in our lives so that we can become productive for the kingdom and reach the lost.

Is your fear worse than having all the guilt, shame, and pain of every sin in the whole world put on you? Is it worse than facing the wrath of God? Jesus loved you enough to go through the worst fear to make sure that your fears were conquered by His. Your fears are very real, but you don't have to face them alone. He will help you because of the magnitude of what He faced to set you free to live a life of faith.

Jesus Identified With Our Feelings

Jesus also faced the emotions that accompany the consequences of our sin. Along with taking our sin and the wrath of God, Jesus also feared the hopeless feelings of guilt and shame that follow sin. He felt the debilitating consequences of oppression and how our sin makes us feel. When I sinned, I was left with overwhelming shame and guilt, to the point I wanted to crawl under a rock and disappear. We all can think of things that we are ashamed of, and many of us allow those things to keep us in bondage as we continually beat ourselves up with the guilt and condemnation that follow. *Sin always has torment.*

Never before had Jesus felt the feelings of shame and worthlessness because He had never blown it. But He knew that you had, and He reached out and took yours.

He suffered and died so that we would be free from the torment of sin.

He chose to feel the self-hatred and the guilt that torment our minds. He had to feel what it does to our self-worth and experience how it robs us of our identity. He faced every paralyzing feeling of guilt, shame, and destruction that accompany us when we do something we despise. The horror of all these detrimental feelings of sin have been utterly and completely for all eternity taken for us so that we could be free from their grip.

Every time we blow it, we need to remember that Jesus faced His fear and took our sin so that we could be free of its torment and obey God like He did. Second Timothy says that the Spirit of Christ will give us the power to face our fears. Overcoming does not mean that we will not still feel fear, but that we will simply not give in to it.

For God has not given us a spirit of fear and timidity, but of power, love, and self-discipline (2 Timothy 1:7).

If you are tormented by the weight of your sin and burdened with guilt and shame, somehow you have missed the purpose of the Cross and its message of love.

Fear is the opposite of faith, and the just shall live by faith. We must see fear as an enemy and refuse to allow it to control our decisions. Whether it is the fear of man, fear of failure, fear of rejection, or fear of pain or loss, we must lay it all down at the Cross. Only then will we be truly free.

Chapter Eight

Dying for the Cross

*So then, since Christ suffered physical pain, you must arm yourselves with
the same attitude he had, and be ready to suffer, too. For if you are willing to suffer for Christ, you have decided to stop sinning (1 Peter 4:1).*

I remember when, shortly after I began to study the Cross and grasp its
incredible meaning, I was so overwhelmed with His love that I pondered
what it would be like to be persecuted and die for Him as He had done for
me. All my Christian life I had wondered what I would do if I ever faced true
persecution because of my faith.

Like anyone, I dreaded the thought of jail, torture, or death. Even the rejection I'd had from witnessing had caused some fear in me, and I never could understand how someone could actually rejoice when persecution came. I recalled days
of depression and feeling sorry for myself when a friend avoided me after I had
shared my faith with her. I had prayed I would never have to face real persecution
that would cost me more than a hurt ego. Jesus talked a lot about persecution, and
in the gospel of Matthew He even told us to be happy and glad about it!

*God blesses those who are persecuted because they live for God, for the
Kingdom of Heaven is theirs. God blesses you when you are mocked and
persecuted and lied about because you are my followers. Be happy about it!
Be very glad! For a great reward awaits you in heaven. And remember, the
ancient prophets were persecuted, too (Matthew 5:10-12).*

It Is a Joy to Suffer for Him

Like you, I don't like pain. I enjoy my comforts, and the thought of leaving my beautiful home and warm, king-sized bed for a jail cell and hard cot is
very unappealing to my flesh.

I had always rationalized that God would give me the grace if persecution came, and hopefully I would do the right thing. However, I seriously doubted my bravery. Since the Cross has been made so real to me, I now hope I get to suffer real persecution. Not that it is something I would look forward to or would try to bring on myself, but it would be such an honor to suffer for Him. I love Him so much that to identify with His suffering would make me more like Him.

If you are willing to suffer for Christ, you have decided to stop sinning!

Because of the Cross, becoming like Him is now a greater desire than that of having pleasure and comfort. I love Him so much that to suffer persecution for Him seems more like a privilege than a curse. The disciples felt the same way.

The apostles left the high council rejoicing that God had counted them worthy to suffer dishonor for the name of Jesus (Acts 5:41).

As we truly understand all that the Cross represents, as the early church did, suffering becomes a blessing to embrace. Unfortunately, that thought is a far cry from much of the North American church. When it comes to suffering, we all need to change our hearts. Only a life centered on the Cross of Christ is able to embrace this with true heartfelt thankfulness. That has been a gift of the Cross to me that has been incredibly freeing.

The Word explains the willingness to suffer in 1 Peter:

So then, since Christ suffered physical pain, you must arm yourselves with the same attitude he had, and be ready to suffer, too. For if you are willing to suffer for Christ, you have decided to stop sinning (1 Peter 4:1).

Wow! When we are *"willing to suffer,"* we have decided to stop sinning. That is so powerful! It also means that if we are not willing to suffer, we have *not* decided to stop sinning.

The day after I told God and truly meant it from my heart that I would be honored to die a martyr's death, He showed me the scripture above. I had never noticed it before, but I realized this is the goal of His desire for us.

Have I stopped sinning? Only when I keep my focus on the work of the Cross.

We can relate everything we go through to the Cross. Every step of Jesus' passion had a purpose that relates to our life, and He covered it all.

There are some awesome scriptures on suffering that few Christians put up on their fridge, but they are written for those who truly understand the work of the Cross. When we only seek God's blessings, we tend to explain away these verses and make God after our own image. I believe that God promises us blessings, but He also promises us persecution. The blessings often follow suffering and persecution.

Like the law of giving and receiving, if you don't give (that's the suffering part), you don't receive. The believer who is centered on the Cross will embrace persecution if it comes, not by running from it or trying to confess it away, but by actually identifying with Christ in it.

I'm not saying it would be easy. Whenever our flesh has to die to anything, there is a battle. But that battle has been won at the Cross. Some believers think that Jesus suffered so we wouldn't have to, and I would like to think that, but the Word says different. The suffering we have been set free from is the wrath of God and the effect of the curse of the law because of our sin. *In Christ we are no longer under the curse.* But as long as we are on earth, the Word guarantees suffering because we live in a world where many people are hostile against God.

This verse in 2 Corinthians promises us that the more we suffer for Christ, the more He comforts us!

You can be sure that the more we suffer for Christ, the more God will shower us with his comfort through Christ (2 Corinthians 1:5).

This means He comforts us with His presence and glory! If suffering brings more of His presence, then it can't be all that bad. I must stress that this kind of suffering is what we go through *for Him,* not the kind that is incurred from our poor decisions and that we inflict on ourselves.

Self-Inflicted Suffering

An example of this type of suffering is when believers marry someone whom their authorities and friends advised them not to. Now they are suffering in a bad marriage with someone who is not easy to get along with. That suffering was self-induced by their disobedience and lack of trust in those whom God had in their lives to advise them. That does not mean you walk out of a difficult marriage. You made a vow to your own hurt, and you must learn from the Cross how to love the unlovable. Unless your life or that of your children are threatened, or your spouse broke your marriage vow by ongoing infidelity or desertion, you are bound to it. Even if you have broken marriage vows because of your own sin, the Cross also offers forgiveness and redemption. Nevertheless, there still may be consequences from man.

As a pastor's wife, I've seen many believers do things in the name of the Lord when they really were being led by their flesh. I recall one young man who witnessed nonstop at work and rarely did the job he was paid to do. He was reprimanded and finally fired for his lack of work ethics, and he went around claiming he had been persecuted for the Gospel.

Many believers suffer not for the cause of Christ, but because of their wrong choices, and they so lack in character that they get mad at God and blame Him for their self-induced problems. Some even backslide because of their lack of maturity, full of misdirected anger at God. We can read about this in the gospel of Matthew when Jesus shared on the sower sowing the seed of the Word:

> *The rocky soil represents those who hear the message and receive it with joy. But like young plants in such soil, their roots don't go very deep. At first they get along fine, but they wilt as soon as they have problems or are persecuted because they believe the word* (Matthew 13:20-21).

If we do not understand that the work of the Cross was to help us face our fears, and even embrace persecution and suffering, we will tend to give up easily.

Dying to Self

We are strengthened when we focus every aspect of our lives on Jesus' passion. Seeing how He suffered can give us the power we need to overcome whatever we are facing. If we do not make it a practice to align what we go through with the work of the Cross, we can easily fall away from our faith or lose our first love. It wasn't until I made the Cross a daily part of my life that I could see how persecution could be a blessing for me spiritually. When we surrender everything to the Cross, God will teach us many things about dying to self, and that will promote our spiritual growth and deepen our love walk even if we created the mess we are in. The Cross turns our mistakes into blessings when we trust in its power to do so. The more we die to the flesh, the more we will experience the mighty power of God.

> *As a result, I can really know Christ and experience the mighty power that raised him from the dead. I can learn what it means to suffer with him, sharing in his death* (Philippians 3:10).

Real suffering for Him produces an experience of His mighty power that can come no other way. Just as we go through labor pains to bring forth a new life, when processed through the Cross pain will always produce life in us. We all want the power, but we don't want to pay the price. Suffering for Him is a big flesh killer, and our flesh does not want to die. However, it is the biggest hindrance that keeps us from the amazing peace and presence of God that we say we want.

The blessings follow as we grow in His character and love.

Let me clarify something here: The suffering I am speaking of is obeying God's will over our own, as well as the persecution that may follow obedience to Him. I do not believe that God wants to harm us, but to bless us. However, His priority is not to bless us as much as it is to see us develop Godly character.

It is not His will that we be sick and broke and continually beat ourselves up with thoughts of defeat and failure. Because we live in a world that is under a curse and we have to deal with our flesh, suffering happens. I firmly believe that God desires to meet our needs and heal us, but at times He can't because our flesh gets in the way. We may want the glory, but we fail to realize that the real glory is accompanied by suffering, which is the death of our flesh. Our flesh dies through persecution or by self-denial of the things that it lusts after. I am not speaking of extreme religious self-denial that literally deprives oneself of all comforts and pleasures, purposely inflicting pain and suffering, but of that which comes from doing what is right.

In countries like China, during the worst persecution of the last half of the twentieth century, the church grew from 700,000 believers to 70,000,000 believers. When the flesh is out of the way, God can truly move supernaturally. The church in China suffered greatly, and many of the pastors were put in jail for 25 years or more. Some even died there. Their families were left without income, but the church came through and helped them. In some cases even angels provided for them supernaturally. The church acts more like Jesus Christ in the height of its suffering than it does in the lap of luxury. Right now the believers in China are training over 100,000 men and woman to go across the Middle East and witness to the Moslem nations, and they are preparing themselves on how to survive in prison, suffer torture, and die for their faith.[16]

In the book of Hebrews we read that we are to identify with the body of Christ that suffers for Him. I have actually heard Christians say that those who suffer are not in faith. That is the complete opposite of what the Cross teaches.

We are in a spiritual war, and we need to begin to act like soldiers in God's army. His soldiers fight with weapons of love and peace and are willing to give up a lot to help and protect one another. They train hard and leave their comforts behind, taking risks and boldly facing their enemies for the cause of Christ.

The book of Hebrews also tells us to share in each other's sufferings:

Don't forget about those in prison. Suffer with them as though you were there yourself. Share the sorrow of those being mistreated, as though you feel their pain in your own bodies (Hebrews 13:3).

Isn't that exactly what Jesus did? Out of love for us, He decided to share in our pain. Even if we are not suffering severe persecutions, we should be conscious of those who are. The Word tells us that we should suffer with them, and that means we have a responsibility to help their families, visit them, take care of their homes, and whatever else we can do to ease their trouble. Colossians says it well:

I am glad when I suffer for you in my body, for I am completing what remains of Christ's sufferings for his body, the church (Colossians 1:24).

The apostle Paul was glad to suffer for the sake of the church. He remembered his focus and concentrated on and preached the Cross of Jesus Christ only. He completely related to it and experienced it as the very wisdom and power of God. He knew this message was foolishness to the world, yet he saw suffering as part of the Cross and of the development of becoming more like Christ. The Cross is a message of dying to self and loving others regardless of how you are treated. In 1 Timothy it says they worked hard and suffered much to spread the Gospel:

We work hard and suffer much in order that people will believe the truth, for our hope is in the living God, who is the Savior of all people, and particularly of those who believe (1 Timothy 4:10).

Suffering Is Not an Option

It is only with our willingness to suffer that we can accomplish the task that God has given us to win a lost and dying world. At times the cost is great. In North America, much of the church is often focused on how to believe for bigger and better for self rather than sacrificing to build the kingdom. Some even get mad if the service is ten minutes too long, or if a second offering is taken. We have had people get angry because they were asked to pick someone up and drive the person to church, or worse yet, give their seat away to a visitor. Offense can come easily to those who are not centered on the Cross, but to those who are, sacrifice and suffering for Him is a privilege and an honor. In fact, in 2 Timothy it says *we will suffer persecution if we live a Godly life.*

Yes, and everyone who wants to live a godly life in Christ Jesus will suffer persecution (2 Timothy 3:12).

This does not sound like it is an option; rather, it is a statement of fact. It is not always the major persecution and becoming a martyr that we have to endure; oftentimes it is the daily price we pay when we have to say no and our flesh is crying yes. Our selfishness thinks nothing of people going to hell, but we suffer when we give up our time and money to rescue them.

We suffer when we have to keep our mouth shut when it screams to gossip, or when we have to be kind to someone we want to hurt. Whether it is loving the unlovable or submitting when we disagree, it's the fear of dying daily that we must face and overcome. The fears of being taken for granted or taken advantage of are real. Our fears of rejection and missing out on something can be difficult to ignore, but only the Cross has the power to give us the desire to suffer for Him by refusing to give in to our self-seeking flesh.

Suffering loves the unlovable, gives what one wants to keep, and focuses on someone else instead of one's self. It is the laying down of our life for another.

We can read in the book of Hebrews that Jesus set the example for us. It was by the things that He suffered that He learned the obedience that qualified Him to be our High Priest and source of eternal salvation.

> *So even though Jesus was God's Son, he learned obedience from the things he suffered. In this way, God qualified him as a perfect High Priest, and he became the source of eternal salvation for all those who obey him* (Hebrews 5:8-9).

Suffering actually helps us see our true identity. Many in the body of Christ are trying to *become* something when the truth is we already *are* something. The more our flesh dies, the more we will see and know who we are, and with His mind-set we will be able to overcome whatever suffering we face. I have seen too many Christians backslide because the God in their image was a Santa Claus, a "bless me only" God, and when trials came they lacked the character to stand firm in their faith.

Only the Cross has the power to give us the desire to suffer for Him.

The blessings are always a byproduct of serving Him faithfully, not something we should seek after. I have learned that we will never be disappointed or moved from our faith if we pursue the work we are called to do and leave the blessings up to Him. It is a fact that many ministers leave the ministry and some even their faith because they failed to understand the full message of the Cross, which resulted in their false expectations of God. As believers we should live to please our heavenly Father, as that is our purpose. It was what motivated Jesus to do all that He did.

In 1 Peter the Word tells us to be patient when we suffer:

> *Of course, you get no credit for being patient if you are beaten for doing wrong. But if you suffer for doing right and are patient beneath the blows, God is pleased with you* (1 Peter 2:20).

Being patient in this verse means enduring pain and annoyance with peace and calmness. It also means to wait for the outcome of something to come to pass. It also says that God is pleased with us when we suffer patiently, not because He likes to see us suffer, but because He knows that when we suffer, we become more like Christ in our character. He also knows the blessings and the glory that will be released because of it. That is our goal, and, as with Christ, the rewards for the suffering will be beyond our wildest dreams.

Could you imagine how pleased God was with His Son when He chose the path of suffering that He had to endure? He saw past the suffering to the resurrection and all that would come because of it. He could see every believer who would ever enter into His kingdom because of Christ's willingness to lay down His life. As with Him, much fruit is produced when we die to self too. If only we could see the glory that awaits us! When we suffer for doing right, so much is accomplished in God's kingdom that has eternal benefits.

> *It was Jesus' willingness to go through the suffering that released His resurrection power.*

It takes faith to please God, and if suffering pleases Him, then it takes greater faith to suffer for Him than it does to believe for His blessings. This is not a message our flesh wants to hear, but if we want great faith, we must choose to suffer for Him when the opportunity presents itself. Keeping our eyes on the Cross will always help develop this mind-set in us.

Suffering is part of our calling in these last days. It is not something to shrink from. It will define the true soldiers of the Cross from those who are deceived and only want to cater to the whims of their flesh. This verse in Revelation reveals the promise to those who do suffer:

> *Don't be afraid of what you are about to suffer. The Devil will throw some of you into prison and put you to the test. You will be persecuted for "ten days." Remain faithful even when facing death, and I will give you the crown of life* (Revelation 2:10).

We will be given the crown of life! When we suffer persecution for doing what is right, we release His Spirit in us to do powerful things. He is asking us to have the same attitude He had and to be willing to suffer and see it as He did. A Cross-centered life sees it as an honor to suffer for Him who gave us everything.

His wrestling in the Garden was His ultimate test of facing His fear, and He won the battle of dying to His flesh so that I could win mine. Whenever I am faced with something that would overtake me by fear, I think of His night of darkness and how He made a way for my victory! He didn't run but pressed on to do God's will, and that shows me I can do the same.

Fears come up often, and when they do we must gaze on the beginning of His passion, when He cried out to God to change His mind and begged for another way. But then He said, "Not My will, but Your will be done" (Mark 14:36).

Let His cry be yours.

Chapter Nine

The Cross and Your Betrayal

But even as he said this, a mob approached, led by Judas, one of his twelve disciples. Judas walked over to Jesus and greeted him with a kiss. But Jesus said, "Judas, how can you betray me, the Son of Man, with a kiss?" (Luke 22:47-48)

Jesus did not have to go through betrayal to redeem us! Rather, He allowed Himself to feel the pain of incredible betrayal so that He could completely relate to ours as a human being.

We have a God who loves us enough that He chose to connect with us in our pain on every level.

Jesus wanted to deal fully with the sin of betrayal, as all of us have to deal with it. We all have betrayed God, and whether we have been hurt by this sin or hurt others, He showed us how to overcome it when He went through His.

The Pain of Betrayal

To be betrayed, you have to have first trusted. To trust is to put your faith in someone, believing that he or she will not hurt you. Betrayal means "to commit treason," "to give over to an enemy," "to lead astray and deceive," "to cheat on," and to "violate one's trust."[17] Betrayal comes when you are totally dependant on someone and that person purposes to do you harm in some way.

Obviously there are different degrees of betrayal, depending on how much the one betrayed suffers from the act. However, every one of us has experienced it in one form or another, and often we are left with the scars that never seem to fully go away. Betrayal has the ability to permanently damage our heart and emotions, and therefore affect our future. Many marriages are destroyed because of a present or past betrayal. When a person has trouble trusting, it will hinder healthy development in a potentially good relationship. As a leader in the church, I frequently hear the tragic stories of betrayal when a spouse leaves his or her covenant partner for another.

Recently a handsome young man came into my office and poured out his heart to me. He had been betrayed. I felt his pain as he revealed to me, with tears in his eyes, the devastating story of his wife's infidelity. He had come home early from work and caught her with another man, and now his marriage was over. She had made her decision and had no desire to end the affair.

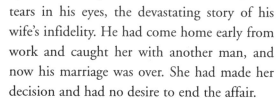

Betrayal is one of the most difficult, humiliating, and demoralizing traumas that someone can face.

I knew the cascading effect this would have on their children, parents, and close friends. The number of people who would feel betrayed and hurt by this was far greater than just the two of them. I knew the days, weeks, and months of heartfelt tears that would be shed from this tragedy. The weeping in the darkness of night on tear-soaked pillows, the wails of loneliness and powerlessness of loss that rips one apart in seemingly unending torment. I had heard stories like his too often…broken hearts, broken promises, love gone wrong; children betrayed by those who were supposed to protect and provide for them.

Betrayal is one of the most difficult, humiliating, and demoralizing traumas that someone can face, and it comes in many forms. I thought of one of our associate pastors whose mother on her deathbed confessed to him that his father was really a neighbor and not the man she was married to and had raised him as his own. Rick and I had felt betrayal when two of our children were molested—one by a babysitter and one by a trusted relative. The faces of numerous women I knew who had been violated by a dad or close family member, and the children left to struggle without both parents, loomed before me. The list goes on.

Years ago a friend of mine tried to take her life because of a betrayal by her boyfriend, and when I went to visit her in the psychiatric ward I discovered that many of the patients were there because of their inability to cope with the pain of betrayal. I could relate to this feeling as I recalled a time years ago when as a teenager I fell in love for the first time and then found out a few weeks later that my heartthrob had left me for someone else. At the time I thought my life was over. I felt like I was garbage to be discarded, and the feelings of low self-worth overwhelmed me. My heart was broken, and I cried for days. My identity, which was already shattered from a childhood of desertion and betrayal, once more was stomped upon and left for dead. So many teens today make serious life-threatening decisions because of the betrayal of someone they trusted, many committing suicide.

As much as we all have been victims to some form of betrayal, we also all have betrayed someone who trusted us. Children break the trust of their parents; we share a secret of a close friend; we lie to our spouses; or perhaps we leave a loved one for someone else. The abused of yesterday are often the abusers of today as sin repeats itself.

I knew the struggle of anger and bitterness that was going to bombard the mind of this young man who bared his heart to me. He had a battle ahead of him, and I knew full well how important it was that he overcome the enemy that would try to use this injustice to destroy his faith in God. The deep wounds of betrayal tug on every ounce of anger and revenge that lurks within us. The desire to kill does not seem so unreasonable when betrayed—or if not to kill, at least to take revenge wherever possible. "I'll get even and pay you back! You hurt me, so I'll hurt you!" is often the cry of a broken heart.

I knew I had to steer this broken man to the Cross, for there lay his only hope of coming through this hurt as unscathed as possible. He needed a renewed hope that God had a plan and was not done with him. God was after his broken heart, and He knew how to win it.

Give Thanks

In our betrayal it is important to think of the communion table. It is a sacred act of remembering and honoring the work of the Cross, and the scripture in 1 Corinthians that we commonly use for communion is so appropriate for overcoming betrayal:

For this is what the Lord himself said, and I pass it on to you just as I received it. On the night when he was betrayed, the Lord Jesus took a loaf of bread, and when he had given thanks, he broke it and said, "This is my body, which is given for you. Do this in remembrance of me." In the same way, he took the cup of wine after supper, saying, "This cup is the new covenant between God and you, sealed by the shedding of my blood. Do this in remembrance of me as often as you drink it." For every time you eat this bread and drink this cup, you are announcing the Lord's death until he comes again (1 Corinthians 11:23-26).

These verses talk about what Jesus did the night that He was betrayed. He took the bread, which represented His body, and He *gave thanks*.

Giving thanks to His heavenly Father was how Jesus handled betrayal!

When Jesus broke bread with the disciples on the night of His betrayal, He knew what was going to happen. It was obviously on His mind when He told them about it two days before.

As you know, the Passover celebration begins in two days, and I, the Son of Man, will be betrayed and crucified (Matthew 26:2).

Jesus was aware of the betrayal; He was in full knowledge of the magnitude of it. He knew that it would end up costing Him His life. On the night it came to pass, He turned to look into the face of His Father and give thanks. He loved His betrayer; if He hadn't, it would not have wounded Him so deeply. Jesus had multitudes that followed Him; thousands of men and women hung on every word He said. People thronged to get close to Him wherever He went. But He had chosen 12 to be His closest friends. Only they would be in His inner circle, the group with whom He would share the secrets of His kingdom. They were the only ones who would know Him more than all other humans. Judas Iscariot was one of them. Jesus even trusted him to take care of the money, and He sat beside him at His table at the last supper and washed his feet.

The Price of a Slave

In Matthew 26:6-13 we are told of the final thing Jesus did that upset Judas. Betrayers will always have a reason to justify their betrayal, and Judas had his.

Judas chose to betray Jesus immediately after he disagreed with something that Jesus had allowed. Jesus was visiting the home of Simon, a man He had healed of leprosy, when a woman came in and poured expensive perfume over Jesus because of her love for Him. Judas was upset at the waste of money, claiming it should have been sold and the money given to the poor. But Jesus honored her for her act of love, and Judas despised Him for it. Jesus didn't meet up to Judas' expectations because of evil in his heart. It was immediately after this that he went to the leading priests and sold Him out, as we can read in the following text:

> *Then Judas Iscariot, one of the twelve disciples, went to the leading priests and asked, "How much will you pay me to betray Jesus to you?" And they gave him thirty pieces of silver. From that time on, Judas began looking for the right time and place to betray Jesus* (Matthew 26:14-16).

What is the price tag *we* put on God? What are we willing to trade Him for?

The 30 pieces of silver was very significant; it revealed Judas' heart of greed. He had obviously put a price on his friend, and the sin in him was willing to exchange his friendship for that amount. We must ask ourselves, what is the price tag *we* put on God? What are we willing to trade Him for? Is it our money or our sports? Perhaps it is another person, success, or even power.

Greed and selfishness are usually the root of a betrayer's heart as he or she thinks of self at the expense of another. Jesus was worth the amount of a slave to Judas, the friend of Jesus. Thirty pieces of silver was the amount that it cost to replace a slave, as Exodus records:

> *But if the bull gores a slave, either male or female, the slave's owner is to be given thirty silver coins in payment, and the bull must be stoned* (Exodus 21:32).

Under the Levitical law, 30 pieces of silver is what you owed a slave owner if you harmed or killed his slave. So not only was Jesus betrayed by an act that would cause Him suffering greater than that of any other man, but He also was devalued by one He had trusted with the secrets of His kingdom and sold for the price of replacing a slave. What an insult! This was the betrayal of all time. The Messiah, the Creator, the Living Word of God, the One who holds all things together, sold for the value of a slave. Why?

Because man had fallen into the slavery of sin, we were slaves to betrayal, slaves to its pain, and slaves to the curse. Jesus was sold for the price of a slave to redeem us from a lifetime of slavery. Judas was His friend, someone He trusted, and it must have been very painful to realize His worth to him was so little. What did Jesus think to be betrayed for the price of a slave? I am sure He pushed past His hurt and thought of the slavery of sin that held us in bondage. He thought of the betrayals we would face that would cause us great bitterness and anger, keeping us from His plan for our lives. His heart was broken for every crushed person who felt the sting of violated trust, and He was focused on experiencing His betrayal to keep you from the destructive effects of yours. But His humiliation didn't end with the price tag that revealed His worth to Judas; that man even went a step further in this eternal act of betrayal. Luke records:

> But even as he said this, a mob approached, led by Judas, one of his twelve disciples. Judas walked over to Jesus and greeted him with a kiss. But Jesus said, "Judas, how can you betray me, the Son of Man, with a kiss?" (Luke 22:47-48)

Jesus seemed surprised that Judas would actually betray Him with a kiss. A kiss was an expression of respect and friendship. It meant giving high regard to someone. It was an act of trust. What was He feeling to be betrayed with such an act of endearment? He seemed perplexed and hurt as He spoke these wounded words to Judas: *"How can you betray me, the Son of Man, with a kiss?"*

Jesus was amazed at the level of betrayal Judas had stooped to. He obviously wasn't expecting that, and I'm sure that it deepened the wound that He felt by the broken trust He was experiencing from His friend. He was feeling the pain you had when you gave your heart to someone who broke it. He cried with you because He knew the humiliation and degradation of your rejection.

He is love, and Jesus loved Judas with the purest love possible. The same pain and rejection you feel in the moment of betrayal from someone you love was as real to Him as yours is to you. He knows how you felt when your husband walked out on you. He knows the pain of your broken promise, the overwhelming hopelessness of finding your wife with another lover. He feels the pain of your betrayal, the secret that was told, the knife in the back—however it came and by whoever it came.

God warns us that humans cannot always be trusted. That is why it is so important that He have our heart above anyone else. Only then can we really be safe from the destruction of betrayal when it comes our way. God knows the human heart. We can read this account in the gospel of John where Jesus knew that people could turn on Him in a minute. Jesus knew that betrayal was a part of the human heart that He had to conquer, and to conquer it He had to go through it.

> *Because of the miraculous signs he did in Jerusalem at the Passover cele-*
> *bration, many people were convinced that he was indeed the Messiah. But*
> *Jesus didn't trust them, because he knew what people were really like. No*
> *one needed to tell him about human nature* (John 2:23-25).

No one needed to tell Him about the human heart. He knew full well how those who are with you today could be your ene-mies tomorrow. How quickly the heart can turn!

Overcoming Betrayal

How do we overcome our betrayal? Just as He handled His: by keeping our eyes on the presence of the Father and giving thanks, then choosing to love and sacrifice self, extending forgiveness for all who betray us. We handle it

We must run to the Cross and lay down our betrayal, looking at His.

by thinking of the pain in those who have hurt us and realizing that they too have suffered.

If Jesus could forgive and continue to worship God in His deepest pain, we can too. Can we look at His betrayal and draw strength from His? Can we trust Him that He will bring glory from ours as His did? He faced His betray-al so that we could ours and because He loves us more than any human ever could. When I am betrayed, I look at His and know that I too can overcome. It helps me when I think about His broken heart and connect with His pain as He does ours. We are not alone; we are with this incredible God of ours who shows us how much He truly cares.

Do you see past the betrayal Judas put Him through and see the pain He bore because of your betrayals to Him? This is how real healing can flood into your heart. Until we all recognize that we are just as guilty, we will cling to our pain. Who have you deceived? Who trusted you with their heart, only to have it hurt?

Jesus did not take on betrayal just to feel your pain, but also to show you the immense magnitude of death betrayal can bring to another. He knew that if you understand that broken hearts are from the sin of us all, He can heal yours when you take responsibility for that which you have inflicted on others. That is how He heals yours and mine.

It takes great humility to see past your pain and weep for those whose hearts you broke.

Can you surrender your betrayal to Him and give thanks? We must call out for love and mercy for those who broke our heart just as we want it from those we have hurt.

The consequences of being the betrayer also can be devastating. Many an unfaithful spouse has regretted the day of his or her infidelity. If people could turn back the clock, they would. The price was higher than they thought. Just like Judas, they regretted the day they fell into the trap of betraying another. It is not easy to regain lost integrity and honor.

Judas could not live with his act of betrayal. Maybe you can, but your heart has hardened, or you've justified it with excuses. Perhaps this whole betrayal thing, whatever side of it you're on, has made you bitter and angry. Maybe you've even taken it out on God, blaming Him for your pain.

Remember, Judas wasn't Jesus' first betrayal by man—Adam and Eve were. All who backslide betray Him, and it breaks His heart every time we allow something else to take His rightful place in our heart. He is our Creator; He is the true lover of our soul who will never leave or forsake us. Nothing can separate us from His love, and yet how often do we discard Him as though He means nothing to us?

Betrayal is the opposite of the character and nature of God. It is the complete opposite of who He is.

He is trustworthy. He cannot lie, and He will not betray you. To betray you have to lie, and it is impossible for God to lie.

So God has given us both his promise and his oath. These two things are unchangeable because it is impossible for God to lie. Therefore, we who have fled to him for refuge can take new courage, for we can hold on to his promise with confidence (Hebrews 6:18).

When our hearts are broken, we can go to His Cross and know that somewhere in the midst of the trial He will come through for us. He went through His betrayal to show us that in spite of how horrible His was, God brought resurrection life because of it. How can we look at the Cross and continue to blame God for those who betrayed us? He hates betrayal with a passion, and He came to destroy its destructive power.

His willingness to go through it proved He will never fail us, as we can read in 1 Peter:

So if you are suffering according to God's will, keep on doing what is right, and trust yourself to the God who made you, for he will never fail you (1 Peter 4:19).

He despises the pain of broken hearts and the destruction of a person's worth. Looking at the Cross helps us see His incredible love for us that was willing to deal with betrayal by going through it Himself. As a human He submitted Himself to God in His darkest hour, knowing what the enemy meant for evil God would turn around for good. With God we cannot lose, but we must guard our heart in our betrayals and walk in love and forgiveness as He did.

When betrayal rips apart your heart, look to Him on the night that He was betrayed and give thanks.

Chapter Ten

Abandonment of the Cross

Then Jesus said to the crowd, "Am I some dangerous criminal, that you have come armed with swords and clubs to arrest me? Why didn't you arrest me in the Temple? I was there teaching every day. But this is all happening to fulfill the words of the prophets as recorded in the Scriptures." At that point, all the disciples deserted him and fled (Matthew 26:55-56).

Jesus knew fully all the suffering that awaited Him as He was arrested in the Garden. The knowledge that His Spirit would always be with us motivated Him to submit to the atrocities He was born for. He faced His abandonment with a passionate desire for our heart to be united with His. He saw and felt our hurts with every heartbeat within Him, longing to deliver us.

Abandonment is when the person you trust completely disappears from your life, cutting off ties with you altogether, as though you meant nothing to them; it is to withdraw support and help in spite of duty, allegiance, or responsibility.[18] When people abandon others, they desert them—often when they are most needed. This is what happened to Jesus.

Jesus Was Abandoned

When He was about to face the most difficult time of His life, those He depended on deserted Him, leaving Him to His fate. In His greatest time of need, His closest followers left Him. His disciples had seen Him as a man of great authority and power, and some had even caught the revelation of who He really was. He possessed incredible wisdom and strength, and they had never seen Him show weakness because there was none to be found. He took authority over the weather, multiplied food, and commanded demons to leave their victims. He had healed the sick and raised the dead and time after time they

91

had been in awe and amazement at what He did and said. Now in the Garden they saw Him differently.

He was stressed beyond measure, wrestling with fear, and pleading for their support in prayer. This man who was the Son of God, full of power, now needed them. They had no idea what He was facing, even though He had repeatedly told them. Their commitment to Him was summed up in the fact that they fled, leaving Him to fend for Himself. Let's read again about the night of His arrest:

Jesus went through abandonment and denial for us, and He didn't have to.

> *Then Jesus said to the crowd, "Am I some dangerous criminal, that you have come armed with swords and clubs to arrest me? Why didn't you arrest me in the Temple? I was there teaching every day. But this is all happening to fulfill the words of the prophets as recorded in the Scriptures." At that point, all the disciples deserted him and fled* (Matthew 26:55-56).

Jesus went through abandonment and denial for us, and He didn't have to. Every step of His passion was planned to touch our pain on every level and win our soul. He came to heal our deep hurts and to forgive us for causing pain in others.

Some of you have been stung deeply by this demoralizing sin. Maybe a parent left you, and you sting with the heartache from someone who was supposed to take care of you. Perhaps you are a young mother abandoned by the father of your children and left to fend for yourself and them. Jesus chose to go through His abandonment to touch the gnawing pain of your heart and let you know that there is a better day for you.

He suffered complete abandonment as He was left alone to face His greatest fear. They all left Him, running for their lives while He was dragged to the illegal trial that awaited Him. He had laughed with them, taught them, traveled with them, and blessed them in countless ways, and now they were gone. Having Jesus, the perfect man, for a close friend had to have been an incredible experience, as He was completely real, loving, and unselfish.

He had truly loved them and trusted them with the secrets of His heart. He valued their friendship, and, like any human, His need for human connection was real. How did He feel when their fear and concern for themselves surfaced and they abandoned His needs when the true test came? What did He think when His best friends couldn't trust in His destiny even after He had told them over and over that He must die, but would rise again? Was He hoping that the warnings of His fate would keep at least one of them by His side? Did He know deep down that what He faced, He faced completely alone?

As painful as desertion can be, most of us have not had everyone in our life take off and leave us when we are in trouble. I've seen even the worst of criminals have a few supporters still at their side.

When I look over my life and think of abandonment, one of the most painful memories for me was the last night I saw my father. I was only a child, but that day remains vivid in my mind as my brother, sister, and I huddled behind a door and watched our parents fight. We felt helpless and afraid, and something told us this was different from the years of abuse my mother had been subjected to. Before we knew it, the police came and my father was forced to leave. I was only five years old that night, and I knew a part of my childhood was gone forever. I didn't see him again until I was an adult. As I grew up I never even heard from him, nor did he assist my mother financially in our upbringing.

The pain of being abandoned by a father was detrimental to everything I felt and believed about myself. I thought that I wasn't worth anything to him, and that reality crippled my esteem. Seeing other children with their dads made me long desperately for one who loved me. I never experienced the secure love of a father holding me on his lap and letting me know that I was his princess. Nor did I have the security of a home that revealed the love of a God who cared. The years that followed were difficult for my mom, who sacrificed greatly to meet our needs. Back in the 1950's, raising three young children alone was not common and there was little help available.

Only God knows how many children have been abandoned by a messed-up parent. I remember crying myself to sleep many nights wondering, why me? The helplessness of children being subjected to the sins of their parents is deeply harmful to their development, and many, like me, grow up believing that they are damaged goods. Children cannot separate the abandonment of their caregivers from their own self-worth. They often believe they were left because something is wrong with them, that somehow they had something to do with it.

Abandonment comes in many ways, whether left by a lover or a friend or just left out of an important event. It is belittling and can leave you feeling inferior and building thick walls of protection around your heart. Just as in betrayal, it can leave lifelong scars. For years, because of the lack of a father's love in my childhood, I struggled with receiving, with absolute confidence, the love of God. My father robbed me of my childhood, and because of the issues in his life he is still in bondage. Today I have reestablished my relationship with him, and my heart longs for his deliverance. I thank God that I now have the love of a Father, but it came through Jesus touching my heart from the abandonment that He too went through. When He was left by all His friends at His arrest, He too felt the total desolation of being alone with no support.

From Abandonment to Denial

But then, to add insult to injury, after His abandonment came the denial of one of His closest friends. Peter was one of the three men Jesus spent the most time with. He was allowed even more privileges in the secrets of the kingdom; he had witnessed the transfiguration and had been given the revelation that Jesus was the Messiah, the Son of the living God. When Jesus went to the home of Jairus to heal his daughter, He allowed only three people to go with Him, and Peter was one of them. Jesus had taken him to be one of the three nearest Him when He wrestled in anguish in the Garden. He loved Peter's boldness and desire to please Him, and he had given Him so much joy when he had figured out who He was! It must have surprised Jesus when Peter rose to His defense, declaring his loyalty, since He knew of the denial to come. When Jesus made the ultimate decision to conquer His flesh, He wanted Peter close to Him because as a human He was emotionally attached to him. It is always comforting for us when we are going through a trauma to have those who are closest to us nearby.

Peter had seen just about everything Jesus did in His ministry. He saw the miracles, healings, and deliverances. He heard the words of Jesus and even knew who He was, yet he deserted Him and denied Him when Jesus needed him the most. Jesus loved Peter, and even though He had predicted his denial, it must have been like a knife in the heart when it came to pass. Luke describes the event:

So they arrested him and led him to the high priest's residence, and Peter was following far behind. The guards lit a fire in the courtyard and sat around it, and Peter joined them there. A servant girl noticed him in the firelight and began staring at him. Finally she said, "This man was one of Jesus' followers!" Peter denied it. "Woman," he said, "I don't even know the man!" After a while someone else looked at him and said, "You must be one of them!" "No, man, I'm not!" Peter replied. About an hour later someone else insisted, "This must be one of Jesus' disciples because he is a Galilean, too." But Peter said, "Man, I don't know what you are talking about." And as soon as he said these words, the rooster crowed. At that moment the Lord turned and looked at Peter. Then Peter remembered that the Lord had said, "Before the rooster crows tomorrow morning, you will deny me three times." And Peter left the courtyard, crying bitterly (Luke 22:54-62).

Notice that immediately after Peter's denial, *"the Lord turned and looked at Peter."* Imagine the deep disappointment and rejection that Jesus felt when He heard from one of His closest, "I don't know Him!"

What was He thinking as He stared hurtfully into the eyes of Peter? Did He see the fear in him and wish that he knew how much He loved him? Did He think of you when the one you loved denied your existence? Did His heart long for all the babies who were denied the right to live or the ones who cry alone at night with no one who seems to care? Peter must have melted when he saw the pain in Jesus' eyes. He knew how deeply he had wounded Him, and he saw it and wept bitterly with shame. When he realized he had abandoned and denied the Messiah, it was too late. He couldn't take back the cowardly words that struck like a dagger in the heart of the King of kings in His greatest hour of need.

> *How often do we break His heart by denying Him because of the fear of man?*

If we look over our lives, we can usually remember a few times where we felt abandoned, but I can't remember a time when I was actually denied. Sure there were the times when some people might walk the other way when they saw me because of an offense. But to tell someone that he or she didn't even know me when that person was actually a close friend would be devastating. To deny you is to act as though you don't exist or ever did; it is a form of treating someone as nothing, like so many do when they treat others as inferior humans.[19] It is the ultimate rejection, declaring someone invalid and inferior.

People suffer greatly from rejection, but we serve an incredible God who loves us enough to connect completely with our pain and identify with us in it in order to heal us.

Maybe you are a parent of adult children, but they are too busy for you. Week after week you sit alone, wishing they would call or show up at your door. You tremble with excitement when the phone rings, praying it is a loved one, but your heart sinks with disappointment when the call is only a telemarketer. In a cutthroat, fast-paced achieving culture, many of the elderly are left by their children.

To abandon a loved one in his or her time of need is a sin.

Perhaps you have aging parents, and you're too busy to ever spend time with them. Think about the pain in their hearts. Hear this heart cry of the elderly in Psalm 71:

And now, in my old age, don't set me aside. Don't abandon me when my strength is failing (Psalm 71:9).

Remember that to abandon a loved one in his or her time of need is a sin. It goes completely against the nature of God. If we are honest and really search our hearts, we all have been guilty of abandoning someone. Whether we ran away from home, left a spouse, or disappointed a friend, abandonment and denial will cause us great pain, regardless of which end of it we are on.

When we gaze on the abandonment of our Savior, we can see that we can still love those who hurt us and that we can be forgiven for the pain we have caused others.

When we go to the Cross and see the abandonment that Jesus endured, we can know that to whatever degree we have experienced this, and whoever we have hurt, He took care of it. He went through His so He could help us get the victory over ours. He allowed Himself to experience abandonment for all the times that we would. He says to us, "I know how you feel; I feel the pain in your heart. Even though they hurt you, you are Mine, and I will not abandon you."

Our Abandonment of God

Ignoring people and treating them as though they don't exist—how many times have we done that to God by refusing to acknowledge Him?

How many times have we questioned His existence in our life when the going got tough? Peter's denial of Jesus was not unique to Peter; nor was his abandonment.

How often do you and I abandon God, only to run to Him when we are in trouble? I cannot tell you how many people give God their leftover time, if there is any, when things are going good. But when a storm hits, they run back to Him pleading for His help. Only then do they have time for God. How would you feel if someone only spent time with you when he or she needed something from you? How devaluing is that? Still, He loves you and waits patiently for you to run to Him like the prodigal son did to his father.

God is very familiar with abandonment. The suffering and death of Christ was an outward manifestation of the abandonment that man puts God through all the time.

Living a life centered on the Cross will change the way you live, and to abandon and deny its work is the greatest sin there is.

It is like taking a treasure that cost someone everything he had and saying to him, "It's worthless to me," "I don't need it," and "I'm good enough without it." That's what God hears from so many who ignore His love for them. How valuable is His sacrifice to you? Are you open to receiving His love? Does it possess you with a passion to reach out as He did to the lost?

I have enough faith in the character of God that He will do everything possible to reach every soul that is open to Him. But does He have your heart so connected to His that you too reach out to them? If He went from heaven to earth, from deity to humanity, from glory and righteousness to the depths of horror and sin to reach you, then He longs to touch everyone who cries out for true righteousness. He said that he who seeks shall find. He knows who they are, and He is more than able to orchestrate their salvation. He needs you and I, His body—His hands and feet—to reach out and bring life to those who are dying. Do you desire what He desires? If not, draw near to the Cross and you will.

The Cross is God's greatest act of love, His greatest triumph over evil. It was to win your heart so that you will not abandon and deny Him. The Cross reveals that He will never abandon those who are His!

In the Psalms God says He will never abandon us; we are His own special possession:

The LORD will not reject his people; he will not abandon his own special possession (Psalm 94:14).

Jesus left His disciples with an awesome promise: He guaranteed that He would send His Holy Spirit. He said He would not abandon them (and us) as orphans. He is with us. It is His Spirit who dwells in our hearts!

Several months ago I was praying and asking God to help me be more aware of Him throughout my day. I was having incredible times in His presence in the morning during my prayer time, but as I got busy doing His work I would seemingly lose the awareness of Him. I was now so in love with Him because of the Cross that I wanted to feel Him all the time. When I was seeking Him about this, one evening I had an incredible experience. For a few seconds I saw an image of the face of Jesus looking into my eyes, and He said these words: "*I am always with you!*" As He spoke, His words burned in my heart and continued to echo in my mind for days after.

It happened so fast initially that I questioned what I had seen, but the revelation from that moment on was so real, and, even though His words were something I already knew, from that moment *I knew He is always with me and will never abandon me.* It dropped from my head to my heart. The ability the enemy had before to make me question His presence is no longer effective. Whenever He seems distant, even for a moment, I think of the Cross and His word to all of us. He is always with us because of the Cross. It forever speaks of how far He will go to always be with us.

Jesus told His disciples that after His crucifixion and resurrection, His Spirit would be released because of what He would accomplish on the Cross. *The Cross made the way for Him to always be with us.* With Him we are never alone, and with Him we will reveal His heart to those who have no hope!

Purpose to think of every time you were abandoned or denied and bring it to His Cross to find your healing. Then think of the times when you abandoned or denied Him or others. Lay it down at the place where He reconciled and justified you. He took the wrath for your offense and those who offended you.

All our sin and pain end at the Cross, and whatever we leave there will turn into the fullness of His life and the empowerment to do what He did. He gave all He had to save the lost, and He gave us His heart so we would do likewise.

Chapter Eleven

The Cross and False Accusation

For God is pleased with you when, for the sake of your conscience, you patiently endure unfair treatment (1 Peter 2:19).

Not everything in life will be fair, and when it isn't we are called to the test of patient endurance. There is never an excuse to do the wrong thing, no matter how loud our flesh may be screaming to do so. Jesus Christ demonstrated to us that we can connect to Him in every trial because He experienced what we go through. During His suffering He withstood the most hypocritical false charges that were ever made, willingly absorbing the accusations and pain of all mankind. But He also went through this injustice to heal all those who have been innocent of crimes and yet were accused anyway.

What was He thinking when they accused Him of blasphemy, knowing that they were guilty of blaspheming God Himself? Was He reliving the eons of time when those He created rose up against Him, accusing Him of all that is wrong in the world? Did He cringe as He thought of the fists of man raised in anger toward Him for the curses they incurred on themselves? Did He battle the raging war of keeping His peace as opposed to retaliating against them? Or did He feel the love and compassion that ruled His heart and with excitement and anticipation see the true sons of God?

Jesus Was Falsely Accused

When Jesus was brought before the high council in the evening, they were looking for witnesses to lie about Him. They couldn't even find one to testify falsely against Him. Then His accusers demanded in the name of the living God that He tell them if He was the Messiah. When He did, they didn't believe Him. In a rage they condemned Him, declaring Him guilty of blasphemy against God. Because of His honesty, they spit on Him and beat Him mercilessly. Now that is injustice. We can read the account in the gospel of Matthew.

Inside, the leading priests and the entire high council were trying to find witnesses who would lie about Jesus, so they could put him to death. But even though they found many who agreed to give false witness, there was no testimony they could use. Finally, two men were found who declared, "This man said, 'I am able to destroy the Temple of God and rebuild it in three days.'" Then the high priest stood up and said to Jesus, "Well, aren't you going to answer these charges? What do you have to say for yourself?" But Jesus remained silent. Then the high priest said to him, "I demand in the name of the living God that you tell us whether you are the Messiah, the Son of God" (Matthew 26:59-63).

While Jesus was being falsely accused, He remained silent. He did not attempt to defend Himself, but stayed resolute to endure whatever they did and said against Him. He had complete trust and assurance in His heavenly Father and what His purpose was.

His heart was fixed on the multitudes of souls that He was born to rescue.

With Jesus there is nothing that He expects us to overcome that He did not first conquer for us. He has gone through every battle known to man, and He did it so we could guard our heart toward others and love them like He does.

In this life things are not always fair, and because of the pride and selfishness of man many people are falsely blamed and accused by others. Maybe you have felt like you were blamed and accused for things that you did not do, and that compounded with the sins that you did commit overwhelmed you to the point of giving up.

False accusations come in many different ways and are usually the result of man's need to blame someone for every bad thing that happens. It can be as simple as someone losing his or her keys and accusing a family member of taking them, to rebellious teens blaming their parents of abuse to justify their behavior. There is something in our sin nature that desires to accuse others for things that go wrong. Now there are times when accusations are true, but I am referring to when the innocent are declared guilty.

When you are falsely accused, the need to defend yourself will rise up, often resulting in your reacting and retaliating in response. This is usually followed by guilt and condemnation for blowing up from your frustration with yourself and your accuser. All of this has the potential to keep you bound and from knowing who you are, robbing you of God's blessings. Jesus purposed to go through His illegal trial and unjust accusations to liberate you from your fears and show you that He will rise to your defense if you trust Him. If you have faith in God, you do not have to attack your accusers because you will know that everything will work out. Despite how it looks and what you may have to patiently endure, you will have a calm assurance of His intervention.

Let's contemplate for a minute the bizarre treatment that Jesus willingly tolerated during His trial leading up to His execution.

When He was brought before Pilate, the Roman governor who had the authority to release or condemn Him, He was found innocent. Pilate announced this verdict to Christ's accusers, but when he saw they were angry with it he condemned Him out of concern for his own neck. Now let's take this scenario into modern-day courts and stand in His shoes.

Imagine that you are completely innocent of something and some leaders falsely accuse you because of their fear and jealousy of your success. That would be painful enough, but then they demand you to reveal to them your true identity. You comply, but they don't believe you and declare you guilty. Then they condemn you to death, calling you a liar, spitting on and beating you as they do. Following all that, they take you to the Supreme Court to get the judge to give you the death sentence. After questioning you and hearing the witnesses, the Supreme Court also finds you innocent. However, your accusers persist in pressuring for your condemnation. Because the judge fears a riot, he tells them that in spite of your innocence, they can kill you anyway. Then, in order to relieve his guilt for condemning an innocent man, he simply washes his hands of the whole matter. You never get to have a fair trial or even a lawyer. You were proven innocent but condemned to die. When you told the truth, they refused to believe it and declared you guilty without evidence.

That is the magnitude of the injustice that happened to Jesus. Could you imagine that playing out in a court of law today? Could you feel how He felt, knowing the absolute absurdity of what He was put through? Everything in me would have been protesting my innocence and pleading for help, but not Jesus.

He knew who He was, and His thoughts were of you coming into His kingdom for all eternity. The Bible says He endured abuse and shame for the joy that would follow, and that joy was seeing you free.

> *We do this by keeping our eyes on Jesus, on whom our faith depends from start to finish. He was willing to die a shameful death on the cross because of the joy he knew would be his afterward. Now he is seated in the place of highest honor beside God's throne in heaven. Think about all he endured when sinful people did such terrible things to him, so that you don't become weary and give up* (Hebrews 12:2-3).

The total feeling of knowing what was being done to Him and that He had the power to stop it at any time, yet submitted to such a contradiction, is beyond our human understanding.

We All Deal With False Accusations

Sometimes as Christians we can look at the sin of false accusation and see it as something that only the unsaved do, but in reality we face it every day, especially in our homes.

Living in a family unit has all kinds of dynamics to it, and when things go wrong it is common to accuse each other out of anger and frustration. Husbands and wives particularly fall victim to the vicious cycle of finger pointing. What they fail to realize is that it slowly eats away at their relationship and hinders their prayers from being answered. Some of you have grown up in your family feeling like you were the one who was always blamed for things whether or not you were guilty. Over the years that injustice has taken its toll on you, and you feel that regardless of what you do you'll be held responsible. There were many times as a child when that was my experience.

As I was growing up, because our family was so dysfunctional and I was the oldest child, I was blamed more frequently for things than my younger siblings. I found myself continually in trouble when I honestly had no realization that I had done wrong. In many cases I had messed up unintentionally, but still would be accused and punished for it. Of course there were the times when I was misbehaving and knew it and would earn my punishment. However, that dynamic created in me tremendous frustration and the feeling that no matter what I did, I would be in trouble anyway. This added to the stronghold already developing that I was wrong and therefore inferior to others.

This core belief ate away at me as I entered my teen years. That stronghold led me to drugs and careless living for several years as I desperately sought acceptance in all the wrong places. My personal history made it difficult for me to process false accusation when it came, and that has led to problems in some of my relationships. It was a trigger point for me when someone alluded to or directly accused me of something that I knew I was innocent of. I would seethe in anger and frustration, as my husband Rick would frequently discover. When I felt falsely accused, I had difficulty processing it reasonably, and it became a "little fox" that spoiled the vine in my marriage. That dynamic easily lends itself to strife and resentment in many homes, which robs us of our peace with God.

> *When we lack in confidence, false accusation can leave us feeling very vulnerable and defenseless and even guilty, though innocent.*

Because we all are flawed and have a sin nature, that feeling of never getting it right can be very real and haunt us our entire lives.

Multitudes of children grow up and act out what has been continually declared over them, whether it is true or not. When we see that life is not fair, we can easily use that as an excuse to do wrong. I'm sure you have heard people say such things as, "Why try? No one will believe me anyway!" or "It's no use; I'll get in trouble no matter what I do!" "It's not fair—he got away with it!" etc. There is a cry in our hearts to seek justice for ourselves, and at the same time there is a willingness to blame others falsely if it absolves us of our responsibility. It amazes me how quick we all are to blame others and at the same time cry, "That's not fair!" when we are the one the finger is pointed at.

False Accusation Is Rampant in the Church

As a church leader, I have been falsely accused of some bizarre things. For instance, people said I murdered my late husband (he died in a car accident while I was out shopping with some girlfriends). I have been accused of having an affair while I went to Bible school (I didn't even go to Bible school). I have been accused of being a lesbian (I am not nor ever have been), and I have been *falsely* accused of stealing from the church. Now I know I am not perfect; there are other things that I have been guilty of, but nothing of moral issues that would disqualify me from ministry.

Has my judgment always been perfect? Absolutely not. Have I ever said anything I regretted? Most definitely! Have I believed the worst of someone? Yes. I have learned that no matter how good our intentions are, we all will miss it at one time or another. However, mistakes can turn into blessings if we learn from them. So when false accusations come—and they will—surrender to the Cross. As hurtful as they can be, it is extremely important we guard our heart as Jesus did.

> *When we respond in love and forgiveness, we move God's hand and healing and restoration are possible even with our worst enemies.*

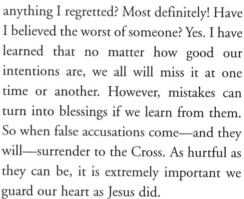

My awesome husband Rick has been accused of even more things than I have, and I have watched in awe as he endeavored to bless the people who purposed to do him harm. One time a minister publicly spoke lies about him and our church. When Rick found out about it, he wrote the pastor a check for $1,000 and invited him out for lunch to get to know him and show him our support. He never mentioned the incident, and now that pastor is a friend of his. He has done things like this more than once, though I must add in our early years of ministry neither of us always responded with the love of Christ.

We have both learned the hard way to trust God and let Him defend us when we are slandered by lies meant to destroy our integrity. I can honestly say God has never failed to come to our defense.

As leaders in ministry, we have learned that when someone accuses us of something, we must ask ourselves this one question: "Is it true?" If it isn't, then we need to forgive and forget it and let God take care of it. If it is, then we need to make our wrong right and ask forgiveness where we need to. Either way we cannot lose. We have witnessed time after time of God turning our accusations into our biggest blessings when we surrendered them to Him.

Because we have chosen to handle such accusations properly, some of those who at one time wanted to harm us are now our friends.

The accuser, the devil, is always there to try and take us out, but the only way he can succeed is if we allow our heart to get bitter and begin to retaliate and attack those who try and destroy us. One of the promises that I claim often is in Isaiah:

No weapon that is formed against thee shall prosper; and every tongue that shall rise against thee in judgment thou shalt condemn. This is the heritage of the servants of the LORD, and their righteousness is of me, saith the LORD (Isaiah 54:17 KJV).

Those who speak lies against us will not prosper, but we must guard our heart and let God deal with them.

Run to the Cross

When Jesus was falsely accused, He did not try to defend Himself; instead, He took it as a man of character and integrity, demonstrating His complete trust in His heavenly Father. What happened to Him was definitely not fair, but it was necessary for our redemption. He knew His false accusation would bring our souls to God. He set the course in His illegal trial to comfort and help us deal with false accusations when they come so we too could win the lost. We are called to follow in His steps, as 1 Peter tells us:

This suffering is all part of what God has called you to. Christ, who suffered for you, is your example. Follow in his steps (1 Peter 2:21).

If you are like me, everything in you will desire to retaliate when false accusation comes. But when I run to the Cross, I see the glory of God in the face of Christ who trusted His Father and *took every false accusation for His enemies*. In these next verses it also says that He did not sin or retaliate when He was insulted, and that is our example to follow:

He never sinned, and he never deceived anyone. He did not retaliate when he was insulted. When he suffered, he did not threaten to get even. He left his case in the hands of God, who always judges fairly (1 Peter 2:22-23).

107

We are tested in our marriages, with children, with parents, at work, and even in the church. Whether you have been lied about, blamed, or condemned because of the sin of someone else, Jesus went through His trial so that you could bring yours to the Cross and find healing.

The trial of Jesus was a visible display of how we attack God for the sins of man.

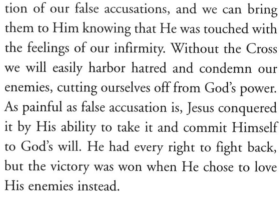

He completely identifies with the devastation of our false accusations, and we can bring them to Him knowing that He was touched with the feelings of our infirmity. Without the Cross we will easily harbor hatred and condemn our enemies, cutting ourselves off from God's power. As painful as false accusation is, Jesus conquered it by His ability to take it and commit Himself to God's will. He had every right to fight back, but the victory was won when He chose to love His enemies instead.

Every day people falsely accuse God for all that is wrong in the world. The trial of Jesus was a visible display of how we attack God for the sins of man.

The false accusations against Him revealed the ugliness in all of mankind who shake their fist at God with anger and hatred because they do not understand their circumstances in light of His kingdom. When we rationalize things in our carnal mind, we are blinded to the truth like the religious leaders who condemned Him. As we look at the Cross, we need to ask the Holy Spirit to reveal to us any areas in our heart where we have accused Him. It is His Spirit who gently nudges us to search our heart and see where we may have been guilty of accusing God.

What have you blamed Him for? Because we all have accused Him, we are guilty of being His enemy. Whenever we falsely accuse God, we exalt ourselves as a god over Him just as the high priest did with Jesus.

Every day when I pray, I look at His work on the Cross and thank Him for everything and blame Him for nothing. He is our awesome and gracious God who does no wrong, and I refuse to let any lies about Him penetrate my heart. Keeping my focus on His Cross makes it easy to know His character, and I am so thankful for who He is! When we cultivate a grateful attitude in prayer, it creates the atmosphere for His presence to show up. It is then that we experience fullness of joy! I purpose to take the circumstances I am in and line them up with what He has done for me. It is then that I am reassured that I have overcome!

When you look at the contradiction of His false accusation, it can put yours in perspective. Mine seems so small when I see His, and even though it is real and hurts, seeing what He so lovingly endured for me gives me the strength to trust Him with mine and forgive those who have come against me. It is there that I find the healing from the pain that would try to destroy me and rob me of my peace and joy. His Cross is our victory!

Chapter Twelve

The Scapegoat of the Cross

Jesus replied, "Yes, it is as you say. And in the future you will see me, the Son of Man, sitting at God's right hand in the place of power and coming back on the clouds of heaven." Then the high priest tore his clothing to show his horror, shouting, "Blasphemy! Why do we need other witnesses? You have all heard his blasphemy. What is your verdict?" "Guilty!" they shouted. "He must die!" Then they spit in Jesus' face and hit him with their fists. And some slapped him, saying, "Prophesy to us, you Messiah! Who hit you that time?" (Matthew 26:64-68)

This sentencing of Jesus fulfilled an act of the priesthood that had been carried on for thousands of years. Those who fulfilled it had no idea of its significance—that it would forever change the destiny of man.

Charged as Guilty

Many people live their entire lives haunted with the guilt of their sins. If we have a moral conviction of right and wrong, we will feel the heaviness of guilt and allow its condemnation to control our lives when we sin. The devil works overtime to keep us reliving our crimes and blinding us from knowing who we are. To be accused and hear the word *guilty* can be one of the most devastating, paralyzing things that could happen to us. It means that we are responsible for committing a reprehensible act deserving of blame and that we have been judged with a price to pay.[20]

Jesus stood before the high priest and was declared guilty when He was innocent of all wrongdoing. When He was falsely accused, He fulfilled prophecy and became our scapegoat; the sins of man were transferred onto Him,

111

never to return. When someone innocent is declared guilty, it is an injustice to the victim, yet Jesus *chose to take* our guilt as the sinless Lamb of God.

> *Then the high priest tore his clothing to show his horror, shouting, "Blasphemy! Why do we need other witnesses? You have all heard his blasphemy. What is your verdict?" "Guilty!" they shouted. "He must die!"* (Matthew 26:65-66)

The verdict over Jesus was decreed: "He is guilty, and He must die!"

Jesus has now become the scapegoat. The carnal minds of the priests blinded them from seeing who He really was. These spiritual leaders were full of pride and envy at the success of Jesus' ministry and the magnitude of His following. He had revealed their hypocrisy by being the truth, and He was not the Messiah they were expecting. They were looking for a majestic king who would come and establish His throne on earth and free them from Roman oppression with His force and power. Jesus said His kingdom was not of this world. Their sin limited their ability to see past the natural realm just as our sin also keeps us blinded to the truth. They did not understand the concept of a spiritual kingdom and had no idea that the kingdom of God involved the death of self and the serving of others. First Corinthians says that if they had understood it, they never would have killed Him:

> *But the rulers of this world have not understood it; if they had, they would never have crucified our glorious Lord* (1 Corinthians 2:8).

The Cross that they were crying out for to kill Him was the very instrument that would be their true deliverance and show them the way to serve others. The guilty verdict they declared over Him was their own and was the fulfillment of the scapegoat offering on the Day of Atonement. They had no idea that they were carrying out the final transfer of man's sin to the Savior of the world!

The guilty verdict they put on Him was the same one Aaron put on the scapegoat for the sins of the children of Israel. Jesus was their scapegoat to remove their guilt by their declaration of His guilty sentence.

In a moment of time, He fulfilled one of the most important things that has ever happened: He was declared guilty of our sin and the death sentence we deserved was transferred from us to Him.

We can read about this exchange in Leviticus when Aaron confessed the sins of the Israelites onto goats on the Day of Atonement:

> *The people of Israel must then bring him two male goats for a sin offering and a ram for a whole burnt offering. Aaron will present the bull as a sin offering, to make atonement for himself and his family. Then he must bring the two male goats and present them to the LORD at the entrance of the Tabernacle. He is to cast sacred lots to determine which goat will be sacrificed to the LORD and which one will be the scapegoat. The goat chosen to be sacrificed to the LORD will be presented by Aaron as a sin offering. The goat chosen to be the scapegoat will be presented to the LORD alive. When it is sent away into the wilderness, it will make atonement for the people* (Leviticus 16:5-10).

The Levitical Scapegoat

The word *atonement* means "at-one-ment," which refers to the reconciliation between God and man.[21] Our sin separated us from Him, and He set up the whole sacrificial process in the Old Covenant as a type of what the Cross would accomplish once and for all. One goat was to be sacrificed to the Lord, and the other was called the scapegoat.

Both goats represented Jesus; He was both the one that took the guilt of our sin and the one that was sacrificed for sin.

Both goats are to be seen as a single sin-sacrifice; the two together of equal importance make a sin offering. Both goats represent two sides of the same thing. The second one represents what the first one doesn't—namely the removal of the sin and its guilt. We can see this described further down in Leviticus 16, in the importance of the laying on of hands. The sin and guilt are transferred when they are confessed over the goat and are then carried away into the wilderness by it. The fact that the goat is accompanied by somebody and that it is taken to an uninhabited place indicates the absolute impossibility of its return. In the same way, our sin and guilty verdict have been absolutely forgiven and erased, never to return.

When Aaron has finished making atonement for the Most Holy Place, the Tabernacle, and the altar, he must bring the living goat forward. He is to lay both of his hands on the goat's head and confess over it all the sins and rebellion of the Israelites. In this way, he will lay the people's sins on the head of the goat; then he will send it out into the wilderness, led by a man chosen for this task. After the man sets it free in the wilderness, the goat will carry all the people's sins upon itself into a desolate land (Leviticus 16:20-22).

All of our sins were put on Jesus; He took them away forever, so we are now innocent of all charges against us. *Now that is the Good News of the Gospel!* It does not matter what you have done; if you have surrendered to the work of the Cross, it is gone!

Your verdict is in, and you are not guilty because of the Cross.

That amazing fact should make you and I eternally grateful to God! If you have ever been caught red-handed doing something wrong and had accusing fingers pointed at you declaring your guilt, it is a very shameful and humiliating feeling. Jesus saw your guilt, but He took your sin on Himself and now looks lovingly at you and says, "You are now righteous and innocent of your crimes; I have taken them and been punished for them so you could be free. Now go and tell others the Good News!"

The Debilitating Feelings of Guilt

When we carry our guilt, it causes feelings that reinforce our sense that we are wrong, producing self-hatred and insecurity in us. As imperfect humans we all have to deal with these feelings that threaten our sense of well-being. In the world most people cope with their guilt by calling evil good and good evil so that that they don't have to feel bad about what they do. People never cease to amaze me as they twist God's law to justify their evil heart. This is called "deception" and doesn't change the consequence of sin. However, if our conscience is *not* seared by deception, then when we do wrong it reinforces in our heart that we are sinners. As a result, out of shame and fear we will be tempted to lie, cover up, or blame someone else if we get caught.

If you have ever been pulled over by a police officer for running a stop sign, or speeding, that sinking feeling of being caught in the act of something wrong is demoralizing and painful. One of my earliest memories of that feeling happened when I was in Grade Two. Because I was bored in class, I took some crayons and ripped the paper from them, letting the debris fall to the floor. My teacher saw the mess on the floor and demanded to know who had made it. Because I had done this absentmindedly, I was terrified when I realized that trouble was brewing, so I denied it. The teacher then checked inside everyone's desk to see their crayons. I was found to be the culprit as mine were the only ones missing their wrapping. I knew there was no way out; I was caught red-handed and was embarrassed that I also had lied. I was guilty and therefore humiliated by being punished with the strap in front of the class.

> *He accepted the guilty verdict so that you would not have to at Judgment Day.*

That day remained an unpleasant memory for me for years. Guilt is a horribly debilitating

feeling that can linger your entire life. Because Christians tend to be more sin-conscious than unbelievers, they are more prone to allowing guilt to dominate their thoughts when in fact they are not guilty in God's eyes because of the Cross. Why? You and I have an enemy who knows if he can keep us focused on our guilt, we will not be a threat to him. Satan's strategy is to accuse you to keep you from seeing that you are now righteous.

Guilt will motivate you to hide and cover things up, and that will prevent you from having genuine and transparent relationships with God and others. You may ask, "What if I have done something wrong? Shouldn't I feel guilty?"

The difference between true conviction for our sins and guilt is that the Spirit of Christ leads us to repenting at the Cross and seeing our righteousness in Him. The accuser leads us to condemnation and hopelessness that we will never be right. One leads the way out of our guilt, which is the Cross; the other leads to self-destruction and hopelessness. That is why it is very important we take our sins to the Cross by repenting and leaving them there in order to receive the forgiveness and freedom that He has purchased for us. At all times and through every step He allowed the guilty verdict to be put on Him. He did it for us, to relieve us of our guilty verdict on Judgment Day of every thing we've done wrong. Our case has been judged at the Cross.

Failure to understand and accept this exchange will result in either a seared conscience or a life lived under the weight of your sin. Too many in the church wear masks because they live out of a guilty conscience, thinking of themselves as failures and hopeless in their weaknesses. They are afraid to let anyone really know them for fear of being seen as imperfect and therefore rejected. If this is you, I have news for you: We all are flawed, if that is what we choose to focus on. That does not mean that we don't face and deal with sin in our life; we do, but at the Cross we know that it is His righteousness that sanctifies us.

Our problem is that we focus on ourselves and our weaknesses rather than on the finished work of the Cross.

How often do we allow the guilt of our imperfections to weigh us down? Because they do not understand the Cross, many of God's children feel condemned. If guilt is dominating our thoughts, we have not embraced Christ as our scapegoat and we will be weak in our witness to others.

This scripture in Acts tells us that belief in Him frees us from *all guilt!*

Everyone who believes in him is freed from all guilt and declared right with God—something the Jewish law could never do (Acts 13:39).

Jesus Made Us Not Guilty!

Let's think through how determined Christ was to take on the verdict for our sins. He was in the Garden praying when He was betrayed by His friend Judas and turned over to the Roman soldiers. The Word says a whole battalion came to arrest Him. That was no small group. Two hundred soldiers came to arrest one man. We can read this account in the gospel of John:

The leading priests and Pharisees had given Judas a battalion of Roman soldiers and Temple guards to accompany him. Now with blazing torches, lanterns, and weapons, they arrived at the olive grove. Jesus fully realized all that was going to happen to him. Stepping forward to meet them, he asked, "Whom are you looking for?" "Jesus of Nazareth," they replied. "I am he," Jesus said. Judas was standing there with them when Jesus identified himself (John 18:3-5).

They obviously knew Jesus had supernatural power if they thought it would take that many to ensure His capture. But what was Jesus thinking? Did

He think of the legions of angels that would come in a moment at His request to defend Him and destroy these men? Or did He see them with determination to set them free from the deceptions they were bound to? Perhaps He was recalling the sacrifices of the scapegoat and was bracing Himself to face the fear of taking on your sin that He had almost recoiled from moments before. Maybe He was thinking of you living your life free from guilt and condemnation and saw you standing before the throne of God with all the angels in heaven watching, as the verdict of your case was announced "Not guilty!"

He wanted you to live every day of your life with the knowledge that your sin was entirely taken and removed forever by Him, the Son of God!

He knew who He was, the power He possessed, and that He had done no wrong; yet He willingly went with His captors. His submission was to His heavenly Father, motivated by a love so great that no natural man could comprehend it. He knew what hung in the balance, and He knew that all the sin and accusations that would ever exist would be His to bear alone.

He was the full expression of righteousness and the complete opposite of those who accused Him. He had flesh like you and I and would have desired to defend Himself, but He knew the guilty verdict we would face and wanted to take it so we could be completely free to love Him. He could have walked away or wiped them all out by a spoken word, but He had been born to bear our guilt.

The purpose of His passion was so that you could identify with Him in your pain, know that your God has been there, and understand that *He has removed your guilt*. When you connect with Him in righteousness, you will find His resurrection power by His Spirit to overcome and do what He has called you to. Don't let your pain destroy you by allowing your sin or others' as an excuse to remain under guilt and condemnation. Jesus, our scapegoat, took it to where it cannot return.

Chapter Thirteen

The Abuse and Shame
of the Cross

The soldiers took him into their headquarters and called out the entire battalion. They dressed him in a purple robe and made a crown of long, sharp thorns and put it on his head. Then they saluted, yelling, "Hail! King of the Jews!" And they beat him on the head with a stick, spit on him, and dropped to their knees in mock worship. When they were finally tired of mocking him, they took off the purple robe and put his own clothes on him again. Then they led him away to be crucified (Mark 15:16-20).

The work of His Cross revealed the worst shame and humiliation that humans can inflict on one another.

The whole purpose of all His abuse was for us to be healed and connected to God. For that to happen, we must go to His Cross and process our pain through it. We relate to Him and know that whatever happened to us, happened to Him and He was victorious over it. To find our healing we must not only know that it happened to Him, but also realize in the depth of our heart that we too caused His pain. The awareness that we contributed to His suffering is essential for our deliverance.

We can read here in Isaiah this prophetic word of how Jesus submitted to those who intended to harm Him:

He was oppressed and treated harshly, yet he never said a word. He was led as a lamb to the slaughter. And as a sheep is silent before the shearers, he did not open his mouth (Isaiah 53:7).

What was He thinking as they hurled abusive words, mocking Him relentlessly? Perhaps His thoughts were of all the men, women, and children who have been violated and shamed by the abuse of incest; perhaps He heard the agonizing cries of humanity that have been raped and plundered. He felt the shame and humiliation of the hatred of man and subjected Himself to it as He looked past what was happening to Him and saw you free.

God went beyond the limits for us, allowing the worst of humanity's atrocities to be inflicted on Himself so we could see how much He loves us and desires to connect with our heart and possess us with His love. He suffered for the rejected and abused of this world.

The Pain of Shame and Abuse

Being treated as an object of ridicule is demoralizing and painful and leaves its victims feeling like trash. Every one of us can go through a time when we are treated without love or mercy and are rejected and left with feelings of humiliation and shame.

Several years ago, a close friend of mine, Krystal,[22] experienced a cruel and bizarre time of horrendous treatment that almost destroyed her. I am telling her story because it is incredibly unthinkable and was inflicted by people she trusted. I'll never forget the day that she showed up at my door following her ordeal and with tears poured out her heart to me.

She was overwhelmed, devastated, and in total despair. The only thing she knew was that she desperately needed help, and God had led her to come to see me. Three weeks earlier she had gotten married to a minister in the United States and had left Canada for her new life in the States. Now here she was at my kitchen table, back in Canada, the marriage over, filled with what seemed like a lifetime of pain obtained in those few weeks. I listened with shock and anger as she unfolded what had just happened to her.

She told me that her new husband was under the extreme control of his senior pastor's wife of the church he worked in. At the wedding this woman had insisted on being in every wedding picture, on the other side of the groom, and accused Krystal of wanting to be the center of attention in her own wedding photos. On the honeymoon, he called this other woman daily and gave intimate details of their relationship at the other woman's request, making Krystal leave the room as he did. The wedding money, mostly from Krystal's family and friends, had been taken by this pastor's wife and used as she wished.

The day they returned from the honeymoon, Krystal was told to leave for a few hours so the other woman could spend time alone with him. It was becoming very obvious that they had an inappropriate relationship going on, and Krystal felt powerless to stop it.

Throughout the second week of her marriage, her new husband and the other woman continually berated and ridiculed Krystal, calling her names and making fun of her relentlessly. She was forced to sit in a chair for hours while they proceeded to destroy her esteem by telling her that anything good about herself that anyone told her was a lie. She was not allowed to call home to talk to her family or friends as they were determined to break her will. Their goal was to be able to control her completely.

Many other cruel things happened, and as Krystal resisted their abuse, they finally decided that they would send her away at the end of the third week. I had been very close to Krystal for many years, and she was a mature Christian, a very Godly person who loved people and gave to all whom she knew. I had known her for many years as a person of honesty and integrity. I ached for her, and as this story poured through her agonizing sobs, I knew it was true.

You may wonder how someone could allow him or herself to go through such ridicule and abuse, but when you are taken away from all you are familiar with and have your mind mentally messed with by threats and intimidation, it can be very overpowering. Krystal is a very intelligent career woman who had traveled across Canada training people in the business world. At the time of her marriage she had been living in another city in Canada, and because of the humiliation and shame she was experiencing, she felt she had to come to us to get help. She wasn't ready to face her friends and family back home, so she stayed with us.

Krystal had kept herself pure and had believed and waited for who she thought was a Godly man. After all, he was in ministry and appeared to be a great catch. Unfortunately their relationship had been a long distance one, and much that could've been detected amiss wasn't. Some signs were there, but like many others in love, she was blinded to obvious clues. Desire can surpass reason, and when Krystal made a decision to marry, she found herself in her worst nightmare.

It was just over a year before she was able to get over the devastation of her brief marriage. My husband and I spent many hours with her as we watched her weep almost daily from the humiliation, shame, and rejection that she had been subjected to. What she went through was not much different than being kidnapped, violated, and held hostage. Our hearts broke for her, and we knew the crippling effect that these debilitating emotions had on her. Slowly Krystal recovered as she processed through the anger and hurt that had damaged her heart and allowed forgiveness to flow. Eventually she was able to return to her home city and back to work. Fortunately she has remarried, and it has been many years since her ordeal.

When people are treated like they are completely worthless and are ridiculed, mocked, humiliated, and shamed, it is absolutely destructive to their esteem. Many women and men have been raped or sexually abused by some-one they trusted. The shame they carry from it does great emotional damage and robs them of healthy relationships.

The amazing thing for all of us is that Jesus, the Creator of all things, also was stripped, ridiculed, and subjected to incredible abuse—all because of His love for us. He knows our pain and understands the extreme indignities we were subjected to. The mocking, rejection, and beating He suffered were all for us. He chose to be touched with all the feelings of our infirmities.

For we have not an high priest which cannot be touched with the feeling of our infirmities; but was in all points tempted like as we are, yet without sin (Hebrews 4:15 KJV).

The point of this verse is that despite what He endured, He didn't use it as an excuse to sin. We all are mistreated at times and are tempted our whole lives to wallow in our pain.

Another friend of mine, Cindy,[23] had been severely sexually, emotionally, and verbally abused by her father after her mother died. Her father was an alcoholic and from the time of her mother's death at the age of four, he had kept her locked in a cabin in the Maritimes in Canada. No one knew she was there until she was discovered at age 12. She was left handicapped and men-tally slow because of the mistreatment, and her pain left her with a negative attitude. Many believers avoided her because of it.

One day God spoke to me to have Cindy over for lunch and get to know her. I asked her to tell me about herself, and she candidly shared her story as though it were normal. As she talked, I had to fight back tears. She did not feel sorry for herself but had accepted her lot in life even though she was not happy. She had no concept of love, as her life had formed around violence and hatred.

God wanted the rest of His body, the church, to love her in spite of her attitude. Our God sees the outcasts of this world and aches to comfort them with His love.

As we connect with His love, we will reach out with His power and touch those who have been used and abused. Humanity can be incredibly cruel, and unfortunately people suffer at the hands of man every day. However, we who know Him will bring them hope!

> *His heart cries out from the Cross to reach out and touch the broken people of this world.*

I remember feeling like an outcast as I was growing up because of my broken family. We were raised in a church where we were treated like second-class Christians because of my mother's divorces. We struggled financially, and my siblings and I were the only ones we knew of being raised in a single-parent home. Needless to say, I was often the brunt of a lot of teasing and name-calling—not to mention feeling shunned and left out of the majority of the other kids' fun and games. As I shared previously, feelings of shame and inferiority were my constant companions because of the continual rejection.

Jesus Understands Your Shame

Shame is an emotion that can completely distort your thinking and strip you of your confidence. It is a feeling of embarrassment, unworthiness, and disgrace that immobilizes you from doing what you were created for.

Let's read again how Jesus was taken out by an entire battalion of soldiers (that means 200 soldiers) who stripped Him and made fun of Him in incredibly cruel and horrendous ways.

> *The soldiers took him into their headquarters and called out the entire*
> *battalion. They dressed him in a purple robe and made a crown of long,*
> *sharp thorns and put it on his head. Then they saluted, yelling, "Hail!*

123

King of the Jews!" And they beat him on the head with a stick, spit on him, and dropped to their knees in mock worship. When they were finally tired of mocking him, they took off the purple robe and put his own clothes on him again. Then they led him away to be crucified (Mark 15:16-20).

Jesus was shamed beyond shame and humiliated to the uttermost. This is God allowing His creation to treat Him atrociously! We really do not know all that was done to Him, but we do know that He identified with everything known to man. I am sure that whatever pain, shame, humiliation, mocking, or ridicule you or I have endured, His surpassed it. He allowed Himself to be subjected to it to win our heart and connect with us in our pain.

Jesus truly knows your humiliation and shame and how it feels to be the object of someone's hatred; He's been there.

During this part of His ordeal, Jesus was stripped of all dignity and forced to endure their abuse naked and defenseless. To strip someone is to deprive that person of clothing or covering.[24] It is to expose the person. Can you imagine Jesus being treated that way? He felt all the unworthiness and embarrassment of the treatment that He was subjected to. He was completely exposed to 200 cruel men, left at their mercy to be hurt, pushed, punched, hit with a stick, and ridiculed. This had to be utterly degrading for Him, as the King of kings and Lord of lords fully experienced the most incredible contempt imaginable—just so He could conquer it for you.

Because of His willingness to submit to it, He can truly say to you, "I know your humiliation and shame and how it feels to be the object of someone's hatred, for I've been there!" He completely understands the underdogs of this life because the Word of God says Jesus was despised and rejected. He knows what it is like to be discriminated against and be judged for something you have no control over, such as your race, social status, and even who you are. He knows the pain of segregation, imprisonment, and isolation as He was treated without dignity and made to feel like the scum of the earth.

Words of hatred echoed in His ears between painful punches and laughing mockery as He stood naked before those cruel soldiers. Maybe the heartless words that ridiculed you still ring true in your mind. What was He thinking as this heartless mob mocked Him? Did He see you weeping as you nursed your bruised emotions from the hurtful words that attacked you? Did He see the countless women who hid in shame after being violated by the wickedness of man? Perhaps He wept inside for those who were treated like animals because of their race, or maybe He longed to comfort the scarred and mutilated from their pain of "Why me?"

Going through the trials of life that cause us humiliation and shame are our opportunities to exercise our faith in the Cross.

In 2 Corinthians we read that He is the God who comforts us in our trouble so that we can comfort others in theirs:

> *All praise to the God and Father of our Lord Jesus Christ. He is the source of every mercy and the God who comforts us. He comforts us in all our troubles so that we can comfort others. When others are troubled, we will be able to give them the same comfort God has given us. You can be sure that the more we suffer for Christ, the more God will shower us with his comfort through Christ. So when we are weighed down with troubles, it is for your benefit and salvation! For when God comforts us, it is so that we, in turn, can be an encouragement to you. Then you can patiently endure the same things we suffer. We are confident that as you share in suffering, you will also share God's comfort* (2 Corinthians 1:3-7).

When we surrender our humiliation and shame to the Cross, we are empowered to bring life into our pain by helping others who are going through the same thing. That is how we find victory over the things that were meant to destroy us.

Trial-Tested Faith

To find and understand the work of the Cross is worth everything. It is the greatest treasure that exists, and if your pain leads you to it then you are greatly blessed! Without the Cross your heartache will only lead you to hardness, anger, selfishness, bitterness, and a life of hurting yourself and others.

Only then can we experience the power that gave Jesus the ability to rise above and so be glorified with Him. Our rejection, and the feelings that come with it, are not the final word. The power of the Cross is! First Peter tells us that the trials in our life are a test of our faith.

These trials are only to test your faith, to show that it is strong and pure. It is being tested as fire tests and purifies gold—and your faith is far more precious to God than mere gold. So if your faith remains strong after being tried by fiery trials, it will bring you much praise and glory and honor on the day when Jesus Christ is revealed to the whole world (1 Peter 1:7).

These trials reveal what is really in our hearts. For example, it is easy for me to love someone when that person loves me. Even unbelievers can do that. But it is the person who has hurt me who will show me how loving I really am.

The more loving and compassionate I can be to those who hurt me, the more I am like Christ. However, without the trial of people doing evil toward me, I will never see if I can truly love my enemies. That is the test! So when someone hurts and shames me, I have an opportunity to show that person the love of God.

A few years after Krystal had remarried, she heard that her ex-husband and the pastor's wife were getting married (the woman's husband had recently passed away). I advised her to send them some money and bless them, not so much for them, but as a test of her heart. She was glad to do so.

The Cross will help us to know the truth of what we really believe. Whatever negative attitudes and feelings are inside of us will come out, and, as we leave them at the Cross, we take on the nature of Christ and His life is produced in us.

It is incredibly freeing to be able to bless an enemy and wish that person well, especially when he or she has rejected and shamed us. We will see whether we are trusting in this life alone or truly believing that eternity with God really awaits us. If a great loss in our life causes us to be so devastated and hopeless that we despair life itself, then our heart is in the wrong place.

That does not mean that we don't mourn loss; we do, but not without hope. To have what we hope for is essential to overcoming what could destroy us. It is a powerful weapon that gives substance to our faith, and it is the greatest thing we have, as 1 Thessalonians tells us:

And now, brothers and sisters, I want you to know what will happen to the Christians who have died so you will not be full of sorrow like people who have no hope (1 Thessalonians 4:13).

It is comforting to know that when we live for Him, there is absolutely nothing that can take our hope away from us. The expectation of being with Him in heaven is the greatest thing we have. There are times when I am in the presence of God, that I so long to see Him face to face that I have to force myself to want to stay here and finish what I am called to do. Seeing Him is what I live for! The Word is clear that we cannot yet see or imagine the incredible things God has waiting for us:

When we choose to think of what God has prepared for us, we will always have great joy!

That is what the Scriptures mean when they say, "No eye has seen, no ear has heard, and no mind has imagined what God has prepared for those who love him" (1 Corinthians 2:9).

Unfortunately, too many believers live by sight. The book of Colossians tells us that heaven is what must fill our thoughts; in other words, we are to live for eternity. That knowledge should supersede our faith in this world.

Since you have been raised to new life with Christ, set your sights on the realities of heaven, where Christ sits at God's right hand in the place of honor and power. Let heaven fill your thoughts. Do not think only about things down here on earth (Colossians 3:1-2).

If Jesus or His disciples had looked at their difficulties as a determining factor of God being with them, they would have given up on Him. It was not their circumstances, but their focus on the Cross that motivated their passion for Him. Before the resurrection, the disciples saw everything through their natural eyes and fled in fear. After the resurrection, they saw the work of the Cross and died for Him. The resurrection revealed to them there is more than what this world has to offer, and that knowledge empowered them to lay down their lives.

We can accurately judge our hearts as we look at the Cross and see God's example of how to respond to our circumstances.

God Is Rejected Every Day

It is also important to know that *the suffering Jesus went through was meant to reveal in the natural realm how we treat God in the spiritual realm.* As I wrote earlier, it is critical to our healing when we acknowledge how we treat God. We can read about this treatment in Isaiah:

> *He was despised and rejected—a man of sorrows, acquainted with bitterest grief. We turned our backs on him and looked the other way when he went by. He was despised, and we did not care* (Isaiah 53:3).

Notice it says *we* turned our backs on Him and *we* despised Him.

To despise is to regard with contempt or scorn, or to treat one as unworthy of interest or concern.[25] To reject is to refuse to submit to, accept, believe, or make use of.[26] Man rejects God every day. When Jesus was going through His passion, He was being treated the way God is treated by untold millions all the time. His passion revealed the hearts of men toward their Creator.

An example of how man feels toward Christ was seen prior to the release of the movie, *The Passion of the Christ.* Mel Gibson, the producer, was subjected to a lot of ridicule because of his belief in the message of the movie. Many were offended at him for producing it, and he was subjected to a lot of false accusation and treated with contempt. Much of the criticism was in direct relationship with the response man has toward the Cross of Jesus Christ.

To reject the work of the Cross is to reject God; yet, because it is offensive to the pride of man, many disregard it as useless, failing to see it is God's greatest gift to them. Man tends to want to believe that what they do has to be a part of their salvation.

The Cross does not appease our self-exaltation and angers those who lift themselves above God. He took on Himself the worst of contempt and hatred and allowed Himself to be completely and thoroughly dishonored by those He created so we could be with Him in honor and glory. Because He responded in humility and faith, willing to take the abuse, He earned the place of highest authority where all that exists bows down before Him. As the soldiers did it in mockery, one day they will do it in honor. Regardless of how people treat Him now, one day they will bow down and worship Him and confess that He is Lord!

> *And in human form he obediently humbled himself even further by dying a criminal's death on a cross. Because of this, God raised him up to the heights of heaven and gave him a name that is above every other name, so that at the name of Jesus every knee will bow, in heaven and on earth and under the earth, and every tongue will confess that Jesus Christ is Lord, to the glory of God the Father* (Philippians 2:8-11).

He went to the lowest place so that He could bring us to the highest.

Whenever I take the work He did for me for granted, I shame Him and myself. The more I remember and focus on what He did for me and on just how incredible it was, the more I desire to honor Him. Honoring the Cross is my delight. It is my privilege and my salvation every day, and it enables me to overcome my flesh. When we honor His work on the Cross, we experience His overcoming power. I make sure that in my pain *I honor His suffering, and that sets me free!*

Now I can honestly look over my entire life and see all the pain and heartache that I experienced and be absolutely thankful for it all, for it led me to the Cross.

My humiliation and shame is now a weapon I have to defeat the enemy just as Christ did with His. What is meant to hurt me will *always* be turned into glory by the power of the Cross.

To see Him in all His glory is impossible now; we can only get a glimpse as our flesh is unable to absorb all that He is. First Timothy says that He is so brilliant that no human can touch Him!

> *For at the right time Christ will be revealed from heaven by the blessed and only almighty God, the King of kings and Lord of lords. He alone can never die, and he lives in light so brilliant that no human can approach him. No one has ever seen him, nor ever will. To him be honor and power forever. Amen* (1 Timothy 6:15-16).

THE CROSS

As I focus on His Cross, I wait earnestly for that day when I will see Him as He is, in all of His glory. Every day I realize that I am better than I deserve because He took what I deserved. I no longer need to feel my shame, for He took it for me.

Chapter Fourteen

The Crown of Thorns
and Purple Robe

Let this mind be in you, which was also in Christ Jesus: who, being in the form of God, thought it not robbery to be equal with God: but made himself of no reputation, and took upon him the form of a servant, and was made in the likeness of men: and being found in fashion as a man, he humbled himself, and became obedient unto death, even the death of the cross (Philippians 2:5-8 KJV).

I f we do not believe who He is, we will never know who we are.

The devil's strategy is to oppress us in our mind. It is there that the battle for our lives is won or lost. Oppression of our mind is the greatest attack because to oppress someone is to keep that person down so he or she cannot do what he or she is capable of.[27] When we are focused on who we are not, what we can't do, and how often we fail, then we are allowing oppression to dominate us. Therefore it is important we understand that it is in our mind we win our battles and have the power to believe for things God has promised, no matter how we feel.

When Jesus went through His suffering, He did not have to subject Himself to the mockery of the crown of thorns and the royal purple robe. They were not necessary to being the sacrifice for our sins. Rather, He submitted to this abuse to show us that He also bore the curse of the battle for our mind, the fight that robs us of our identity and righteousness.

That means that instead of thinking like victims, He has given us the ability to think as conquerors who rule over whatever comes against us because of who we are in Christ. The crown of thorns Jesus wore represents the oppression of the mind that stripped us from the reality of who we really are. He took that mockery of His identity in order to win back ours.

The royal purple robe represents the robe of righteousness that He restored to us in exchange for the guilt and condemnation of our sin. We have been made righteous, and to see ourselves any other way is to turn away from the Cross. What was done to Him forever sealed *who we are.* Because of the Cross, we now have entrance into the throne room of God! We are called kings and priests to rule over sin, establish His kingdom on the earth, and rule over the enemy of our mind!

What was done to Him forever sealed who we are.

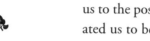

The purpose of His suffering was to restore us to the position of kings and priests that He created us to be. We must remember that Jesus gave up the crown He wore in heaven for a hideous crown of thorns. Thorns represent the curse of the ground that came as a consequence of sin when we were stripped of our position and authority in the Garden of Eden.

> *And to Adam he said, "Because you listened to your wife and ate the fruit I told you not to eat, I have placed a curse on the ground. All your life you will struggle to scratch a living from it. It will grow thorns and thistles for you, though you will eat of its grains"* (Genesis 3:17-18).

Mankind now had to work against the curse of thorns and thistles to produce their livelihood, and it would not be easy. The thorns would crowd out the fruit of what should be without any hard work to remove them. It was the original sin that stole our identity and robbed us of our position and authority. When Eve chose to eat the fruit of the tree of the knowledge of good and evil, the serpent told her that she would become just like God. The truth was she was *already* like God, made in His image and likeness. She was His child, and just as our children are like us, she was like Him—but Satan caused her to doubt who she was.

A Story of Oppression

With the fall of man came the consequence of our sin and the oppression of our mind, which limits all we do. Many Christians live with oppression when they do not have the revelation of what was done for them on the Cross.

As leaders, we too can be victims of negative thoughts, and we often experience the backlash in our churches of men and women who live in defeat. As a pastor's wife, I have witnessed much of this. One of the most dramatic testimonies I have seen was of a man in our church who, for more than 30 years as a believer, was still under the strongholds of his mind—until the day he finally caught a greater revelation of the Cross.

I will never forget the evening when I looked down the hallway of our church in amazement as Bob ran toward me. "Pastor Cathy, I got my miracle!" he shouted as he got closer. "I got my miracle!" I could hardly believe what I was hearing! This man had been attending our church for years, and I had never once seen him show an ounce of emotion. He had just returned from one of our men's encounters, which is a weekend we hold quarterly that is centered on teaching on the Cross. It was obvious that he had experienced an incredible breakthrough from the strong oppression that had held him in bondage all these years.

Bob's walk as a Christian was very turbulent because of the trauma he endured as a child—trauma that left him unable to show his emotions. His father was a violent alcoholic who abused him most of his life. As a young boy, he also was traumatized when hit by a car at the age of five. That experience caused him to cry uncontrollably at almost anything. This incited his father to abuse him by dragging him out of bed to stand in front of his drinking companions while they relentlessly made fun of him. They used him as an object of their cruelty and took sport in seeing him cry. They would force him to smile, and when he couldn't, his father would beat him severely. The father and his drunken friends would revel in seeing him cower in fear, and their abusive antics continued often over several years.

Bob recalled one incident when his father blamed him for something he didn't do, and, taking a fly swatter, beat him so severely that he bled profusely and was left so battered and bruised that he almost died. Only his mother's intervention saved him from being killed that day. When he was eight years old, his father started threatening his life, and Bob knew he would be killed. He would lie awake at night in terror, planning how he could kill his father first. Once, with fear and trembling, Bob mustered up the courage to sneak his father's shotgun and was actually going to attempt to murder him. His mother intercepted him without ever revealing his plan to his father.

After years of beatings and constant threats on his life, Bob finally ran away at the age of 14. He'd had enough. Soon he became involved in drugs and lived a life of continual violence that almost left him dead several times. After several years away from the area he was raised in, he came back and that summer his father took a knife and stabbed his mother to death while she slept. He had told Bob's six-year-old brother to tell the police that Bob had done it, threatening him with his life if he didn't. Bob was picked up by the police for the murder of his mother, but fortunately they were able to get a confession from his father and Bob was released. His father was charged, convicted, and sentenced to only five years in prison because he was drunk when he committed the crime. He was released after 30 months, and on Christmas Eve in 1974 he committed suicide.

Bob's life was very isolated and guarded because of his inability to show emotion, which hindered him in his relationships. He had very few friends he trusted and spent most of his life avoiding contact with others. At the age of 24, as a very angry and bitter man, he asked Jesus into his life and for the first time experienced some healing and was filled with joy. However, he still struggled with the ability to show his emotions. Being around people made him constantly nervous, and when he got nervous or upset he would look angry. Because he always looked mean, he was not accepted by most believers. As a result, he spent the next 30 years avoiding any interactions with others and situations that would make him nervous. Attending church on Sunday was a challenge for him, and he kept to himself. Sadly, at times he overheard hurtful comments about how miserable he looked. The hurtful words reinforced his oppression, but he was mature enough to forgive in his heart.

When we started doing encounter weekends on the Cross, all Bob could think of was that he would be in a crowd of up to 80 men and would have to share a room with a stranger. Everything in him wanted to avoid going, and if it had not been for his wife's persistence he would have stayed home.

On the weekend he spent both Friday and Saturday evening in the hotel lobby reading his notes, and he began to seriously meditate on Jesus and what He did on the Cross. His thoughts were riveted to His beaten flesh and the severe cuts and bruises that Jesus bore, which brought back memories of his own. He thought of how most men would have died from their injuries long before they made it to the Cross, and slowly the reality of the suffering of Jesus for his freedom began to sink in and unlock the chains of bondage over his oppressed mind. He finally acknowledged that Jesus took his hurts and fears, and anything else that would hinder him from being who he was made to be.

He began to daily take his problems and lay them down at the foot of the Cross. For Bob, doing that every day replaced his sickness with health, anger with love, and sadness with joy. He knew his life would never be the same, and he shared with us that for the first time he felt great. His oppression was gone, and he no longer felt nervous around people. Bob found the key in keeping his eyes on the work of the Cross and remember-

Oppression of the mind afflicts almost everyone in varying degrees.

ing what Jesus did for him. He is so thankful that today he is a new man free from the fears that held him captive.

Bob's deliverance is an incredible tribute to the power of the Cross in our church, as many knew of him and witnessed the incredible change. Now he smiles often and is excited about the things of God and shares His goodness at every opportunity.

Our natural mind is filled with negative self-talk all day long, and it is our responsibility to replace those thoughts with the truth of the Word. Jesus felt the fullness of our oppression when He was pierced with the thorns of defeat and mocked mercilessly for every truth that He was. He knew Satan would do anything to keep us from believing who we are!

The Core Beliefs of the Heart

This scripture in Proverbs is one I love and quote often because it holds a great truth about how important the beliefs of the heart are.

Above all else, guard your heart, for it affects everything you do (Proverbs 4:23).

Notice it says our heart affects *everything* we do! Therefore it is critical that we know what we believe in our hearts. Our core beliefs will motivate everything about us. Those beliefs set the boundaries in our life and determine our course.

Whatever you allow yourself to believe will be a core belief in your heart, and like it or not, that belief will shape your future. That is why this heart issue is so important.

Whatever you allow yourself to believe will be a core belief in your heart, and like it or not, that belief will shape your future.

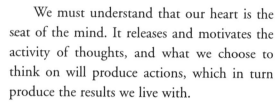

We must understand that our heart is the seat of the mind. It releases and motivates the activity of thoughts, and what we choose to think on will produce actions, which in turn produce the results we live with.

When our mind limits us and keeps us from what we should believe, we are oppressed. Whether we realize it or not, we are in a spiritual war and the battle is won or lost by what we allow ourselves to think on. But Jesus won that battle with His crown that shed the blood that set us free!

Another thing many do not realize is that our wrong beliefs unwittingly invite demonic activity to work in our lives. The demonic entities that exist in the spirit realm strategize many of the thoughts that pop into our mind, hoping that we will embrace them as our own. The Bible says that our enemy is not other people but the spirits in the demonic realm of principalities and powers that can and will use other people to affect us negatively. We can read about this in Ephesians:

> *For we are not fighting against people made of flesh and blood, but against the evil rulers and authorities of the unseen world, against those mighty powers of darkness who rule this world, and against wicked spirits in the heavenly realms* (Ephesians 6:12).

Few people acknowledge that this realm actually exists, and that sets us fighting one another rather than our real enemy. When our focus is on ourselves—on our needs, our hurts, our wants, our weaknesses, etc.—then we will be quick to react in the natural realm instead of recognizing the spiritual battle we are in.

The message of the Cross is to focus on *others.* Doing that will make it easy to discard the negative thoughts that come into our mind. While Jesus was humiliated, He did not consider Himself, but us, knowing we would soon have possession of His mind—a mind that would focus only on what it can do for a lost and dying world.

Often, because of our overly great concern with self, many people can go quickly from oppression to depression. Why? Selfish thinking is never happy or satisfied and is the opposite of righteousness, peace, and joy. Depression leaves a person with extreme feelings of hopelessness, sadness, guilt, helplessness, and even suicide. The devil works overtime to get us to believe something that will weigh us down, and then he adds more things until eventually we are overwhelmed and he has a foothold in us. He is constantly looking for those who will fall prey to his tactics, for those who judge God's love for them by their circumstances instead of by His work on the Cross. We can read this warning in 1 Peter of how the devil goes around looking for whom he *may* devour:

Be sober, be vigilant; because your adversary the devil, as a roaring lion, walketh about, seeking whom he may devour: whom resist stedfast in the faith, knowing that the same afflictions are accomplished in your brethren that are in the world (1 Peter 5:8-9 KJV).

Seeing the Cross will help us see who we are in Christ by keeping us free from the guilt and condemnation of our sin and showing us how to live for others.

The Enemy Can Only Try

For a Christian, the enemy can only *try* to get us to believe *lies*, such as, "You'll never make it," "You'll fail if you step out," or "Nobody really cares about what happens to you." These thoughts appear real and can determine our core beliefs about ourselves and others. They are like fiery darts, as Ephesians says:

Above all, taking the shield of faith, wherewith ye shall be able to quench all the fiery darts of the wicked (Ephesians 6:16 KJV).

This means we must use our faith to quench these negative thoughts that pierce us like darts. A dart is like a slender, pointed missile that can pierce or penetrate its target.[28] The fiery darts of the devil are the thoughts he puts in our mind to oppress us with. So it is important that we guard what we allow ourselves to see and hear as we can help him along by the evil we expose ourselves to.

The Crown Pierced His Mind

The crown of thorns that Jesus bore had razor-sharp points that were approximately two to three inches long. The Roman soldiers roughly and mercilessly pressed this crown into His skull, drawing blood as it pierced Him. His blood was shed, and it was absolute agony for Him as the oppression and depression of the human mind pierced into His. All the thoughts of hopelessness, fear, powerlessness, guilt, condemnation, hatred, and anger penetrated deep inside of Him.

We can read about Him bearing this painful crown in the gospel of John:

The soldiers made a crown of long, sharp thorns and put it on his head, and they put a royal purple robe on him. "Hail! King of the Jews!" they mocked, and they hit him with their fists (John 19:2-3).

The thoughts of being nothing, no one, a victim, without purpose, were screamed into His ears and heart by that ruthless mob that beat Him. What was He thinking as the lies echoed relentlessly in His mind? Was He angered by the great deception that held those He loved in slavery? Was He thinking of the countless believers who would wear the crown of life and the robe of righteousness with Him? Was He appalled at how low man would go, knowing the beauty and riches of a kingdom He came to give them? The Roman soldiers who took sport in ridiculing Him represent us and what we do to Him when we question His power and authority.

These negative thoughts create boundaries that hinder us and lead us to believe lies that rob us of our authority and keep us from preaching the Good News of the kingdom.

Whenever we think that God didn't come through as we thought He should, we fail to see the big picture and reveal how little we understand eternity. Living our lives for what this earth has to offer will strip us of our hope and faith. The Cross forever speaks of who He is and strengthens our understanding of the purpose of suffering. It was when He wore the crown of thorns that He took the oppression of our mind and restored us to our rightful place as God's children.

We need to expose the negative beliefs, such as fear of failure, that subconsciously keep us from stepping out in faith to do God's will. In that scenario, our core belief is that we will always fail. That fear will stop us in our tracks and leave us feeling defeated and discouraged, with circumstances in control of us instead of us in control of them.

For years I struggled with feelings of inferiority, even after I was saved. Those feelings kept me from speaking out publicly even when I was asked to do so. I recall years ago attending a friend's wedding, and, when asked to give a short speech about the groom, I stood up to speak and froze, unable to utter a sound. With all eyes on me, I stood there embarrassed and had to sit down humiliated by my fear. For years I also believed that I would not be able to finish anything I started, and that kept me from doing many things. Now I refuse to believe that lie and purpose to finish whatever God tells me to do. When discouragement or lies bombard my mind, I run to the Cross and think of Him wearing the crown of thorns to assure me that I now have His mind in me, and I speak God's Word to overcome them. I choose to think of Him as He stood before Pilate declaring that He was a king and that His kingdom was not of this world.

Jesus desired to change the belief systems in our heart until our mind is renewed in the understanding of what He has done for us.

> *Then Jesus answered, "I am not an earthly king. If I were, my followers would have fought when I was arrested by the Jewish leaders. But my Kingdom is not of this world." Pilate replied, "You are a king then?" "You say that I am a king, and you are right," Jesus said. "I was born for that purpose. And I came to bring truth to the world. All who love the truth recognize that what I say is true"* (John 18:36-37).

Jesus was a joke to the Roman soldiers, and they humiliated Him relentlessly, crowning Him roughly with the crown of thorns and the royal purple robe, mocking His kingship.

Who We Are

Just as the King of kings and our High Priest was ridiculed, so our enemies try to undermine our knowledge of who we are in Him. The Word of God says a lot about who we are! We can read in Revelation that we are called kings and priests:

And hath made us kings and priests unto God and his Father; to him be glory and dominion for ever and ever. Amen (Revelation 1:6 KJV).

Now, having *that* revelation will definitely change your core beliefs about yourself! You are called to rule and reign in His kingdom. You have been made royalty by Him to rule in a realm under Christ. You are called to rule over the works of your flesh and conquer your circumstances, as He did for you.

> *We obtain the kingdom through understanding the work of the Cross.*

Our role as priest means we have been divinely appointed and anointed to do a work for God Himself. We are here with a purpose, and it is an important honor that has been bestowed upon us to see ourselves as called and set apart as His priests representing Christ to those without hope. It is through us that He will reveal His kingdom to others, by our work as priests, and it is an awesome responsibility to enter into the throne room of God on behalf of others.

Our kingly nature rules over sin, over the ways of this world, and over all the circumstances and difficulties we face. It also rules over the negative, doubting, fearful thoughts of our mind that cause us to see ourselves as mere men without power.

When I look at Jesus wearing His crown of thorns and royal purple robe, I see that I have been given back what was lost in the Garden of Eden.

We are His offspring and there will be a day when I will see Him face to face! In 1 John we can read that we will be just like Him when He returns, and that fact alone should motivate our lives to preach the Good News!

See how very much our heavenly Father loves us, for he allows us to be called his children, and we really are! But the people who belong to this world don't know God, so they don't understand that we are his children. Yes, dear friends, we are already God's children, and we can't even imagine what we will be like when Christ returns. But we do know that when he comes we will be like him, for we will see him as he really is (1 John 3:1-2).

The more we keep our eyes on the Cross, the more we see Him as He really is: obedient, pure, loving, selfless, and powerful enough in His humility to rise from the dead!

We really only have two options. We can look at His work on the Cross and let it determine who we are, or we can look at ourselves and our circumstances and let those determine who we are. It's not about thinking of what we can't do as Christians, but of who we are and what we can do.

Those who are dominated by the sinful nature think about sinful things, but those who are controlled by the Holy Spirit think about things that please the Spirit (Romans 8:5).

When we are led by the Spirit, we will think like He did and cast down the oppressive thoughts that would satisfy our flesh. Second Corinthians tells us that we must bring every thought to the obedience of Christ and destroy the thoughts that oppose God:

Casting down imaginations, and every high thing that exalteth itself against the knowledge of God, and bringing into captivity every thought to the obedience of Christ (2 Corinthians 10:5 KJV).

That spiritual renewal of our thoughts and attitudes can only come from the perspective of the Cross. Philippians says this:

Let this mind be in you, which was also in Christ Jesus: who, being in the form of God, thought it not robbery to be equal with God: but made himself of no reputation, and took upon him the form of a servant, and was made in the likeness of men: and being found in fashion as a man, he humbled himself, and became obedient unto death, even the death of the cross (Philippians 2:5-8 KJV).

The Word says you can know the actual thoughts of God! Can you imagine being able to think like God does? According to 1 Corinthians, you and I have that ability!

No one can know what anyone else is really thinking except that person alone, and no one can know God's thoughts except God's own Spirit. And

God has actually given us his Spirit (not the world's spirit) so we can know the wonderful things God has freely given us (1 Corinthians 2:11-12).

Just a few verses later we see that we also have the mind of Christ by His Spirit, which means we now have His attitude, His love for the lost, His authority and power to overcome, and His righteousness.

We who have the Spirit understand these things, but others can't understand us at all. How could they? For, "Who can know what the Lord is thinking? Who can give him counsel?" But we can understand these things, for we have the mind of Christ (1 Corinthians 2:15-16).

Jesus in His passion wore a crown of thorns and a royal purple robe so that you would no longer be deceived in your mind with oppression but would possess His mind, knowing who you are, and wear His crown of life and robe of righteousness.

You are His king and priest, called to rule and reign over sin and circumstances by allowing His Spirit to lead you. When oppression attacks your mind, think of His crown of thorns. When guilt and condemnation attack your thoughts, think of His royal purple robe and know that it is a mockery to believe the lies that undermine who you are and strip you of your authority as king and priest. Looking at the Cross gives you the power to conquer your flesh so you can rule and reign over your circumstances and obey His commands.

Chapter Fifteen

The Scourging

He was despised and rejected—a man of sorrows, acquainted with bitterest grief. We turned our backs on him and looked the other way when he went by. He was despised, and we did not care. Yet it was our weaknesses he carried; it was our sorrows that weighed him down. And we thought his troubles were a punishment from God for his own sins! But he was wounded and crushed for our sins. He was beaten that we might have peace. He was whipped, and we were healed! (Isaiah 53:3-5)

Jesus was tied to a whipping post and beaten mercilessly before cruel and mocking Roman soldiers. He was mutilated beyond human endurance as the destruction of the deeds of man's flesh were taken out on Him. By this horrendous act we were healed; we receive our healing by faith as we trust Him with our lives. Though our bodies age and die, He left us with a great and precious promise of new resurrected bodies that will be ours forever when we shed these earthly ones. When we look at what He endured during His passion, we must realize that it was our sins and our sorrows that were inflicted on Him. With every painful lash that penetrated His flesh, He purchased our peace and healed our wounds!

Our sins destroy our flesh, and when we look around at the wickedness of mankind we see endless examples of this. Time and time again, man destroys man by the wickedness that drives people to inflict pain.

I recall a day that I went to work and was shocked to see a newlywed we had just married two weeks earlier standing in the foyer of our office, beaten and bruised. I looked in horror at this beautiful young woman standing timidly in front of me, hanging her head in shame, desperate for help. "What happened to you?" I asked, upset at her discolored and swollen face. I thought she had been in a car accident, but I was surprised to hear her say, "My husband beat me up."

She had married an abuser, a man so full of anger that he thought nothing of beating her relentlessly. I knew her husband, and he seemed like such a nice, gentle, quiet man, and my mind wrestled with the very idea of him doing such a barbaric thing. The evidence was obvious, though, and I knew the physical and emotional pain this devastated woman felt was agonizingly real and would deeply damage her esteem.

People Can Be Mean

Domestic violence is just one of many cruel ways man destroys the heart of those they were created to love. Sexual abuse, rape, robbery, assault, murder, pimps, street gangs, and drug lords are rampant in our world. Such evil knows no boundaries. These abominations are in every class, culture, race, and country. Professionals, executives, blue collar workers, and the unemployed all have committed cruel crimes toward others, and in many cases escalated things into full-blown war. Every moment of every day there are untold thousands, perhaps millions, of people who are living in deplorable conditions being physically hurt or even killed at the hands of others.

The majority of us are not likely cruel people; however, there can be a mean streak that arises in all of us at times. I have witnessed the seemingly sweetest people in church turn ugly on a moment's notice if they're offended in some way. If we are honest with ourselves, we all have done something cruel to someone at some point in our lives. Whether intentional or not, we caused pain.

When hatred, threats, envy, or fear preside, man will go to great lengths to destroy one another. Over and over again we hear news emerging of the outrageous afflictions man can put on others. The genocide in Rwanda in 1990, which was featured in the film *Hotel Rwanda*, was one of many examples of how far men will go when hatred dominates their hearts. Numerous refugees from that war-torn country found refuge in our city and came to our church, sharing their unimaginable horror stories. To survive, one young man we came to know had to hide in the sludge of a septic bed for two days to escape death. This resulted in burns of more than 80 percent of his body. Others escaped by running for their lives and hiding for days in the dangers of the African jungle. They were petrified of being pursued by the butchers who sought their death.

Even in the United States we witnessed the cruelty of man when we heard the reports and saw the photos of the U.S. military treating their prisoners of war in despicable ways. Many people saw no problem with that form of inhumanity and hated those who exposed these atrocities, seeing them as traitors. The hatred of our heart performs the deeds of unthinkable wickedness that knows no limit when unleashed.

The work of His Cross shows how much the world hates Him.

The demonstration of the cruelty of man was fully manifested when Jesus Christ suffered at their hands.

We must ask ourselves, why? Why does man hate Him so much? The Word answers in the gospel of John, telling us that it is because they love their sin.

They hate the light because they want to sin in the darkness. They stay away from the light for fear their sins will be exposed and they will be punished. But those who do what is right come to the light gladly, so everyone can see that they are doing what God wants (John 3:20-21).

When we have evil in our heart, we will despise true light and love darkness.

Sinful man wants the depravity of his evil. Jesus, though, accused the world of its corruption as His Cross revealed it for what it is. He exposed their jealousy, lies, and hypocrisy because He is the truth. Those who love sin hated Him because He revealed the true nature of their hearts.

The world can't hate you, but it does hate me because I accuse it of sin and evil (John 7:7).

Unspeakable Pain

The scourging that He endured was to take the full wrath of God for all the cruelty committed by man and for the healing of our diseases.

He did not come to establish a kingdom with force and power, but with lowliness and humility, taking the wrath that was meant for those who hated Him.

In Isaiah's tremendous prophecy we can read about Jesus and His willing-ness to take on what was meant for us:

He was despised and rejected—a man of sorrows, acquainted with bitter-est grief. We turned our backs on him and looked the other way when he went by. He was despised, and we did not care. Yet it was our weaknesses he carried; it was our sorrows that weighed him down. And we thought his troubles were a punishment from God for his own sins! But he was wounded and crushed for our sins. He was beaten that we might have peace. He was whipped, and we were healed! (Isaiah 53:3-5)

Jesus had to suffer extreme torture to take the punishment for sin because God, who is just, absolutely hates evil. Those who desire and do evil are His ene-mies, and part of that punishment was flogging. The gospel of Matthew tells us that Pilate ordered Jesus to be flogged before He was crucified:

He was wounded, crushed, beaten, and whipped to give us the peace and healing that we lost because of sin.

So Pilate released Barabbas to them. He ordered Jesus flogged with a lead-tipped whip, then turned him over to the Roman soldiers to crucify him (Matthew 27:26).

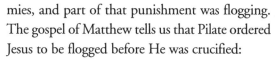

As with many of the other horrors He endured, Jesus didn't have to undergo flogging. But He chose to do so because everything in Him longed to heal us completely. This one small verse carries the weight of all the pain and sorrow inflicted on man. A flogging was a legal practice that preceded execution by the Romans. The whip they used is called a flagellum, and it consisted of a wooden handle with several strips of leather thongs with small iron balls or sharp pieces of glass, bone, or metal attached to the tips. Jesus would have been stripped naked and His hands bound securely to an upright post. The Roman soldiers inflicting the blows were called "lec-tors," and the severity of the flogging would depend on their demeanor. The only restriction they had was to not kill their victim. The lectors were not lim-ited to 39 lashes as the Jewish law dictated; the Romans had no limits.

Due to the hatred and cruelty that was already abounding toward Jesus, they would have shown no mercy. They thought He was a joke, claiming to be a king, and they took great pleasure in mocking Him. The blows would come down on Him hard and fast. The back, buttocks, and legs would be flogged relentlessly, bruising, tearing, and pulverizing the exposed flesh. Jesus would have felt searing, burning, sharp piercing pain permeating through His body, every nerve ending screaming for relief. He would find none; He had to pay the full price for all mankind. The wrath of God was being demonstrated through the cruelty of man on Himself, so that justice would be satisfied for every atrocity ever committed.

As the beating continued, His flesh would begin to come off in strips, similar to flaying a piece of meat. The underlying muscle and bone would be exposed in raw pain. The blows would come again and again, sometimes wrapping around His body and piercing His chest; sometimes His neck and face would be penetrated by the ends of the whip as they continued to fall. It was customary for the Romans, during a flogging, to turn their victims over and then begin beating them on their chest, loin, and leg area. The intense pain and blood loss would send Him into circulatory shock, and, as He weakened, He would collapse just short of death.

What was He thinking as each blow struck Him? Was He seeing the multitudes of people ravaged with pain in their bodies being set free and healed? Did He see the throngs of worshippers rejoicing in heaven with their new incorruptible bodies? With each blow did He think of the destruction of the evil He hated so much, and the believers who would be filled with His Spirit? Did He love His persecutors and pray for their deliverance as He did later on His Cross? Did He see you in your hour of darkness, suffering and in pain, and touch you with His unlimited desire to hold and heal you? Did He pray that you would see how far He would go to win the lost so you would too?

The sins of the flesh would be destroyed and the pain of disease forever abolished by this act of obedience, of Jesus submitting to the punishment we deserved. Remember, this scourging followed a night of relentless torture, having been rejected, betrayed, deserted, denied, falsely accused, spit on, beaten, mocked, ridiculed, shackled, shamed, and humiliated. We must think of how He felt, the fatigue and pain that racked His being but that He endured out of love for us. The Bible describes how He appeared after this ruthless torture:

> *Many were amazed when they saw him—beaten and bloodied, so disfigured one would scarcely know he was a person* (Isaiah 52:14).

After His scourging Jesus had to face the mob again, beaten, bloodied, disfigured, standing in total humiliation with the mockery of the crown of thorns and the royal purple robe ridiculing His kingship, as He carried the evil of man on Himself before all.

> *Pilate went outside again and said to the people, "I am going to bring him out to you now, but understand clearly that I find him not guilty." Then Jesus came out wearing the crown of thorns and the purple robe. And Pilate said, "Here is the man!" When they saw him, the leading priests and Temple guards began shouting, "Crucify! Crucify!" "You crucify him," Pilate said. "I find him not guilty"* (John 19:4-6)

Through His entire passion He never lost sight of *who He was or why He was subjecting Himself to such hatred.* This prophetic word in Isaiah declares His determination to do the will of God:

He became the highest by becoming the lowest.

The Sovereign LORD has spoken to me, and I have listened. I do not rebel or turn away. I give my back to those who beat me and my cheeks to those who pull out my beard. I do not hide from shame, for they mock me and spit in my face. Because the Sovereign LORD helps me, I will not be dismayed. Therefore, I have set my face like a stone, determined to do his will. And I know that I will triumph (Isaiah 50:5-7).

He was determined to do God's will, and He knew He would triumph.

Perhaps you are a victim of a crime; maybe you were sexually abused, raped, beaten, or robbed. Some of you may be war survivors and witnessed the atrocities that have been committed against others while defending your country. Maybe you were beaten mercilessly by an abusive parent or by the bullies at school. Whether you survived a concentration camp or a brutal rape, had your home robbed, or been violated in some other way, your hurt has the potential to destroy you if you do not receive healing. Your pain is very real, and it has to be dealt with. Jesus went through the scourging to take it away and help you see that there is peace, deliverance, and comfort in Him. He literally went through hell to redeem you of your sorrows. However, in order to find the healing you and I desperately need, we must bring our pain to the Cross.

His heart ached for us the entire time He suffered, praying, hoping, believing that we would love Him back. He knew it would not be in vain. He saw you and He saw me. His only goal was to glorify His Father and win our heart.

Jesus had been mentally, emotionally, and physically abused and was now left in critical condition to carry out His final victory. *"With his stripes we are healed"* (Isaiah 53:5 KJV). He was critically wounded and His flesh was flayed for us.

Unfortunately, many things happen that we do not understand, and if we judge them from simply an earthbound viewpoint, we will wonder what God is up to.

Seeing things through our natural eyes will always cause us to question God's character and integrity. Because I keep my eyes on the work of the Cross, it is easy for me to trust God even when circumstances would dictate that God is not for me, may not love me, or want to meet my needs. Sometimes unknown to me there is a higher purpose that I cannot see in the natural. If I judge God by a situation that seems unfair or wrong and think He should have done things differently, I am doing one of several things. I am either blaming Him for something that was a direct consequence of sin—and that is unjust toward God—or I am exalting myself over Him thinking I know better, which is the ultimate of pride.

We Are Healed!

While Jesus walked the earth fulfilling His ministry, everything He did reflected His character and how He feels toward man. Throughout His entire public ministry and His passion, He continually demonstrated His will to heal and deliver us.

Physical healing was a major part of what Jesus did wherever He went. The four gospels are teeming with accounts of His healing power. The gospel of Matthew records that He healed all that were sick:

That evening many demon-possessed people were brought to Jesus. All the spirits fled when he commanded them to leave; and he healed all the sick. This fulfilled the word of the Lord through Isaiah, who said, "He took our sicknesses and removed our diseases" (Matthew 8:16-17).

To take something means to seize with authority, or to confiscate, to impose on oneself or to subject oneself to something.[29] To remove means to take off, take away, eliminate, do away with, or dismiss from position.[30] Jesus literally confiscated, seized with authority, and subjected to Himself our sicknesses and diseases, eliminating them and dismissing them from their position in our lives. In other words, they have departed!

The Word tells us that He took our sicknesses and removed our diseases.

I have had several very supernatural healings in my life. The first time occurred shortly after I was saved. I had fallen on some ice and broken my pelvic bone. A few days after the injury, I was put in a convalescent hospital for six to eight weeks while it healed. I was completely bedridden and could not move my legs without extreme pain. The very day I was admitted to the hospital, some people from my church came to visit me while another group of believers stayed back at the church to pray for my healing. During their visit, God completely healed me. The pain left instantly and I could walk, jump, and do somersaults!

Since then I have experienced God's healing power many times. Through my 34 years as a Christian I have witnessed many supernatural healings of those who stood in faith besides my own. I also know that there are times people believe for a healing and it doesn't happen here on earth. Even though I believe healing is God's will, I also know that there are things I do not know or understand that only God knows. I cannot always understand the whys, but because I know God's character I trust Him regardless of what happens.

We live in a fallen world, and man does many things aside from sin to provide opportunities for sickness and disease to attack us. Years ago people smoked and were unaware of the dangers. However, even in their ignorance they still died from smoking. In our modern day of technology with cell phones and microwaves, along with the chemicals put in our food and drinks, we could be inadvertently harming our bodies. In our city alone the number of people who line up every morning at the local coffee shops to fill their bodies with strong doses of caffeine is amazing. Between environmental exposures, unhealthy eating, and stress, along with the sin of ourselves and others, our aging bodies are subject to attack.

It is not our place to judge others if they get sick or whether or not they receive their healing here or by obtaining their new bodies. We overcome by faith, and whatever we believe we must be fully assured of to receive. Our problem is that we always try to figure out why and find someone or something to blame for everything.

How could we ever know more than God does? Our perspective of God is very important; how we see Him will determine our faith.

My judgment of God must always be grounded in the Cross.

If we need to know what God is like, we simply need to look at Jesus and all He has done for us.

Every day we are faced with circumstances that require faith on our part. God is not a respecter of persons, the Word says, which means He will never favor one over the other (Acts 10:34 KJV). But God *is* a respecter of *faith*. In fact, in the book of Hebrews the Word tells us that without faith it is impossible to please God!

> *So, you see, it is impossible to please God without faith. Anyone who wants to come to him must believe that there is a God and that he rewards those who sincerely seek him* (Hebrews 11:6).

People continually thronged Jesus because of the needs they had; they believed He could heal them. There are numerous accounts of Him commenting that it was *their faith* that produced the healing they received. Look at this example from the gospel of Matthew:

> *Jesus turned around and said to her, "Daughter, be encouraged! Your faith has made you well." And the woman was healed at that moment* (Matthew 9:22).

"Your faith has made you well,*"* He told her.

In the gospel of Luke is an account where Jesus told a blind man He healed that it was *his* faith that healed him.

> *When Jesus heard him, he stopped and ordered that the man be brought to him. Then Jesus asked the man, "What do you want me to do for you?" "Lord," he pleaded, "I want to see!" And Jesus said, "All right, you can see!*

151

Your faith has healed you." Instantly the man could see, and he followed Jesus, praising God. And all who saw it praised God, too (Luke 18:40-43).

In the book of Acts it says that *"Faith in Jesus' name has caused this healing before your very eyes."* Note that *faith* caused the healing!

The name of Jesus has healed this man—and you know how lame he was before. Faith in Jesus' name has caused this healing before your very eyes (Acts 3:16).

Another scripture in the gospel of Mark tells us that because of lack of faith, He couldn't do any mighty miracles:

And because of their unbelief, he couldn't do any mighty miracles among them except to place his hands on a few sick people and heal them (Mark 6:5).

In every account of Jesus healing someone, there was faith involved. Thus it is very important that we understand the principles of faith. Faith has a lot to do with our receiving healing. Many *hope* for healing and think it is faith. Faith and hope are two different things. Hope is what gives purpose to your faith, and faith is what gives substance to your hope. *Without hope there can be no faith, but without faith your hope will not produce results.*

When you are in faith, you are absolutely assured of what you hope for regardless of what you see or when it happens. Faith simply believes what it cannot yet see, and what is seen doesn't affect what it believes. The first verse in Hebrews 11 describes it well:

What is faith? It is the confident assurance that what we hope for is going to happen. It is the evidence of things we cannot yet see (Hebrews 11:1).

Sometimes we believe that because the object of our faith doesn't manifest here in this natural realm, it didn't happen. That is not true, as we can read on in Hebrews 11:

…But others trusted God and were tortured, preferring to die rather than turn from God and be free. They placed their hope in the resurrection to a better life. Some were mocked, and their backs were cut open with whips. Others were chained in dungeons. Some died by stoning, and some were sawed in half; others were killed with the sword. Some went about

in skins of sheep and goats, hungry and oppressed and mistreated. They were too good for this world. They wandered over deserts and mountains, hiding in caves and holes in the ground. All of these people we have mentioned received God's approval because of their faith, yet none of them received all that God had promised. For God had far better things in mind for us that would also benefit them, for they can't receive the prize at the end of the race until we finish the race (Hebrews 11:35-40).

This portion of scripture tells us that many stood in faith yet didn't receive their promise until the resurrection life. Some of the saints in God's Word are still waiting in faith because God has far better things for them. The prize they suffered and believed for can't be received until *we* finish the race.

God has a plan so much bigger and better than we could ever imagine, and sometimes we simply have to trust Him with the timing and magnitude of the outcome. The Cross convinces me of that. When we are absolutely assured of His love, it is easy to rest in His promises in spite of how things appear around us.

My Sister's Story

This next story I am going to share is very difficult for me. It is still fresh, and I still occasionally weep when I think about it. However, I don't weep just with sorrow, but also with gratitude for God's goodness, even when I do not understand everything.

Approximately nine years ago my younger sister, Jennifer, was diagnosed with a brain tumor. When it was first discovered, the medical profession operated and removed most of it. They said it was not life-threatening as it was very slow growing and the cancer was not very dangerous. (I didn't know there was such a thing.) They were unable to get it all since it was wrapped around a major artery in her brain and it was too dangerous to remove it completely. For several years she seemed fine, and she took the treatments recommended. Then symptoms returned. They operated again, and, following their recommendation, she chose to have extreme doses of radiation and chemotherapy. As time went on, the tumor became more and more aggressive. Eventually another surgery left her paralyzed on one side. Finally there was nothing more the medical field could do. They could only keep her as comfortable as possible until she passed away.

Jennifer was a very vibrant, loving wife and mother who served God, leading the praise and worship with her husband in her church. She was well known for her encouraging words and hugs. She was only 40 years old and had three children. Throughout the course of her illness, she desired to be healed but was not afraid to die. She continually encouraged those who came to see her that she felt sorrier for those who would be left than for herself, and she was absolutely confident of where she was going. Even her doctors and nurses were often compelled to visit her room, for she had an amazing ability to encourage others. They were impressed by her lack of fear and her faith in an afterlife. She chose to place her faith in where she was going more than in being healed.

> *God has saved, healed, and delivered us all. And as it says in Hebrews, some died believing for their miracle.*

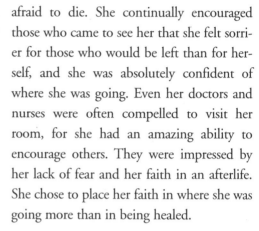

To my knowledge, based on what she told me, she never embraced a place of being assured of her healing in this life, but rather she accepted whatever happened, hoping for healing. I personally questioned that it was God's best for her to die so young; however, Jennifer was ready and willing for whatever happened. I respected her in where she placed her faith and confidence of her eternal destiny. So in spite of the prayers and fasting of many for her healing, she passed away January 9, 2003. She died the same day my late husband had died 14 years earlier. Whenever I would visit her in the hospital, she would tell me she was going to see Jim soon. It was portentous to me that she died the same day.

Some people, because of their insecurities, had to have a reason for her death. Some blamed her for sin in her life—nothing they could name—they simply believed it just had to be there. If that were true, we all would be dead since none of us are perfect outside of Christ, and she was in Christ. Some say such things because they do not understand the Cross or eternity. Even though I believe it is God's best to heal, because of the law of love, it is never my place to judge another. I am not so insecure in my faith that I need an explanation for what someone else goes through. The Cross teaches me that. Jennifer was always willing for whatever happened, and, regardless of how things looked, she kept the right attitude. What was going on *in her* was far greater. Her faith was in eternity more than in her healing. She had confidence in her God and what awaited her in heaven.

It would be incredibly tragic if this life is all there is, and thank God it isn't! We all have been healed by the stripes of Jesus because by the power of faith it is already done. The more these truths become real to us, the more we will see the manifestation in our lives. Perhaps you live with the physical pain of infirmity in your body. Some may have chronic back pain, arthritis, migraines, or pain from a progressive disease that has ravaged them. Physical pain can be excruciating and torturous, and it has the potential to drive a person mad when it is.

This life is short, and in light of eternity we all will experience the full manifestation of all healing.

Jesus knows the depth of your pain, and regardless of whether it is emotional or physical, He dealt with it all. He understands the feelings of hopelessness and the searing fire of physical pain that throbs through your being. He prays for you and waits for you to take it to Him at His Cross, for it is only there you find life, heal-

ing, and wholeness for your life. Place your trust in Him and rest confidently in the healing power of His Word as you focus your attention on Him. He's already done it all. First Peter tells us that we have been healed by His wounds!

> *He personally carried away our sins in his own body on the cross so we can be dead to sin and live for what is right. You have been healed by his wounds!* (1 Peter 2:24)

I have noticed that the older I get, the more this next scripture is true in 2 Corinthians. It says that our bodies here make us sigh and groan and that they are humiliating compared to the new ones that await us.

> *Our dying bodies make us groan and sigh, but it's not that we want to die and have no bodies at all. We want to slip into our new bodies so that these dying bodies will be swallowed up by everlasting life* (2 Corinthians 5:4).

The book of Romans says that the Holy Spirit within us has been given as a foretaste of future glory and our full rights as God's children are coming, including the new bodies He has promised us:

And even we Christians, although we have the Holy Spirit within us as a foretaste of future glory, also groan to be released from pain and suffering. We, too, wait anxiously for that day when God will give us our full rights as his children, including the new bodies he has promised us (Romans 8:23).

The Cross forever declares that all the pain and destruction set against mankind has been destroyed. He took the brutal scourging to heal and deliver us spiritually, emotionally, and physically. In Isaiah it describes so well the promise of the Christ to come and how through Him our chains will be broken and we will live in His peace forever!

The people who walk in darkness will see a great light—a light that will shine on all who live in the land where death casts its shadow. Israel will again be great, and its people will rejoice as people rejoice at harvesttime. They will shout with joy like warriors dividing the plunder. **For God will break the chains that bind his people and the whip that scourges them,** *just as he did when he destroyed the army of Midian with Gideon's little band. In that day of peace, battle gear will no longer be issued. Never again will uniforms be bloodstained by war. All such equipment will be burned. For a child is born to us, a son is given to us. And the government will rest on his shoulders. These will be his royal titles: Wonderful Counselor, Mighty God, Everlasting Father, Prince of Peace. His ever expanding, peaceful government will never end. He will rule forever with fairness and justice from the throne of his ancestor David. The passionate commitment of the LORD Almighty will guarantee this!* (Isaiah 9:2-7, emphasis added)

The scourging whip is broken and by His stripes we are healed! That is our promise from His work on the Cross.

Chapter Sixteen

The Road to the Cross

Then Jesus said to the disciples, "If any of you wants to be my follower, you must put aside your selfish ambition, shoulder your cross, and follow me. If you try to keep your life for yourself, you will lose it. But if you give up your life for me, you will find true life. And how do you benefit if you gain the whole world but lose your own soul in the process? Is anything worth more than your soul?" (Matthew 16:24-26)

After taking every sin known to man and enduring the destruction of His flesh, Jesus picked up His Cross and walked down the road of suffering. Today, we know that road in Jerusalem as the Via Dolorosa. The name means "a difficult course." I have been there, and it is approximately six football fields long. As Jesus stumbled along it, He was in physical agony and surrounded with the jeers of an angry mob as well as of the soldiers who were determined to see Him to His fate. Because His love for us was so immense, He carried the Cross and struggled under its weight, determined to complete our redemption.

What was He thinking as He bore the horrors of this world on His wounded shoulders? Was He weeping inside for the suffering of humanity that He was now experiencing? Was He overwhelmed with the depths man had fallen to from the glory we were created for? Or perhaps He was seeing the broken men and women who discovered their spouse had left and now faced a painful road alone. His heart must have ached for the starving people in lands that had been corrupted by the selfishness of man. His thoughts filled with a love so powerful that it drove Him to continue, even as He felt the breath of death awaiting Him. For beyond, He knew, was the hope of the resurrection that would follow. And not just His, but ours.

Whatever He thought, we know that His heart was bursting with compassion for those He had created to live in His glory for eternity. It possessed Him so completely that nothing could keep Him from that hill He was heading to.

It has been said that Jesus fell several times along the way from exhaustion and physical pain, and like Him we too at times may collapse under the pressure of going down a long and difficult road.

When we truly see Him, we will know that every step of His suffering was to identify with ours, so He could touch us heart to heart, making us one to set us free.

We also must never forget that we too were the cause of His pain, breaking His heart and abandoning Him as though He meant nothing to us. We all have caused Him to weep as every parent does over a rebellious, runaway child. We have murdered those He loved by our selfishness and hatred. Our addictions and bondages drove Him to deliver us, sparing no cost. We forced Him who loved us so immensely to watch us in our affliction ignoring His outstretched arms of mercy and grace.

I have now come to realize that the suffering we go through when we lose someone by death, desertion, or a life-threatening addiction is what He feels every time we turn from Him. He was so compelled by a love for us that He would die rather than see us perish. He desired to show us that, as He walked the Via Dolorosa, He understands and knows what we feel and how difficult it is to bear our pain. Because of what He has done, we will always have the Cross to run to when life gets tough. To meditate on that fact is to connect with His heart and receive the strength we need to overcome and keep going. As we go through life, we will encounter trials that will test us to the limit, and as many have discovered, everything can change in a moment of time.

My Own Via Dolorosa

As I look over my life, one of those life-changing moments was the day I came home from shopping with some girlfriends and found the police waiting at my door. They were there to tell me that my husband had just been killed in a car accident. He had been on his way to pick up a friend for a men's prayer breakfast when it happened.

As the police officer approached me, I saw our associate pastor pull up and knew that something was terribly wrong. My heart raced and I felt like the blood drained from my body as they told me to go into my house so they could talk to me. I felt sick and dizzy and could barely make it inside. Once we all were settled on my sofa, the police officer gently began to explain to me what had happened. When I heard the words "your husband didn't make it," I couldn't believe what I was hearing. I was shocked and numbed, and I knew that I was about to begin the most difficult time of my life.

I had never lost someone that close to me—only my grandfather when I was a young girl. A hundred thoughts flooded my mind. *How could this happen? How am I going to tell our girls? Do his parents know? If not, how am I going to tell them? Why didn't he drive more carefully? Why? How can I make it without him? WHY? HOW? WHERE? WHAT?* The thoughts continued to bombard my mind, and I couldn't imagine my life without him.

I was asked to go to the hospital to identify his body, which took every bit of strength I had. Only God enabled me to get through the horror of seeing him lifeless in that cold sterile room in the hospital basement.

As the day of Jim's death progressed, dozens of calls began flooding in from acquaintances and fellow ministers from around the world, and within hours my home filled up with friends and family. I felt overwhelmed; everything seemed surreal. It was difficult to think clearly and process my thoughts.

My three daughters were at the home of a friend of mine when I found out about Jim's death, and when they came home a few hours later, telling them was the most difficult thing I had to do. Their lives would never be the same either, and looking into their eyes and having to let them know that the father they adored was gone was almost more than I could bear. They too were devastated and wept with grief.

In spite of the entire trauma I was going through, deep inside, because of my strong faith, I knew somehow we all would be okay, but it would not be easy. I had a difficult road ahead of me, and for a while I struggled to live one day at a time. To think beyond that was unbearable. And as anyone knows who has had a great tragedy in his or her life, sometimes living one minute at a time is enough.

As the days dragged by, my emotions came and went in waves. I would start to feel a little better, then something would trigger my grief and I would feel like the world had ended for me. I had never wanted to die before, but now at times I did, and felt part of me already had. When the Word of God says a husband and wife are one, they really are. So when death or divorce separates them, it is a dying process for both.

There was no way out, no turning back the clock; this was something I had to walk through, but not alone. Praying and worshipping God was my greatest solace, and that is what kept me sane at times. I thank God I knew His Word as well as I did back then; however, I wish I had known the revelation of the Cross that I now have since it would have made things so much easier.

I would get to the other side, and, fortunately for me, I had a tremendous support of Godly people who poured out their love for me in many ways. For weeks my home was filled with meals prepared with love, and though I couldn't eat much, the constant flow of company greatly appreciated it. Many pastors and their wives called and met with me, and the leaders in my church surrounded me with affirmation and ongoing support. Never had I experienced such an outpouring of love, and yet I felt I walked alone. At night when the people left and the children were asleep, it was just me, and it was then that I would weep with grief. Yet, when I stopped to listen, I could hear the gentle voice of my loving Savior whispering comfort to me. "I've been there; I know your pain. I feel your heartache, and I suffered with you and for you."

I was not one without hope, and even though I lacked the knowledge I now have, He carried me through the darkest days of my life.

Carrying a Heavy Cross

Jesus knows that lonely, difficult walk we face when we have to go down a road of suffering. When there is no escape from a trial, it is a cross we must bear.

Technically speaking, the Cross Jesus had to bear, which took our sin and God's wrath, He bore by Himself. However, Mark records that He was assisted by a man named Simon from Cyrene when He required help to carry the physical Cross because of the weakness of His beaten flesh.

A man named Simon, who was from Cyrene, was coming in from the country just then, and they forced him to carry Jesus' cross. (Simon is the father of Alexander and Rufus.) And they brought Jesus to a place called Golgotha (which means Skull Hill) (Mark 15:21-22).

Whenever we go through suffering, we will either die to self or we will become selfish, angry, and bitter. Many believers mistakenly think that they will never be touched by trials and that the Christian life is a life of blessing only. Unfortunately, bad things will happen since this world is full of tragedy. Yet, we who believe will have blessings that follow every test we face. The trials of our life help us to become more like Him when we keep our heart right and trust Him through them. Although there are many things we don't want to walk through, when we do so with joy, using our authority to conquer our flesh, we will be ready for anything, as James tells us:

Dear brothers and sisters, whenever trouble comes your way, let it be an opportunity for joy. For when your faith is tested, your endurance has a chance to grow. So let it grow, for when your endurance is fully developed, you will be strong in character and ready for anything (James 1:2-4).

This means that we will have everything we need because trials produce Godly character in the same way our muscles grow stronger when built up by resistance. Growing and strengthening is usually always a painful process in all areas of life. The old saying, "no pain, no gain," is very true.

Those who believe we are exempt from suffering often backslide when it comes. Many people get angry with God and blame Him because He did not pamper them as they desired. We all go through devastating circumstances. When we are not prepared for them, we will not likely survive when they show up. God never promised that our lives would be easy and stress-free. In fact, He said in the Psalms that we would have many afflictions—*and* that He would deliver us out of them! Our response when all hell breaks loose determines the outcome and the blessings to follow!

Many are the afflictions of the righteous: but the LORD delivereth him out of them all (Psalm 34:19 KJV).

The Cross creates in us a desire to go through whatever it takes to be like Him.

When we really acknowledge that He got what we deserved, any trial we go through doesn't seem as difficult as what He faced. Knowing this produces gratefulness for our redemption. The apostle Paul in 1 Thessalonians went as far as to say that we were *"appointed"* to afflictions. Now that is an appointment we don't often brag about or desire, but it comes hand in hand with reaching the lost!

> *The work of the Cross enables and prepares us to be ready for anything.*

That no man should be moved by these afflictions: for yourselves know that we are appointed thereunto (1 Thessalonians 3:3 KJV).

When we keep our eyes on Him, we will be led by His Spirit and able to conquer the worst of circumstances. Like Him, we too will keep our heart completely right with God through it all.

Our faith in His work on the Cross is what empowers us to the other side!

Victory is accomplished when we process our suffering through the Cross and keep the same attitude Jesus had. When His life is produced in us, we experience His glory and overcome our pain!

Releasing Life in the Midst of Death

Just as He focused on the incredible joy that would follow His suffering, so we always receive life-giving power when we look and believe for the good in a bad situation.

We must be prepared spiritually for any major curve that changes our lives in order to receive the glory from it. It only takes a moment for our circumstances to completely change forever. A natural disaster, the death of a loved one, an adulterous spouse, a diagnosis of cancer, or even a job loss are life-changing moments. It only took a few minutes on September 11, 2001, to change the world as we knew it. That one event altered our travel, freedom, and national security.

There is immense suffering almost everywhere, most of which gets blamed on God. Unfortunately, the curse of sin abounds, and no country is exempt. It takes no faith to trust God when we get what we want, when and how we want it. Real faith is obedience when nothing makes sense. When we know God's character, we will not be moved but be willing to trust Him whatever the cost. *Only the Cross can give us that type of trust.*

The apostle Paul acknowledged it this way in his letter to the Corinthians. He said his suffering for the Gospel revealed Christ in him. Just as the death of Christ on the Cross released the life of His Spirit, so the daily dying to our flesh in the troubles we encounter and living to win others will release His life in us.

> *But we have this treasure in earthen vessels, that the excellency of the power may be of God, and not of us. We are troubled on every side, yet not distressed; we are perplexed, but not in despair; persecuted, but not forsaken; cast down, but not destroyed; always bearing about in the body the dying of the Lord Jesus, that the life also of Jesus might be made manifest in our body. For we which live are alway delivered unto death for Jesus' sake, that the life also of Jesus might be made manifest in our mortal flesh. So then death worketh in us, but life in you* (2 Corinthians 4:7-12 KJV).

Rejected for a Murderer

Just prior to the excruciating walk to Golgotha, Jesus experienced one of the worst cases of injustice recorded. Pilate knew that Jesus was innocent and sought a way to release Him by offering His life in exchange for a murderer. His plan failed because the absolute hatred and envy toward Jesus was beyond reason. The gospel of Mark records the incident:

> *Now it was the governor's custom to release one prisoner each year at Passover time—anyone the people requested. One of the prisoners at that time was Barabbas, convicted along with others for murder during an insurrection. The mob began to crowd in toward Pilate, asking him to release a prisoner as usual. "Should I give you the King of the Jews?" Pilate asked. (For he realized by now that the leading priests had arrested Jesus out of envy.) But at this point the leading priests stirred up the mob to demand the release of Barabbas instead of Jesus* (Mark 15:6-11).

Imagine the absurdity of a known convicted murderer being released by an angry mob despite the proof of innocence by the governor. The hatred of the crowd demanded that Jesus be crucified. How did their hatred for Him make

Him feel? Did He question why He had to endure this for them? Did He dwell on the magnitude of hypocrisy toward Him? Was His heart pierced again as the reality of their love for evil was driven home? These were the people He came to save; He knew and loved them. He birthed their nation and set up their laws. He wept for them when He saw their evil deeds.

Jesus took our place—the place of a murderer and leader of an insurrection—and went to Golgotha.

Barabbas was a known murderer; a cross had been prepared for him for his heinous crime. Murder is one of the worst of crimes because it destroys man made in the image of God. To take a life is to take everything. Jesus' life was given for all those who have robbed others of the abundant life God intended. When we harbor hatred and ill will toward others, we taken something from them. Sin causes us all to be murderers are guilty of taking a part of their life from them. If you have ever been stopped in your tracks and robbed of time and productivity because you were consumed with a hurt inflicted by another, you have lost a part of your life.

It is interesting to know that the name *Barabbas* means "the son of any father."[31] He was spared the punishment he deserved because Jesus took His Cross that day. He represented all of us, the son of any father; he was guilty just as we are; and the cross prepared for him was also the one we deserved. Barabbas was guilty not only of murder, but also of leading an insurrection, which is a revolt against a constituted authority or government.[32] That is exactly what man did to His Creator. We revolted against God and rebelled against His rule and authority in our lives.

He carried our suffering so that we would walk in freedom from pain's destruction.

One of the most difficult trials occurs when our children are attacked and have to suffer. The following story is an example of how God can work in the midst of the worst of ordeals on a road of suffering.

One Wrong Choice

My heart wept with compassion as I looked into Carol's eyes, so full of pain mixed with hope as she bared her heart to me about the tragic circumstances she was walking through. She is such an attractive, intelligent, and Godly woman, admired by many. To look at her, one would never imagine the pain she carried. Her speech is articulate, and she has written several successful books and travels extensively as a national speaker. A few years ago, everything in her life changed in a moment with one phone call in the middle of the night. (I will briefly summarize her unthinkable ordeal; however, you can read the entire account in her own words in her book, *When I Lay My Isaac Down.*)

Carol and her husband Gene had one child, a son. Like any doting parents, they had great expectations of him. Their son Jason was raised with Christian principles and grew up with a desire to serve God and his country. He graduated from the U.S. Navel Academy and married a Christian woman who had two daughters from a previous marriage. The Kents had prayed through Jason's entire life that he would marry the right girl. So with reservations at first, they loved and accepted his new wife and her children. Their son and daughter-in-law and their new grandchildren were serving God and active in their church in Florida where they lived.

Things seemed to be wonderful until the night of that call. It came at 12:35 a.m. It was a chilling and horrible message concerning their son. The caller informed them that Jason had just been arrested and charged with first-degree murder for killing his wife's ex-husband. This man had been threatening Jason and his wife with taking the girls in a custody battle. Because this man had been abusive, Jason feared for the safety of his stepdaughters, until he snapped and shot the ex-husband in cold blood and in public.

Receiving news like that for good, upstanding Christian parents is not a nightmare that ends quickly. Nor was there a happy ending anywhere in sight. Their lives were forever changed, and they were forced to walk down that difficult course, the road of suffering. There was no way out of it or around it. Their son faced the death penalty, and at the very least life imprisonment. Either way, his only way out of prison was in a body bag.

After much prayer by many supporters, Jason was spared the death penalty and given a life sentence without parole. He is now in a very high security prison, all because he had cracked in a moment of time under extreme stress, fearing for the well-being of his family. His actions cannot be taken back or changed.

Through this unimaginable journey, Gene and Carol have had to learn to keep their eyes on their Savior through every painful step of the way. Because they have guarded their hearts and adopted the Spirit of Christ in all they do, God has been using this tragedy for good.

The Cross tells us that resurrection life is ours to take by faith in Him.

Carol and the other women she frequently ministers with had never been active in prison ministry, but now they are very involved. God is bringing good through it all as Jason is also serving Him inside the prison, assisting the chaplain. However, his life and the life of his parents, wife, and stepdaughters are on a difficult road. Is their suffering the fault of God? Absolutely not! But He does take our mistakes and turn them into something to build His kingdom and give us victory when we surrender them to the Cross.

For Carol and Gene it has been heart-wrenching to see their only child spending his life locked behind bars, never to get out alive. To endure, they have claimed as their hope the following scripture:

That is why we never give up. Though our bodies are dying, our spirits are being renewed every day. For our present troubles are quite small and won't last very long. Yet they produce for us an immeasurably great glory that will last forever! So we don't look at the troubles we can see right now; rather, we look forward to what we have not yet seen. For the troubles we see will soon be over, but the joys to come will last forever (2 Corinthians 4:16-18).

This speaks of the victory of the Cross and gives us the message of an eternal hope to all mankind that resurrection life is ours to take by faith in Him.

This world does not dictate the final word for us, though some things have to be endured for a season. We can hope and believe in a definite outcome that will deliver us from all that afflicts us.

Many who have gone before us sold out to God, and the book of Hebrews tells us of the people of faith who, looking past their lives here on earth, were willing to die for what they believed.

Women received their loved ones back again from death. But others trusted God and were tortured, preferring to die rather than turn from God and be free. They placed their hope in the resurrection to a better life (Hebrews 11:35).

This means that, as Christians, all that this life offers is not what we live for. So many focus most of their hope on what is here rather than on eternity. Unless Christ takes us at His return, we will die. That is certain. Our destiny is not for this world but for the kingdom of God. The only thing we can take with us is souls. Jesus lived and died with passion to win the lost, drawing from the knowledge of God and the kingdom that awaited Him, seeing past this natural world. We are called to follow His example.

The road to the Cross may be a difficult one, but it leads to life. Isaiah told us about how we can be overcome with joy and gladness on it:

> *And a main road will go through that once deserted land. It will be named the Highway of Holiness. Evil-hearted people will never travel on it. It will be only for those who walk in God's ways; fools will never walk there. Lions will not lurk along its course, and there will be no other dangers. Only the redeemed will follow it. Those who have been ransomed by the LORD will return to Jerusalem, singing songs of everlasting joy. Sorrow and mourning will disappear, and they will be overcome with joy and gladness* (Isaiah 35:8-10).

The road of suffering may lead us to the Cross, but the *"Highway of Holiness"* flows from it and leads us to the end of our pain and sorrow.

We will never be disappointed when we put our hope in the work of the Cross and see our resurrected life!

Chapter Seventeen

Nailed to the Cross

And they brought Jesus to a place called Golgotha (which means Skull Hill). They offered him wine drugged with myrrh, but he refused it. Then they nailed him to the cross. They gambled for his clothes, throwing dice to decide who would get them (Mark 15:22-24).

"*Then they nailed him to the cross.*" These seven words in the Scriptures culminate the most important and revolutionary event that ever happened among men: It made all things new.

It was not nails and ropes that held Him on the Cross, but His will. He couldn't help but love us no matter what we did to Him. Because of this amazing moment in history where God died for man, we now have the ability to stand pure and holy in His very presence. Jesus lived to die shamefully, nailed to a Cross while bearing the entire sin of man and the full wrath of God.

Many people still feel bound by their sin, unable to change the things they face in their life, and live frustrated and defeated in chains from their personal history. We must have the revelation that the Cross made all things new in order for us to be free. That means our lot in life can only be changed by His power when we lay it down at the foot of His Cross.

Christ was willing to let go of all the status and power He held in heaven and submit to the hatred of a mankind controlled by the powers of hell itself. Because of the Cross, we who were stained with the stench of sin are now holy and blameless, forever able to be with our God.

Is that how you see yourself? Or do your weaknesses and mistakes continually rehearse their guilt in your mind, robbing you of your peace? Are you confident in your purity or shamed by your sin?

We all had a record of our sins past, present, and future, and that record was nailed on the Cross with Christ. He deprived sin of its means to victimize or condemn us.

Not only do we overcome our sins, but we also overcome the sins committed against us. Unfortunately, many still see themselves as victims, in circumstances where they feel bound with nowhere to go and no way out. If that describes you, Jesus knows that feeling. For a few hours in time He was fastened by piercing nails and cords of love, captive to the powers of hell, in order to defeat them.

Many people despair in being a victim; they feel they are destined to hopelessness because of their inability to stop the evil around them. They are unable to move. One of our associate pastors, Robert, lived through the horrendous drama of powerlessness at the hands of the man who should have protected and cared for him.

Growing Up in Fear

At the age of ten Robert watched in horror, unable to stop the fit of rage, as his father mercilessly beat his younger brother. He was terrorized in fear in the backseat of a car while beside him, his three-year-old brother received blow after blow until he lost consciousness and died. That was the final event that ended a lifetime of severe abuse.

Because of the murder of his brother, Robert was finally removed from his home of terror and became a ward of the court. He never knew his mother, and throughout his childhood he had lived a nightmare that is only seen in horror movies. It was not uncommon for his father to hold a shotgun to his head and threaten his life in fits of rage. Living in extreme poverty, he and his various stepmothers had been subjected regularly to severe mental, emotional, and physical beatings at the hands of this demon-driven man.

During his time as a foster child, Robert continued to live under a constant cloud of terror because his father, who had escaped conviction, was trying to locate him. He was moved from home to home out of fear for his life as he and his caregivers were convinced that his father intended to kill him too.

As he grew into his teen years, he was tormented by the memories of his childhood and was left with the feeling of powerlessness, unable to ever feel a sense of security or control in his life. All he had known was abuse. For a while he lived with his grandparents, the parents of one of his stepmothers. Needing desperately to find the acceptance that always seemed to escape him, he ended up getting into crime, and they had to let him go.

Driven by the relentless pain, at the age of 15 he was involved in gangs and violence and eventually was arrested for breaking and entering, putting him back into the custody of the courts. Then he had a divine intervention. He was at a youth hostel waiting to be sent to a youth detention center in northern British Colombia, when his high school counselor obtained permission to take him home for the weekend. That weekend turned into weeks, and eventually they adopted him at the age of 16. Although he now had a new life, a new name, and a new family, his old life continued to control him. In spite of the love of his adoptive family, his teenage years were filled with extreme turmoil, drugs, violence, promiscuity, and depression.

Robert was damaged goods. The evil voice of his past tormenter was controlling his future. He felt hopeless and destined to a life of violence and pain. Then the Cross came into his life—a weapon that was able to change every act of evil into a life-giving force. After a night of drinking, he was sitting on a mall bench when he heard a voice telling him to go and buy a Bible. Immediately he obeyed the voice and began to devour the Scriptures. Hope, excitement, love, and joy began to flood into him. Having no understanding of how to get saved, he went on a search until someone prayed with him as he surrendered his life to Jesus Christ in 1983. God's power was more than enough to free him from the hell of his lost childhood! Today he testifies of how the Cross can make a testimony out of someone's worst nightmare.

Shortly after he moved to Windsor and began to attend our church. As he grew in the Lord and was filled with the Holy Spirit, the power of God began to flow more abundantly in his life. He was set free from alcohol, tobacco, and a life controlled by tormenting demons of fear and powerlessness. The hopeless cycle of abuse was nailed to the Cross forever!

Robert serves God with a passion for prayer and a commitment to help others discover the Cross.

The Reality of the Crucifixion

It is amazing to know that Jesus possessed all the powers of the universe, yet chose to be the victim of powerlessness as He hung nailed to a Cross. Little did

His executioners know that it was the very power that He possessed that kept Him subject to the cruelty of their hands. His amazing wisdom knew that the ability to submit and obey is far greater than giving in to the pressing urge to destroy their evil deeds in a consuming rage. He would not escape the evils that surrounded Him because He was fixed on the work that He was born to do.

He knew the Cross He was impaled on would seal the eternal salvation of all man.

What was He thinking as He absorbed the sin of man and the powerlessness that it rendered? I know He saw a little boy name Robert, beaten and abused, crying out for someone to help him. I know He saw the end of the law that defeated man, and He knew that He would make all things new! His eyes were fixed on the joy of outpoured grace that would heal our wounds from the curse, never to return.

He saw you free for eternity, standing with Him in the presence of His Father, bursting with adoration and worshipping before the throne. As His body ached and shook uncontrollably with the stench of your sin and the bondage screamed for a way out, He saw you on your knees weeping from the transgressions and deliverance that you now have. As demons mocked Him, He saw the joy of your redemption overtaking you with unspeakable love and peace. He was dying for those who in cruel delight ridiculed Him and marveled in the light that would burst through the darkness and change your hate into surrender to God. He knew the Cross He was impaled on would seal the eternal salvation of all man, by His blood for all who would receive its power! Through His bloodstained brow and beaten face, He saw your righteousness purchased by His death, and He rejoiced that it would soon be over and you and I would be forgiven forever.

I will not medically explain the crucifixion, but I will describe it in simple layman's terms. Jesus was stripped naked and thrown roughly to the ground on His back, thus ripping open the scourging wounds and exposing them to the dirt. His arms were then outstretched forcefully onto a patibulum (Latin), which is the crossbar of the Cross. The pain of that alone would have been horrendous! The open wounds on His back bled as they rubbed against the rough wood. As they held His hands down, large, thick, 9- to 11-inch nails were hammered into His wrists, piercing the large median nerve and producing sharp bolts of searing pain in His arms. Blood began to flow from His wrists. Next, they placed His feet on a wooden support and drove a nail through them, again piercing nerves, tendons, and muscles that inflicted unbearable agony on Him.

Then they lifted and dropped the Cross into the ground, and the weight of His body drove the pain to intolerable limits. As He hung there, He was forced to continually push Himself up to keep from suffocating, for His lungs would have been crushed by the full weight of His bleeding body. The Word says that *we* are His body, and it is interesting to note that when crucified, the weight of the body crushes a person. He was crushed by His body, which we now are, taking the full punishment for our sins just as Isaiah prophesied.

> *But he was wounded and crushed for our sins. He was beaten that we might have peace. He was whipped, and we were healed!* (Isaiah 53:5)

The short, shallow breaths He was forced to take did not suffice, and with an inadequate air supply hypercarbia would set in, resulting in severe muscle cramping. As He became more fatigued and unable to continue lifting Himself up, He would slowly suffocate. The word *excruciating* means "out of the cross" and is derived from the word *crucifix*.[33] It is a word to describe that it was as painful as it could get. As Jesus hung on the Cross, nailed there by His hands and feet, we need to understand what He must have felt as well as the significance of every part of His agony.

> *My enemies surround me like a pack of dogs; an evil gang closes in on me. They have pierced my hands and feet. I can count every bone in my body. My enemies stare at me and gloat. They divide my clothes among themselves and throw dice for my garments* (Psalm 22:16-18).

His Hands Are Our Hands

As they drove the nails into His hands, they were being driven into ours. Let's think about what He created our hands for. He gave us hands first and foremost to worship Him, to lift them up toward heaven in adoration and praise. To raise them before Him in prayer and faith, to serve Him, and to clap with joy at all He has done. They were given to search the Scriptures, anoint and bless others, to bestow mercy and love. With our hands we were to meet needs, serve others, lay them on the sick, feed the hungry, provide, and comfort. Our hands were to hold, caress, and stay pure and holy before God. They were to be creative and skillful, building and accomplishing the tasks assigned to us. But man fell, and God watched in sadness at what we did with the hands He had created to glorify Him.

Now the hands of man have nailed the hands of God to the Cross.

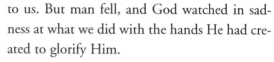

Instead the hands of man have murdered, destroyed, beaten, and robbed. Our hands have been used to serve ourselves, take from the needy, and build lifeless idols to worship instead of our God. Our hands are guilty of unspeakable crimes, like what Robert witnessed at the hands of his father. Hands that were meant to hold and comfort him instead were tools of terror. Man's hands shed innocent blood, take vengeance against others, and do vile, perverse things. The hands that were made to heal instead strike and inflict pain. They devise wicked schemes and take bribes, picking up the alcohol and drugs that hold them in bondage. They use them to create new ways to sin. They form weapons and develop chemicals that endanger mankind. Some hands refuse to work, always looking for a free ride. Their fingers are filthy and tainted with sin.

The hands that created, healed, and delivered them were the object of their hate. The corruption of our hands was nailed there—nailed to where they can no longer sin against Him. His hands were destroyed for our hands. Those hands that had manifested unlimited power were now held powerless. Yet, they were outstretched for all to come to Him, identify with them, and use theirs to glorify God and be restored with the power they had lost.

In the gospel of Mark, Jesus said He would destroy the temple built with human hands and build another with His. He knew that whatever man did with his hands was corrupted with sin.

We heard him say, "I will destroy this Temple made with human hands, and in three days I will build another, made without human hands" (Mark 14:58).

It was not only the will of man that nailed Jesus to that Cross; it was the will of God. He willed to forgive and destroy the work of our hands. As the thud of the hammer bore down, driving the nails through His flesh, He cried out, "Father, forgive them" over and over! Grace was declared between each blow, echoing into the realm of eternity, forever establishing His purpose for us!

His Feet Are Our Feet

The hands of God pierced the hands of the Son of God. It was His plan, but not just His hands. Jesus' feet also were nailed to the Cross.

These were the feet that just a few days before had been washed with tears and kissed with love and gratitude. They were anointed with expensive perfume to demonstrate the worth of worshipping at His feet, as the gospel of Luke tells:

Then she knelt behind him at his feet, weeping. Her tears fell on his feet, and she wiped them off with her hair. Then she kept kissing his feet and putting perfume on them (Luke 7:38).

Now they are crushed with a Roman spike. The blood flowing from them was for the sins of our feet. Like our hands, our feet were created to glorify God.

He had taught His followers to wash each other's feet with humility and honor as He had washed theirs. He knew that to honor the feet is to honor the man.

Our feet were given to us to run to Him in times of need, to go into His presence, to jump and dance before Him with exuberance and joy. They were to go and conquer for Him, to stand firm in His promises and spread His peace. They were to step on the neck of the enemy and keep him subdued under us and to stand on solid ground, walking a straight path. They were to avoid the appearances of evil and keep from stumbling. Our feet were to walk in the light as He is in the light and take us into places that are His.

Instead we chose to walk into the darkness and do evil. We run to do mischief, listen to gossip, hurt and devour others. Our feet race to attack, kill, steal, and betray. They slip and fall into the miry clay and are easily sidetracked, going their own way. They run blindly to the sin and perversion that woos them. They kick and step on the necks of the oppressed, binding the weak, and run to consume what they can on themselves while ignoring the cry of those in need. They dance with lust and jump for power, demanding the worship of man. And now they are nailed to His Cross—stuck with nowhere to go. His feet were ours, destroyed with the evil they pursued, cursed on that tree. Jesus was nailed to the Cross, hands and feet; the One with all power was left powerless, unable to move.

The nails that pierced Him fastened our sin secure on the only place that could destroy sin's power over us.

That's what sin does to man. Sin holds us in the chains of bondage and keeps us from the power and authority that is rightfully ours as God's children. The nails that pierced Him were meant for us; now they destroy the evil deeds of our hands and feet; they fasten our sin secure on the only place that could destroy sin's power over us.

Honor in Dishonor

If we look with our natural eyes at what He did, we will scoff like those who stood watching Him helplessly nailed and bleeding on the Cross. Luke described the scene:

The crowd watched, and the leaders laughed and scoffed. "He saved others," they said, "let him save himself if he is really God's Chosen One, the Messiah" (Luke 23:35).

Their laughs taunted Him to save Himself and prove who He really was. Little did they know that what He was doing was just that. As He hung there naked, beaten, and helpless at their hands, it was the greatest demonstration of power to overcome the absurdity of what He endured while knowing the power of which He denied Himself of. It was humility's greatest hour: *the All-powerful becoming the scum of the earth.* It was His humility that conquered the pride of man. He, the Lord of all, became the servant of all.

His actions showed us how we too can defeat the darkness that lurks around us, taunting us to prove ourselves. Having to prove who we are is the pride of man. Man runs around endlessly trying to prove his own significance. When we know who we are, proof is not necessary. But it is during the taunting of His enemies that God had the final say. It was the custom of the Romans to publish the crime of the malefactor above his head on the cross. It was here that another nail penetrated the Cross above the head of Jesus with a bold declaration of truth. It boldly declared, *This is the King of the Jews.* The proof they were demanding was written by the authority of man and nailed to the Cross. God had Pilate the governor decree it. Pilate, who had found Him innocent, had written on the placard what he had decided, as recorded in the gospel of John:

It is the blood of Christ shed on the Cross that sealed our redemption.

> *And Pilate posted a sign over him that read, "Jesus of Nazareth, the King of the Jews." The place where Jesus was crucified was near the city; and the sign was written in Hebrew,*

> *Latin, and Greek, so that many people could read it. Then the leading priests said to Pilate, "Change it from 'The King of the Jews' to 'He said, I am King of the Jews.' " Pilate replied, "What I have written, I have written. It stays exactly as it is"* (John 19:19-22).

God honored Jesus with the dignity of declaring the truth of who He was in the depth of His shame and reproach. The religious leaders were forced to read it as they watched the blood of their promised Messiah flow before their eyes. The blood that flowed from Him was the blood that washed our evil deeds and turned us into His instruments of righteousness. We cannot separate the blood from the work of the Cross any more than we can separate the resurrection from it.

The Power of the Blood

Our evil thoughts and actions separated us from God; we were charged guilty and condemned to a life of hopelessness as God's enemies. But His blood made peace between us. Years ago I used to wonder why it took blood to redeem us. The Word says in the book of Hebrews that without the shedding of blood there is no forgiveness of sin:

> *In fact, we can say that according to the law of Moses, nearly everything was purified by sprinkling with blood. Without the shedding of blood, there is no forgiveness of sins* (Hebrews 9:22).

Our blood was corrupted; God could take no part in us because of it, or it would corrupt Him and everything would be destroyed. We needed new blood, and He provided it for us. Its power is greater than our sin. It drives out the wickedness that lurks within us when we abide in His presence, receiving His as our own.

If I give you a gift, that is nice; but if I give you my life, that is love.

Our blood speaks and determines who we are. It carries our history and our sustenance and identifies our ancestry. To give it away is to give our life to another.

We can read in the Old Testament that the sacrifices necessary to deal with sin were ongoing. The blood that carried the life of Christ secured our eternal destiny forever and was far better than the blood of animals, as Hebrews tells us:

Once for all time he took blood into that Most Holy Place, but not the blood of goats and calves. He took his own blood, and with it he secured our salvation forever (Hebrews 9:12).

This means we are not powerless, but powerful. The power we have been given by Him is to rule over sin. We are no longer slaves to sin, but to righteousness. If we feel powerless, then we do not yet understand the work of the Cross.

The only weapons the devil has against us are accusation and deception because Christ has destroyed his power. In other words, he can do nothing to us unless he can convince us of lies that contradict what the Word of God says about us. In the book of Revelation he is called the deceiver of the nations:

The angel threw him into the bottomless pit, which he then shut and locked so Satan could not deceive the nations anymore until the thousand years were finished. Afterward he would be released again for a little while (Revelation 20:3).

He only has the ability to deceive us, but when we use the power of the blood of Christ by declaring the work of the Cross, we defeat him.

And they have defeated him because of the blood of the Lamb and because of their testimony. And they were not afraid to die (Revelation 12:12).

His strategy is to keep us from seeing who we are in Christ by getting us to focus on anything but the Cross. But the Cross reveals the truth-shedding light so we will not be deceived. The devil would love the church to ignore the Cross; he hates it because it destroyed him and took back from him what he had stolen, our heart. So if we allow guilt and condemnation to control us, then we negate the work of the Cross.

I now realize that honoring the Cross on a daily basis is the unlimited power to live for others as Christ did.

Jesus suffered slowly and purposefully, identifying with our pain, and revealed the ugliness and truth of how we treat God. He was offered a painkiller, but He refused it because He wanted to experience every bit of what sin does. He wanted to thoroughly know our hopelessness without Him.

What Christ did for us was so powerful that we must never take it for granted.

Jesus understands the times we were held in bondage unable to move our hands or feet under the grip of fear and powerlessness. He laid down His power on the Cross to give us ours. Because of Him our hands and feet are now covered in the His blood to go and do what He has called us to.

From the beginning to the end of His passion, His blood flowed from Him to give you an incorruptible blood transfusion, so that you can live completely whole and free from the slavery of sin forever. We must treasure the blood of the Cross and make it our hope and source of power.

To humble yourself and love God and others is the message that resonates from the Cross to all who will hear.

Jesus overcame with humility, obedience, and love. He was sin *and* perfection on the Cross as He brought together the evil with the righteous. Only there can the two meet, and meet they must.

We must run to the sacrifice of the Lamb of God with our feet and outstretched hands and embrace our righteousness and the destruction of our sin nailed with Him on His Cross.

Chapter Eighteen

The Forgiveness of the Cross

Jesus said, "Father, forgive these people, because they don't know what they are doing." And the soldiers gambled for his clothes by throwing dice (Luke 23:34).

Because of the depravity of man, we all desperately need forgiveness from God. To provide that forgiveness cost Him the life of His only Son, a cost that is dearer than we could ever pay.

Can you imagine offering the death of your only child to forgive your enemies? To comprehend His willingness to do that for me is mind-boggling. Yet, Jesus prayed at the worst of His suffering that His death would accomplish what He was dying for.

He alone had the right to pray for our forgiveness as He alone bore the consequence of our sin. As His Cross was thrust into the ground by the Roman soldiers who were commissioned to kill Him, He submitted Himself to the injustice of their assignment and repeatedly cried, *"Father, forgive them; for they know not what they do"* (Luke 23:34 KJV). These are the greatest words for those who know their guilt and bondage to sin.

Jesus chose to see past His pain and repair the unrepairable. As His voice permeated the heavens, He was the bridge of forgiveness and mercy because God's holiness demands justice. His cry of mercy was not just for those who drove the stakes through His battered body, or for the religious leaders who sought His death out of envy; it was also for the disciples who denied and abandoned Him and the government that condemned Him. It was extended to all who had or would be born of a woman. His heart was burdened with a love so immense for those who committed the crime of the ages, and He ached for their forgiveness. What He bore was greater than any man could bear, and yet while feeling the magnitude of destruction tearing His limbs apart, He forgave. Though He had a right to condemn, He prayed for mercy upon all those who committed injustices.

Every sin against man is a sin against God Himself and requires His wrath to justify it. Jesus did not say, "Who do you think you are? Don't you know that I am God?" He so desired to completely identify with us that He stripped Himself of His rights as Deity and allowed those He created to do with Him what they willed. He did this to prove His love for us. The cruelty of His enemies and the weaknesses of His followers did not discourage Him from calling on His heavenly Father. He did not run from Him but to Him; He did not blame and curse the Father but embraced Him in His darkest hours. We all experience injustices in our lives that are painful and crushing to our hearts, but He is there to experience the worst of what man can do. We cannot easily forgive others until we understand the magnitude to which we ourselves have sinned and need forgiveness.

Forgiveness Is the Key

Years ago I had the privilege of interviewing David Meece, who shared passionately about how forgiveness was the key to freedom. He is well known in the body of Christ as a contemporary Christian artist, having traveled the world and sold millions of records. God has given him incredible revelation on forgiveness because of his own personal history that had held him in bondage for most of his life.

Growing up as a young boy, David was a child protégé in the music world, but he and his mother were often beaten and abused by his father, an alcoholic and drug addict. In spite of his success, the scars from words spoken over him by his father were affecting how he saw himself. He shared with me a time when, at the age of ten, his father, in a drunken stupor, pulled a gun on him, threatening to kill him, and said these words that haunted him for years: "You are worthless! Nothing you ever did is good, and I am going to kill you!" Fortunately his grandmother heard the commotion, rushed into the room, and wrestled the gun away. David, who had been a confident classical pianist performing concerts, was left shaking during performances by the impact of those words.

He had many difficult years following that, and at the age of 16 he attempted suicide twice. Later in his teen years he gave his heart to the Lord and soon became a famous musician because of his incredible talent. However, few knew the demonic assault that still continued to torment his mind. He struggled with forgiving his father and cried out to God for help. Then one day he was given a vision. In the vision he saw a young boy who was being physically and emotionally abused. The little boy was helpless and unable to defend himself. David wanted desperately to help him, and then the Lord revealed to him that the boy was his father.

God showed him that the pain inflicted on him by his father was a result of what his dad had endured as a child. Suddenly the anger and hatred toward his dad that had consumed David melted away and was replaced with love and compassion. David was finally healed and set free from the bitterness that almost destroyed him. Throughout the following years, he shared openly about the power of forgiveness. God revealed to him that his father was a victim too, and his own healing came when he looked past his pain to see his father's.

The opportunities to forgive are constant; the sting of hurts often lodge deep in our heart. Unfortunately, many don't know how to release forgiveness and so remain captive to its suffocating grip. Jesus took forgiveness even as far as to say, "Love and pray for your enemies," which He then demonstrated on the Cross. He didn't just tell us to do something; He showed us how. It is liberating for us when we see that we all are victims of sin and in need of forgiveness.

Just as you have been hurt, there are those whom you have hurt. Someone somewhere bears the pain that you inflicted on him or her because of your sin. Whether it was a parent, a sibling, spouse, lover, or friend, you and I both have disappointed and broken hearts.

We tend to justify our wrongdoing and have double standards since we usually are much easier on ourselves then on those who hurt us. It is interesting to see how man so quickly desires forgiveness and yet struggles to give it. Here in the gospel of Matthew it is very clear that we cannot be forgiven if we refuse to forgive others:

If you forgive those who sin against you, your heavenly Father will forgive you. But if you refuse to forgive others, your Father will not forgive your sins (Matthew 6:14-15).

That passage is about as straightforward as you can say it, yet so many find it difficult to do and rationalize their way around it.

The pain Jesus felt at the betrayal, abandonment, lies, and torture was as real as ours. The desire to hold that sin against them would have been as strong in His flesh as it would be in ours. It is His forgiveness for our sins that enables us to extend it to others. As we understand His mercy, we will see it is a privilege to forgive and will realize that hanging on to our offenses will produce a root of bitterness in us. It is impossible to truly know God and hate others, for bitterness hardens our heart and creates hostility toward others and God. To allow unforgiveness to stay in our heart is like allowing a poisonous spider to crawl on us and watch its venom permeate our bloodstream as it bites us.

The immense grace and mercy God shares is as much for our offenders as it is for us.

Throughout the Old Testament there are many allegories of the Cross. I love this one in Exodus that demonstrates its ability to change our hard heart to love.

> *So Moses brought Israel from the Red sea, and they went out into the wilderness of Shur; and they went three days in the wilderness, and found no water. And when they came to Marah, they could not drink of the waters of Marah, for they were bitter: therefore the name of it was called Marah. And the people murmured against Moses, saying, What shall we drink? And he cried unto the LORD; and the LORD shewed him a tree, which when he had cast into the waters, the waters were made sweet: there he made for them a statute and an ordinance, and there he proved them* (Exodus 15:22-25 KJV).

When something is bitter, it is poisonous to those who partake of it. When Moses threw the tree into the bitter water, it was made sweet. The tree represents the Cross. By going to the Cross we turn the bitterness in us into sweet water. When we forgive, it brings healing and deliverance from the damage done to us by our offenders. When we refuse to forgive, their intent to harm us continues to succeed.

The Cross represents forgiveness to all who trust in it, but there are some who have trouble forgiving themselves. They feel that hanging on to their guilt and punishing themselves for their sins will help their redemption. When they try to pay for their sins, they actually are in idolatry and fail to understand the Cross.

Many misconceptions exist about forgiveness. I want to address three of them.

Number One: Forgiveness Is Not a License to Sin

Some have taken the message of forgiveness to the extreme of believing that anything goes. Because of legalism, which is the other side of the coin, the extreme grace movement has become popular and the freedom to sin embraced. Those who believe this have strayed far from the Cross. We can read here in Romans what Jesus did to defeat sin and free us from it:

The purpose of the Cross was to destroy the works of sin, not perpetuate it.

> *He died once to defeat sin, and now he lives for the glory of God. So you should consider yourselves dead to sin and able to live for the glory of God through Christ Jesus. Do not let sin control the way you live; do not give in to its lustful desires. Do not let any part of your body become a tool of wickedness, to be used for sinning. Instead, give yourselves completely to God since you have been given new life. And use your whole body as a tool to do what is right for the glory of God. Sin is no longer your master, for you are no longer subject to the law, which enslaves you to sin. Instead, you are free by God's grace* (Romans 6:10-14).

At the Cross, sin expressed itself completely, revealing the true horror and ugliness that it is. Those who desire to sin have not truly embraced the Cross, but their limited interpretation of it. The forgiveness they seek is not real; what they seek is permission to sin without consequences. They believe that, once saved, they can live how they want to because God has to forgive them. Often people who believe that way have a desire in their heart to live in some form of sin they are not willing to surrender. Their desire to sin is focused on self and not on God. When we sin, forgiveness is offered out of love, and if that love is appreciated or valued, sin will be hated for hurting the one who loved us.

Many believe that the definition of grace is unearned favor, but that is only part of its meaning. In actuality grace means *divine enablement*,[34] which is God's power given so that we might do what we normally could not. God does not give us power to play with anymore than we would give dynamite to a toddler. It is given that we might overcome sin. These verses in Titus tell us that the grace of God teaches us to live Godly:

> *For the grace of God that bringeth salvation hath appeared to all men, teaching us that, denying ungodliness and worldly lusts, we should live soberly, righteously, and godly, in this present world* (Titus 2:11-12 KJV).

The crucifixion of Christ was a full manifestation of the sin in man's heart, revealing his opposition to what is pure and holy. As I love God, I will hate sin and turn from it.

The other end of the spectrum is the legalism that negates the work God has done for us.

Legalism is a set of dos and don'ts that vary with the opinions of those who set them. In some camps wearing makeup and blue jeans is a sin. I've heard that how long you pray and how much you study the Word measure your righteousness. Some believers think that poverty makes you holy, and others prosperity.

Legalism measures righteousness by how we look on the outside and how we perform to get right with God. It is judging spirituality by external things. God, however, judges us by what our heart does with His Cross, and a heart that loves Him is a heart that loves others.

Even without the desire to sin we will sin enough, and fortunately we will find grace and mercy because the Cross has justified us before God. The apostle John wrote a letter to the church so that we would not sin, but if we do, Jesus is there to plead on our behalf:

> *My dear children, I am writing this to you so that you will not sin. But if you do sin, there is someone to plead for you before the Father. He is Jesus Christ, the one who pleases God completely* (1 John 2:1).

If you ask me, my sin put Jesus through enough; my love for Him does not desire to send Him purposely pleading to the Father on my behalf any more than is necessary.

Those who see the forgiveness of the Cross and still desire to sin have missed its purpose.

To see Him is to want to be like Him! The Scriptures tell us this in 1 John:

And you know that Jesus came to take away our sins, for there is no sin in him. So if we continue to live in him, we won't sin either. But those who keep on sinning have never known him or understood who he is (1 John 3:5-6).

Obviously our flesh will still want to sin, but our heart will not, and God knows the difference. The more my heart loves Him, the more I love others and the stronger I am to overcome the flesh. *Sin always hurts us and others*, and when we are full of love we will hate it. When we abide in His love, our lives will be characterized by repentance.

The Word of God also warns us in the book of Jude of the fate of people who say it is okay to sin:

I say this because some godless people have wormed their way in among you, saying that God's forgiveness allows us to live immoral lives. The fate of such people was determined long ago, for they have turned against our only Master and Lord, Jesus Christ (Jude 4).

To say God's forgiveness gives us permission to sin is a mockery of the crucifixion. Its purpose was to destroy sin and make us holy. If I have been set free from the bondage of sin, why would I want to keep it?

Sin will always be a struggle in our flesh, and we will be free from condemnation and guilt when we hate it and repent at the Cross. I do not purpose to sin, but when I do, I go to the Cross and deal with it immediately. My sin has been nailed there, and I am so incredibly thankful that I can be cleansed from that garbage.

Some believe that it is God's responsibility to forgive us. The only responsibility that He had was to bring justice. Forgiveness is His choice! Keeping that before me does not make me feel that I'm unrighteous; on the contrary, it makes me see how valued and loved I am by God, and I love Him more for it. When we love Him, we will not desire to drive the nails into His hands and feet again as the book of Hebrews says some do:

And who then turn away from God. It is impossible to bring such people to repentance again because they are nailing the Son of God to the cross again by rejecting him, holding him up to public shame (Hebrews 6:6).

Number Two: Forgiveness Is Not Giving Someone the Right to Abuse or Use You

I do not have to compromise justice to forgive people. I can still forgive them when I confront them and set appropriate boundaries and consequences to protect myself from their wrongdoing—provided that the motive in my heart is for their benefit as well as mine. If your motive is to harm them instead of help them, you are not forgiving.

You may say that Jesus did not protect Himself. That is true for the time that He had to be the sacrifice for the sins of man, but He did not stay on the Cross. Instead He rose again into power and will never again have to subject Himself to that kind of treatment.

If someone does something serious to hurt me, I will forgive that person. But if he or she continues, I will set up appropriate boundaries and consequences for the violation, still forgiving the person in my heart. If the harmful behavior still persists, than I will implement the necessary consequence. If that fails, I will withdraw myself from that person until repentance comes, with prayer and faith for his or her deliverance and with a desire for restoration and wholeness. That person's choice to sin is the choice to become a slave, and it robs him or her of the power and glory that God has for him or her.

Number Three: Forgiveness Is Not Denial

Denial is the refusal to accept the truth about something[35] and is a major problem in families. Often in the dynamics of a family structure there can be a member with a serious problem. Everyone in the family knows about it, but because of fear of rocking the boat, losing that loved one, or breaking up the family, the problem is ignored. It is the family secret, so to speak, and kept hidden from the outside. It's like the pink elephant in the room that everyone walks around and pretends is not there. However, its presence slowly eats away at the fabric of the family and inside anger, frustration, resentment, and bitterness are brewing and destroying everyone.

Some Christians believe that to forgive is to ignore, but that only enables and damages the offender along with themselves. Maybe you were raised in a home where the sin of a parent was destroying your sense of security and well-being.

Perhaps you were the victim of sexual abuse that was ignored, or a drug addiction. Whatever the problem, to forgive is not to deny but to confront and seek help with a heart to reconcile and restore relationships when it is safe to do so. Forgiveness does not deny justice. If it did, then every prisoner should be released from jail. So, what is forgiveness?

Forgiveness Is Justice and Mercy

Forgiveness is justice and mercy together. That is what was demonstrated on the Cross. Justice was done as Jesus bore the full wrath of God for the sins of man. Mercy was done when He called out for forgiveness for those He died for. We must see forgiveness as a power that we have the right to exercise. It is our privilege to forgive!

Forgiveness is a power and a privilege!

When I forgive, I desire to see the people who violate me be free from the sin that binds them. When their offense threatens my safety and well-being, I need to set boundaries with appropriate consequences. In order for them to be free they must understand the severity of their actions and desire the help they need to change; otherwise I enable them, and that is damaging to them and myself. Forgiveness offers both.

This is where repentance comes in. To forgive someone means you are willing for reconciliation if it is possible, or healing of the relationship if true repentance is shown. The turning away from sin with sincere regret and remorse for the harm done to another is true repentance. Some are only sorry for the price they have to pay for their actions and not for how they hurt another. The forgiveness that Jesus offers involves repentance. Being sorry for your sins without repenting can result in death, as 2 Corinthians states:

> *For God can use sorrow in our lives to help us turn away from sin and seek salvation. We will never regret that kind of sorrow. But sorrow without repentance is the kind that results in death* (2 Corinthians 7:10).

The gospel of Luke tells us that the message of the Cross is a message of repentance, and that turning to Jesus means turning from sin and finding His forgiveness.

And he said, "Yes, it was written long ago that the Messiah must suffer and die and rise again from the dead on the third day. With my authority, take this message of repentance to all the nations, beginning in Jerusalem: 'There is forgiveness of sins for all who turn to me.' You are witnesses of all these things" (Luke 24:46-48).

For those who do not repent, they remain in their sin because the forgiveness they seek is not sincere.

For instance, your spouse can have an affair and be sorry for the consequences but not turn away from the sin. God faces that same thing every day. There are two kinds of sin: deliberate sin and inadvertent sin. One is planned and purposely done, without remorse; the other is not. We can read about this in the book of Numbers:

If the unintentional sin is committed by an individual, the guilty person must bring a one-year-old female goat for a sin offering. The priest will make atonement for the guilty person before the LORD, and that person will be forgiven. This same law applies both to native Israelites and the foreigners living among you. But those who brazenly violate the LORD's will, whether native Israelites or foreigners, blaspheme the LORD, and they must be cut off from the community. Since they have treated the LORD's word with contempt and deliberately disobeyed his commands, they must be completely cut off and suffer the consequences of their guilt (Numbers 15:27-31).

Notice in this scripture that there was no sin offering for the brazen sin against God; instead, the people were cut off. Brazen sin is sin that is done with insolent audacity, or shamelessly, meaning there is no concern that sin is done.

God knows the motives of the heart, and He judges us according to our motives and knowledge of sin. We need forgiveness for all of our sin—even that done out of ignorance since His standard of perfection is inflexible. He cannot lower it; instead He provided the way for us to escape the eternal penalties when we sincerely seek it. Excuses of ignorance do not stop consequences. The Cross of Jesus Christ is always there for us, and there is no excuse to ignore who He is and what He did for us. It is for the sincere in heart and those who hunger and thirst for righteousness.

When it comes to forgiveness, I must abide in Him daily; otherwise, I will be deceived by extreme grace or legalism.

Forgiveness Loves the Unlovable

Forgiveness is the ability to love the unlovable. As humans, we all have things we do that irritate each other. Whenever we deal with people on a personal level, we discover differences in opinions, quirky harmless habits, or behavior we dislike. The things that irritate but are not harmful must be forgiven without boundaries or consequences.

There are a few things my husband does that irritate me, and vice versa. It is not my job to change him in these areas as they are not harmful; they just simply bother me. I have learned to take these things to the Cross and let God deal with them. It is then that I usually discover I'm the one who needs dealing with. Sometimes we put expectations on others that are unreasonable and controlling, and that is not love. First Peter tells us that love covers a multitude of sins:

> *Most important of all, continue to show deep love for each other, for love covers a multitude of sins* (1 Peter 4:8).

To cover means to overlook.[36] The book of Colossians says we must make allowances for and forgive each other's faults:

> *Since God chose you to be the holy people whom he loves, you must clothe yourselves with tenderhearted mercy, kindness, humility, gentleness, and patience. You must make allowance for each other's faults and forgive the person who offends you. Remember, the Lord forgave you, so you must forgive others* (Colossians 3:12-13).

Have you ever really thought about how much you hurt God when you sin? One common way you and I cause Him grief occurs when someone wounds us badly and we blame Him because somehow we feel He should have prevented our pain! It amazes me at how many leave churches angry and bitter, refusing to even attempt reconciliation or properly confront an offense. These people do not realize that their anger and bitterness separate them from the victory of the Cross and its purpose to receive and extend forgiveness. They are willing to forfeit the forgiveness of God toward them in favor of their hurt feelings. They fail to understand that what they are saying is, "I am righteous, and they are not." That attitude is self-righteousness, something Jesus despised

> *To forgive when our wounds are fresh is a dynamic power that glorifies God and sets us free.*

in the religious leaders. I have seen Christians hate a pastor for teaching about tithing, or leave a church because of the pastor's emphasis on soul winning and discipleship. In contrast, I have seen a mother forgive the man who raped and murdered her daughter and subsequently lead him to the Lord. She now visits him in prison.

"Where was God when this happened to me?" is a common cry. When we ask this, we undermine His character with accusation, just as they did Jesus at Calvary. Jesus could have said the same thing as they pounded in those nails, but He didn't. Instead He clung to His Father and depended on Him even when all hell was literally breaking out around Him.

What was He thinking when He was being blamed for the sins of man? He thought of your evil deed done in secret forever being thrown in the sea of forgetfulness as you cried with tears of repentance before Him. He hid His eyes from your shame and covered you with His spotless robe of dazzling white and held you as His own. When His wounds were raw with pain and hurt the most, He anguished in His suffering and called on God to forgive you. He didn't wait until after the resurrection and say, "Well, I made it through and now I'm okay, so I can forgive you." He forgave at the height of His pain, and He did it so you could forgive those who hurt you while you still hurt.

The Cross is my remembrance of the forgiveness He so graciously bestowed upon me. It enables me to say, "Father, forgive them, for they know not what they do." When Jesus said those words, He was pleading for mercy for you and for your enemies as He bore your sin.

Several years ago one of my children did something that deeply hurt us and our family. We were devastated and wept for months. We prayed and pleaded for her to get right with God, and we never stopped loving her or desiring her restoration. Our love for her is eternal, but God's love for us is even greater. As much as we loved her, her sin at the time kept a great wall between us and true heartfelt intimacy was impossible without condoning the sin. Since then true repentance has come and the relationship is restored, but my love, forgiveness, and willingness for reconciliation was always there, as is God's.

Jesus lives today at the right hand of the Father making intercession for you, pleading mercy for you when you turn from Him, like a Father does a rebellious child.

When Jesus cried, *"Father, forgive them; for they know not what they do"* (Luke 23:34 KJV), they knew what they were doing. They just did not know the enormity of it. As you see His final act of incredible mercy, allow His love to heal your hurts, then flow onto your enemies and the lost.

This awesome psalm sums up what His forgiveness has done for us:

He forgives all my sins and heals all my diseases. He ransoms me from death and surrounds me with love and tender mercies. He fills my life with good things. My youth is renewed like the eagle's! The LORD gives righteousness and justice to all who are treated unfairly (Psalm 103:3-6).

Forgiveness cries from the Cross with healing for all who seek it!

Chapter Nineteen

The Thief and the Truth on the Cross

Pilate replied, "You are a king then?" "You say that I am a king, and you are right," Jesus said. "I was born for that purpose. And I came to bring truth to the world. All who love the truth recognize that what I say is true" (John 18:37).

Jesus referred to Himself as truth. That means He is the one absolute of all that exists and that He alone is the determining factor of what is real or deception. All that we believe must be anchored in who He is and what He has done. So when Jesus was on the Cross, *truth* hung between two criminals. There is great significance with this aspect of His crucifixion.

At the onset of the actual crucifixion, many were yelling and throwing insults, mocking Jesus. Once again this was an audacious insult to His deity. The criminals on both sides also were part of the cruelty that added to His humiliation and suffering, according to the gospel of Matthew:

And the criminals who were crucified with him also shouted the same insults at him (Matthew 27:44).

However, somewhere in the midst of this historical event, something happened. We do not know what changed the heart of one of the criminals, but something caused him to see Jesus differently. Perhaps he suddenly realized his need for God and had heard that Jesus was a prophet. Or it could have been when he heard the religious leaders say, "You saved others!" acknowledging that He had indeed saved some, as we can read here in Mark's gospel:

The leading priests and teachers of religious law also mocked Jesus. "He saved others," they scoffed, "but he can't save himself!" (Mark 15:31)

Those words *"He saved others"* may have echoed in this man's ears as his hunger for God grew. Perhaps he heard of the miracles Jesus had done or read the sign posted above Jesus' head declaring who He was.

He Saw the Truth[37]

He definitely knew he needed saving; he was dying and he was guilty. Being a Jew, he also knew of a coming Messiah. He saw that they were so vehemently against this dying man accused of calling Himself the Messiah, and yet He prayed for them. Perhaps it was the pure love that Jesus returned for their hatred that revealed the truth to this wretched thief. Christ by His nature acted saved; His innocence became obvious, and he saw it! The deception lifted from him, and he could see his Savior dying with him. The gospel of Luke tells of this man's transformation:

> *One of the criminals hanging beside him scoffed, "So you're the Messiah, are you? Prove it by saving yourself—and us, too, while you're at it!" But the other criminal protested, "Don't you fear God even when you are dying? We deserve to die for our evil deeds, but this man hasn't done anything wrong." Then he said, "Jesus, remember me when you come into your Kingdom." And Jesus replied, "I assure you, today you will be with me in paradise"* (Luke 23:39-43).

What was it about this dying man that caused him to see and not the other? We know that the foolish malefactor was demanding something from Jesus: *"Prove it by saving yourself—and us, too!"* he mocked. He needed to see proof. He wasn't showing any remorse for his crime, either, and his concern was for himself. We can find the key to how the repenting criminal found truth in his response to the ongoing scoffing. *"Don't you fear God even when you are dying?"* he said. Obviously somewhere deep inside of him there was a fear of God, and that fear opened his eyes to see truth.

Deception is all around us, and if there ever was a time the truth was hidden, it was at the time of the crucifixion. Just think of the absurdity of this thief calling on Jesus, a dying man, to remember him in His kingdom. Calling upon someone who is dying and cannot move to help you appears to be as ridiculous as it can get, but his perception had changed. He had seen the truth because he had the fear of the Lord, and that is the beginning of knowledge.

> *The fear of the LORD is the beginning of knowledge: but fools despise wisdom and instruction* (Proverbs 1:7 KJV).

Knowledge is the perception, discovery, and awareness of something. Where there is no knowledge, there will be deception. Deception is being ensnared by what is not true. Acknowledging his sin was important; it demonstrated his realization of his need for God. To fear God is to have concern or respect for Him, knowing that our response to Him determines our fate. To fear Him is to honor and recognize His all-encompassing power. We are righteous in our own eyes when we believe we do not need Him. It is our awareness that He is the final authority that will protect us from deception.

> *Whenever we are unwilling to embrace truth, we are open to be deceived.*

Jesus often talked about spiritual blindness and deafness, and He made the claim that because of hardness of heart we can be deceived from seeing the truth. To be deceived is to be tricked or trapped into something.

Unfortunately, many people live their lives in unrealities that they perceive to be real. Some find that the truth they see is too difficult to handle, so they create an imaginary world or fall prey to someone who promises things that they wish were real. Whenever we are unwilling to embrace truth, we are open to be deceived.

The following story is one of the worst deceptions I have witnessed in my ministry—and I have seen a lot. Although all names have been changed, the events are as accurate as my knowledge and experience of them.

A Devastating Deception

Michael and Emily attended our church and were seemingly solid Christians involved in leadership. They had recently sold a lucrative business and were living off the interest, which freed them to be very active in numerous areas of the church. They had a passion to serve God and were faithful to do so. One Sunday a stranger showed up at our church service claiming to be a government representative of a South American country. "Thomas" went forward at an altar call and gave his heart to the Lord. Afterwards he shared with one of our elders that he needed some temporary financial help as a check from his government was late arriving. The elder loaned the money and spent time getting to know him, helping him in his new walk with the Lord.

For several weeks Thomas was faithful to attend services, weeping with appreciation at how blessed he was and how desperately his country needed to hear the Gospel. His tremendous gratitude and continuous tears impressed most who met him. However, there were a few, myself included, who sensed something was amiss. At some point during those first few weeks Thomas had befriended Michael and Emily and ended up staying with them in their home. They quickly bonded and began to spend most of their time with him, impressed with his stories and desire to help his poverty-stricken country.

Meanwhile, the leader who had loaned him money told us he had not repaid it. When the man asked him about it, Thomas told him that he had used the money to help the needy in his country and couldn't repay him. Another of our leaders came and shared that he had picked up some serious discrepancies in his stories. As the concern about Thomas increased, our prayer leader approached me and disclosed that Emily had come and told her some disturbing things. Emily had shared with her that Thomas was a great man of God who had deep spiritual insight and needed her help to secretly get his teaching into our church. She was asking our prayer leader and her husband to assist them in accomplishing this behind our backs.

Obviously my spiritual alarms were sounding, and my husband and I called a meeting with Michael and Emily and the prayer leader. When confronted, Emily was enraged and told us that Thomas loved them like no one else and that he was going to use them to help him run his country. She informed us that they would be moving there with him, and our church needed to back him financially. She went on about how spiritual he was, next to God Himself, and how we could learn from him. She also shared how God had told them to give him a large sum of money to help his country. We tried to reason with them that Thomas could be a con and just after their money, but they claimed he had not asked for the money; God had told them to give it.

My husband Rick warned them that a good con would not ask but create a desire to give by promising something in return. Our reasoning went unheeded, so we had to step them down from their positions in the church. We knew that somehow this man had managed to win their trust and was undermining us.

I quickly did a background check on him and learned from the embassy representing his country as well as the FBI in the United States that Thomas was a very dangerous and wanted criminal and to be feared. He did not work for the government; instead, he had in fact tried to overthrow it with violence and was known as a con with a criminal record dating back to the 1950's. Armed with this new information, I felt convinced that Michael and Emily would see the light, but Thomas had warned them that there was a conspiracy in his government and that lies about him were part of their plan to destroy him. They believed him over us.

Meanwhile several of Michael and Emily's close friends and family also were beginning to trust Thomas, and we warned them about our concerns. Most of them heeded and began to question him, resulting in Michael and Emily being forbidden by Thomas to associate with them any longer. Slowly Thomas isolated them from anyone who questioned him.

Unfortunately, a few others also were enthralled by his promises and withdrew from the church, despite our warnings. Slowly and deliberately Thomas began to drain their finances, promising them leadership in his country. He also had them send down their cars and possessions in preparation for their move there. Within a week of their arrival to his country, he sent them back, claiming the timing was off. But he kept their belongings. Upon returning from this trip with him, Emily called to inform us that Thomas was so respected in his country that people would run and hide when he walked by them. She also informed us that he carried a gun, and whenever he spoke to people they would jump at his command. This obviously impressed her, but it horrified us. We were very concerned for their safety, but our reasoning continued to fall on deaf ears.

Over the next year Thomas had them deposit all their money into a Swiss bank account he had set up. He had them sell their homes and cash in retirement plans and give him the money. Close acquaintances of Michael and Emily, Chris and Erica, were near retirement and had given him everything they had as well. Then as promise after promise fell through, Chris began to question Thomas. The moment he did, his wife was given an ultimatum by Thomas to choose him or her husband, and she chose Thomas. Chris, realizing he was thrown out of his marriage and had lost all he had to a con, was devastated. He had given Thomas his retirement savings, his home, and his business, and now he was ostracized from those he had loved and trusted.

The husband of a third couple involved also began to question Thomas, and his wife was given the same ultimatum. Fortunately she made the right choice and stuck with her husband. Their eyes were opened. With the help of Chris and this other couple, we were able to get the Royal Canadian Mounted Police involved. Unfortunately by then Thomas had moved back to his country, and they were powerless to do anything other than keep him out of Canada.

Sadly, Michael and Emily were still convinced that Thomas would eventually allow them to help him run his government, even though he continually forbade them from living there, citing it was too dangerous. Chris and the other enlightened couple shared with us how this man controlled and used them to continually run back and forth from Canada to his home to bring him whatever he demanded. They had trained killer dogs for him and worked menial jobs to supply whatever he desired. He also pushed them to recruit others to get money for his cause. We also were told that he forbade the husbands and wives from sleeping together, claiming it was sin unless to procreate, and that they had to live in extreme simplicity or they were carnal. The women could wear no makeup and anyone who questioned him would be cut off from him and God.

Many other bizarre things took place that would take too long to disclose, and I wish I could say there was a happy ending for all involved. We may be shocked at how these believers were so deceived, but the devil tricks people all the time through sin we refuse to acknowledge and repent of. That is why it is so important to know the truth. Jesus said that He is the truth, and all who seek it would hear His voice. In John's gospel He also says His purpose was to give us fullness of life and keep us from thieves.

Those who heard Jesus use this illustration didn't understand what he meant, so he explained it to them. "I assure you, I am the gate for the sheep," he said. "All others who came before me were thieves and robbers. But the true sheep did not listen to them. Yes, I am the gate. Those who come in through me will be saved. Wherever they go, they will find green pastures. The thief's purpose is to steal and kill and destroy. My purpose is to give life in all its fullness" (John 10:6-10).

Jesus also said that the purpose of the thief is to steal, kill, and destroy. Many believe that the thief Jesus is referring to here is the devil. He is a thief, no question about it, but the thief referred to is those who try to get to God apart from the Cross. Those who justify and make excuses for the evil they do are blind and cannot see the truth; they will fall prey to being robbed of what God has for them.

Jesus is the gate for the sheep. That gate is the Cross.

Two Thieves, Two Responses

There were two thieves, one crucified on either side of Jesus. When enshrouded in the darkest horror, God gave Him a gift of the first reward of what His death would accomplish:

one of the thieves saw the truth that hung on the center Cross. What did Jesus think when somebody recognized His glory when He was exposed in such shame, sin, and death? Even before He breathed His last breath, He knew that it was not in vain and the joy of that repentant sinner was a ray of light in a sea of hopelessness. It was then He received the promise manifest that some would find truth and forsake the deception of evil. The devil must have been irate when he saw that one could see the majesty of the heaven he thought he'd destroyed. One saw the light and repented; the other continued to mock, demanding He prove Himself. These two criminals represent mankind and the two responses that we have toward the work of the Cross.

Like all of us, both criminals are guilty and condemned. The one who feared God said, *"We deserve to die for our evil deeds."* He acknowledged his guilt and the punishment he deserved. The other did not. The good thief recognized that Jesus had done no wrong. He may have heard Pilate's verdict of His innocence and believed the truth over the jeers of the angry mob. However he came to know the truth, he saw Jesus holy and blameless. His eyes were opened to see in His emaciated, bloody body, the glory of hope and healing for mankind.

This thief did not blame Him for the mess he was in and he did not ask to be saved even from the death he faced; he simply asked to be remembered in His kingdom. (To remember someone is to keep that person in mind as worthy of consideration or recognition.)

One criminal wanted instant relief; the other eternal. They both saw the Cross and responded according to what they believed in their heart. One was under the deception of sin; the other was enlightened with the fear of God. Notice the response that Jesus had: *"I assure you, today you will be with me in paradise."*

Two thieves hung on either side of the Cross, each representing one of two responses of mankind.

Jesus was saying He would make certain, without any doubt, that that day the man would be with Him in paradise. Paradise is the resting place of righteous souls awaiting the resurrection. Other than repenting for his sins and acknowledging that he was getting what he deserved, this man could do nothing to get saved except trust in this dying Savior on the Cross. This demonstrated that it is not what we do but who we trust in that saves us. In God's immense plan, two guilty, condemned men representing all mankind hung on either side of the Cross. One response leads to Him; the other leads to death. One rejected the Cross of God's love and redemption, but the other saw it as the gateway to salvation.

What was done to Jesus during His passion was incomprehensible; we could never imagine or understand the full magnitude of what He endured. But in the midst of all the demons of hell, a common criminal saw the light. It shone brightly before him, radiant and powerful enough to take him from the depths of evil to the height of righteousness.

The miracle of the thief is proof of what God can do to the soul of a condemned man on his way to hell, if he believes.

Deception is all around us and without His light it blinds us to the truth. Like Michael and Emily, if we do not focus on the Cross we can easily be deceived by wrong desires. The motives of our heart will mislead us if we do not process them through the truth of the Cross. Its power and light will penetrate deep inside of us and reveal the lies that would lead us astray. Daily I must approach it, allowing its truth about God, myself, and others to fill me.

Also in John's gospel Jesus said, *"I am the light of the world."* He was referring to His work on the Cross:

> *Jesus said to the people, "I am the light of the world. If you follow me, you won't be stumbling through the darkness, because you will have the light that leads to life"* (John 8:12).

To stumble means to make a mistake or blunder and fall into evil ways.[38]

The one criminal saw the brightness of the glory of God that is seen in the face of Jesus Christ. When I gaze upon the Cross, I too see, and it is awesome. There is nothing better. It fulfills me and satisfies me with every good thing. He is the lover of my soul, and I am overwhelmed with His glory that is seen there. Second Corinthians describes it so well:

The Cross will keep you from stumbling in a world filled with darkness.

> *For God, who said, "Let there be light in the darkness," has made us understand that this light is the brightness of the glory of God that is seen in the face of Jesus Christ. But this precious treasure—this light and power that now shine within us—is held in perishable containers, that is, in our weak bodies. So everyone can see that our glorious power is from God and is not our own* (2 Corinthians 4:6-7).

Because of the Cross, we can now be a light bearer and shine His light to reveal the darkness that holds others in bondage. Like the deceived criminal, some may not see; but others will. We are called to live in the light of the Cross, and, like the good thief, we will be rescued from the kingdom of darkness and brought into the kingdom of light:

> *Always thanking the Father, who has enabled you to share the inheritance that belongs to God's holy people, who live in the light. For he has rescued us from the one who rules in the kingdom of darkness, and he has brought us into the Kingdom of his dear Son. God has purchased our freedom with his blood and has forgiven all our sins* (Colossians 1:12-14).

We all were represented by those two men who hung on either side of Him. There were two criminals, two choices, and two sides to the Cross.

Chapter Twenty

The Responsibility of the Cross

When the soldiers had crucified Jesus, they divided his clothes among the four of them. They also took his robe, but it was seamless, woven in one piece from the top. So they said, "Let's not tear it but throw dice to see who gets it." This fulfilled the Scripture that says, "They divided my clothes among themselves and threw dice for my robe." So that is what they did. Standing near the cross were Jesus' mother, and his mother's sister, Mary (the wife of Clopas), and Mary Magdalene. When Jesus saw his mother standing there beside the disciple he loved, he said to her, "Woman, he is your son." And he said to this disciple, "She is your mother." And from then on this disciple took her into his home (John 19:23-27).

Jesus died to meet needs; thus the Cross gives us the responsibility to meet the needs of others.

The passage in John 19 describes one of the most touching moments in the agony of our Savior's passion. Here Jesus did something that was incredibly endearing and typical of His unselfish nature.

Jesus Took Care of His Mother Mary

Just prior to being nailed to His implement of torture, the soldiers stripped His clothes from His battered body. They were then divided between four of the Roman soldiers carrying out His execution. However, His undergarment was a seamless robe, and they cast lots for it. Usually this undergarment was given by a loved one; very possibly the mother of Jesus had given it. Perhaps seeing the confiscation of that robe transferred His thoughts to her. It is immediately after their casting lots that Jesus acknowledged her as she stood near the Cross.[39]

Jesus' mother Mary was accompanied by Mary Magdalene, Mary the wife of Clopas, and one of His disciples, the one He was closest to: John. With agonizing strength He uttered words that characterized His incredible nobility and complete desire to care for others more than Himself. He gave an assignment to John to care for His mother, and He gave His mother a son. Through parched lips and barely breathing, He uttered, *"Woman, he is your son,"* and to John, *"She is your mother."* He was moments away from finishing His assignment on earth, and He was going to complete every last part of it without neglecting anything.

What was He thinking as He watched her heart break for His broken body that was so mutilated it was unbearable to behold? Did He also think of His Father who was losing His Son to gain multitudes more? He knew the devastation that was tearing her apart to watch Him tortured and die before her eyes. Did He long to hold her in His arms and comfort her as He would all the other mothers who have lost those closest to their hearts?

Losing a child is the greatest loss of all for humans. Flesh of flesh, bone of our bone, a part of us, born of our seed and now being taken all too soon. Many are the tears of mothers who lost children—children torn from them mercilessly through miscarriages on through adulthood. The pain is almost too much to bear and is as agonizing as any means of torture. Mary bore that pain, and somehow Jesus, in the midst of torture upon torture, took His eyes off His pain and took care of hers. He tried to give her back what she was losing: a son, perhaps symbolic of the new birth of many who would be part of His family.

But even beyond that He was simply taking care of His responsibility. It was the Jewish custom for the oldest son to take care of his mother if the father was deceased. It is understood that Joseph, the stepfather of Jesus, had died, as there is no record of him after Jesus was 12 years old. Therefore Jesus was responsible for her care. It was not common for women to work outside the home at that time. They were dependent on the provision of the man of the house. Jesus was that man, and He had taken care of her every need up to His crucifixion.

Now with His mission on earth accomplished, He would not consider abandoning the care of her who was entrusted to Him. He loved John and depended on him; he was the only disciple brave enough to come back to witness the culmination of all times accomplished on the Cross. He had fled from the Garden, but now he had returned and stood at the feet of his Master, ready to hear His dying words.

Jesus was about responsibility. He always did what He was assigned to do, and He did it perfectly. John knew that, and the Word that burned in his heart had drawn him back to the place of fulfillment. John encountered the Cross, and with it an assignment.[40]

It is our duty to go to the Cross and seek that which the Father would have us do. He must be able to trust us to carry out what He desires of us. As we see the Living Word on the Cross and know His heart, we realize it is about serving others. *The Cross speaks the message of living to meet the needs of others.* Many live their entire lives focused on "I need, I feel, I want." Their world centers on them and whatever they are going through. However, it's not about us!

> *The Cross always has an assignment for us—a responsibility to take care of the things of God.*

Shirking responsibility is an enemy of the Cross because it causes pain and disappointment in those who depend on us. People do not realize that when we purpose to live for others, we experience the

love, peace, and joy of the kingdom. There is nothing like it; it satisfies the soul so immensely that gratefulness abounds. Those who seek their own, on the other hand, are never satisfied. They complain and bear the marks of disappointment, seeing only what they do not have.

I recall, when my husband passed away, the thing that helped me through my grief the most was when I focused on helping someone else. There is something so powerful about doing for others. It is how the kingdom operates.

Seven Assignments From the Cross

The Cross has entrusted assignments to us with His dying for us. Though there are more, I want to briefly discuss seven of these assignments.

1. We Are to Seek the Kingdom of God Before Anything Else

One of our first assignments is to seek the kingdom of God. If we do, then He promises to take care of us. We can read about this in the gospel of Matthew:

And he will give you all you need from day to day if you live for him and make the Kingdom of God your primary concern (Matthew 6:33).

Notice that it says *"if"* we focus on His kingdom, He will give us all we need. To make the kingdom our primary concern or to seek it means to diligently discover, search for, and endeavor to obtain or grasp the understanding of it. The gateway to the kingdom is the Cross. All we need to know about His kingdom we can learn from the Cross. Upon learning, we are then assigned to share the Good News we discover there. That brings us to the second responsibility.

2. We Are Given the Mandate to Preach the Gospel

Mark's gospel tells of Jesus' giving the assignment of what He desires us to do.

And then he told them, "Go into all the world and preach the Good News to everyone, everywhere" (Mark 16:15).

It is obvious that His heart is to see the lost won, and we all have a responsibility to fulfill what mattered to Him. It was why He died.

I am convinced that many believers are not faithful to the mandate of preaching the Gospel because they have not yet discovered the richness of its meaning. The more I keep my focus on the Cross and discover the greater depths of its treasures, the more I desire to shout it from the rooftops. There is nothing I would rather do than help others discover His riches. Before I understood the revelation of the Cross, I shared my faith out of obligation rather from than a driving passion motivated by my love for Him. Now there is nothing more important or real to me.

When you are in love with someone, you can't help but talk about that person. Your loved one is always on your mind; you think he or she is so wonderful you must let everyone know. That is how it is when the Cross becomes your life. For me, my interest in this world has diminished. Building the kingdom is my desire.

Jesus did not leave us without a mandate. The gospel of Luke tells of Jesus' declaring that it is our duty to preach the coming of the kingdom of God:

Jesus replied, "Let those who are spiritually dead care for their own dead. Your duty is to go and preach the coming of the Kingdom of God" (Luke 9:60).

This is not just a job if we feel like it. It is why He went through all of His suffering. It was His plan from the beginning of time. All He had done in the Old and New Covenants was to display and announce to the world His love for them and His desire for their heart. His torture and abuse was for the lost; but first they must hear about it, and that is where our responsibility starts. The Word tells us that people will not know the good news of the Cross unless they are told by someone.

When we meditate on all that Christ went through, we will be driven to tell others about it.

When we meditate on all that Christ went through in His passion and truly appreciate it with all our heart, we will be driven to tell oth-

ers about it. He will guide our steps and lead us to those whom He wills. He is simply looking for those who truly value what He has done and will yield to Him regardless of the personal cost to them.

The apostle Paul understood the responsibility of his assignment, and he preached the Cross only. Once when Paul was discouraged, Jesus spoke to him. At the time he was in jail and many were plotting his death. He was beginning to feel like he would never make it to Rome where he believed God had called him to go. Jesus appeared to him and told him that he would preach the Gospel in Rome.

Rome was the center of the world at that time, and the Romans were known for intolerance of anything that threatened them. To preach in Rome was like being sent into the lions' den, but Paul was unafraid. In fact, he could not rest until he fulfilled the mandate placed on him. Acts 23 describes Jesus' assignment to Paul:

> *That night the Lord appeared to Paul and said, "Be encouraged, Paul. Just as you have told the people about me here in Jerusalem, you must preach the Good News in Rome"* (Acts 23:11).

Jesus said Paul *must* preach the Good News in Rome. It wasn't an option but a command. Paul lived for the Good News of the Cross; it motivated his every move. He did not shrink from his responsibility; nor did he take on anything that wasn't his to accomplish. He was not ever ashamed of the One who saved him from the wrath of God and made him righteous.

The Cross gave him the power he needed to accomplish the assignment given to him. It will do the same for you.

3. We Must Love Our Spouse

Time and time again I feel the anguish of Christian marriages falling apart. It is the selfishness of men and women that rip apart their homes and destroy what God intended for them.

Recently I felt righteous anger boiling inside me as I listened to an attractive young woman crying uncontrollably as she shared her plight with me. Her husband had left her and their four children for another woman and disappeared. She knew that he would not be assisting her financially or even have an interest in seeing his children. I knew her husband; he had been attending church for several years and had been faithful in serving. He seemed like a strong believer with a conviction to do what was right. I had even witnessed their vow renewal a few years earlier, but something had gone wrong.

It had started slowly with his job requesting him to do some work in bars, and it somehow grew into an obsession to frequenting them and all that goes with it. Before long he had met someone and deserted his faith and family. Several months had passed, and she was penniless and brokenhearted with four hurting kids.

This was not the first time I had heard a story like this; rather, it was the third time in less than a few months. I could not comprehend how low and selfish some people would stoop to gratify their flesh at the expense of their families.

Before I discovered the amazing truths of the Cross, my marriage was comfortable but at times disappointing and frustrating. Resentment toward Rick would take over when I felt hurt by him, and I would seethe in silence, making him suffer. Eventually we would argue over whatever the issue was that caused my anger. As my passion and thankfulness for Jesus grew, so did my passion and thankfulness for my husband. The times of disappointment have decreased greatly. Since my life has centered on the Cross, I can freely without fear or reservation love my man. I still do not agree with him on everything; however, because the Cross is now the center of our marriage, I choose to walk in peace. When I need to confront something, I do it with love and honor.

One of the biggest killers of a good marriage is pride because its focus is on self. Working on a marriage cannot be achieved with formulas, but with a heart like Christ's—a heart that willingly sacrifices and humbles itself for the object of its love. The Cross is about humility and dying to self, and the most difficult place to do that is in our homes. Jesus told us to center our marriages around the work of the Cross in the book of Ephesians:

> *And further, you will submit to one another out of reverence for Christ. You wives will submit to your husbands as you do to the Lord. For a husband is the head of his wife as Christ is the head of his body, the church; he gave his life to be her Savior. As the church submits to Christ, so you wives must submit to your husbands in everything. And you husbands must love your wives with the same love Christ showed the church. He gave up his life for her* (Ephesians 5:21-25).

My spouse will inadvertently help me discover what lies in the crevices of my heart by my response to him when I disagree with what he says or does.

To give you an example, recently Rick and I were leaving late to be somewhere and he was in a hurry. As we were about to leave I realized I had forgotten something and had to run upstairs to retrieve it. I had difficulty finding it, and suddenly I heard Rick expressing in frustration his concern for my tardiness. Instantly anger welled up in me; the old feelings of resentment began to rise up. *I'll give him the silent treatment,* was my first thought. I knew what would transpire. We would get in the car and I would sit there silently brewing. My mind would fill with thoughts like, *He is so impatient, He doesn't care about me,* etc. He, in turn, would feel my anger and be uncomfortable and would try to defend his reason for being upset. That would trigger an argument and our day would be ruined. That is not a good place to be in to hear God's voice. I am sure you get the picture and can relate, especially if you're married!

Now here is how the Cross has changed me. When I hear Rick's impatient yell to hurry up and feel the resentment rising inside me, I purpose to bring it to the Cross. I then think about how much Jesus endured of my sin and how far He went to forgive me, and I compare what I am going through with what He did. I then find it easy to lay my resentment down, swallow my pride, and choose to walk in love. When I get in the car I will then be able, through the power of the Cross, look at my husband, smile, and apologize for being late, letting him know what a patient man he is to put up with me. He, in turn, will affirm me and apologize as well, and we will have a great day full of love and peace.

What an incredible responsibility of love and humility the Cross has given to us for our marriages. Furthermore, it is impossible to fulfill that responsibility without focusing on what it is to be patterned after. As I love the work of Christ on the Cross, I will honor it enough to obey the responsibility it gives me in every part of my life. I am no longer my own, but His.

Acknowledging the Cross in the difficulties of life will always change your perspective and your response.

4. We Are to Care for Our Children

I can recall a time as a child when my mother, desperate for a new start, had moved from Toronto to Montreal to begin a new job. She had three hungry mouths to feed and somehow the move caused her to fall so far behind financially that we did not have enough money for food. I recall days when she went hungry and fed us homemade soup with whatever she could scrounge up. That was a low time in my childhood that was filled with need. I can recall another time when I desperately wanted a bicycle. So my mother picked up old parts of discarded bikes and built one for me, painting it a shiny green, for there was no other way she could afford one. It was my Christmas gift, and to me it was brand-new. I treasured that bike and rode it everywhere.

I thank God for my mother who kept her responsibility to care for her family when everything was going against her. Unfortunately she bore that burden alone. I often wondered where my dad was, the daddy who was supposed to help, but he had disappeared. I wondered if he thought about the pain and lack we had as children because of his abuse and addiction to alcohol and gambling. As a child it is difficult to understand when you bear the ridicule of your peers at school because you lack the things they have.

As sin abounds in our society, the increase in parents' neglecting their responsibilities to their families is staggering. This is not how God intended it to be. Fathers are meant to be the providers and mothers the nurturers. Sadly, the perversions of greed, selfishness, and immorality have ripped apart the family unit at the core.

God loves children and says that we must become like a child to enter the kingdom. A child surrenders to the love and care of his or her parents, trusting them to meet his or her needs. God has put a natural desire in us to care for, nurture, and provide for those needs. Sin, though, perverts even the most basic of human instinct for survival. I cannot tell you how many children have been abandoned, neglected, and abused by those who were meant to love them. Over and over again I hear the atrocious stories of broken hearts from irresponsible parents.

Early on in my ministry, I too fell into the trap of pursuing a successful ministry and for a few years my children were left in the care of others more than they should have been. That has been one of my regrets. I can't turn back the clock or restore the time I stole from them, but I have repented to them. Fortunately today they all are serving God, and my sins have been forgiven.

The Word instructs the women to teach others to care for their families:

These older women must train the younger women to love their husbands and their children (Titus 2:4).

As the need for more and the desire to impress others to satisfy our own egos grows, women are forsaking and minimizing the importance of their role as mothers. They are more concerned about meeting their own needs than their children's. They have to have, be, and do those things that satisfy their desires while their children are abandoned to fend for themselves or be cared for by others who have little interest in their well-being.

This is due to dissatisfaction, and the Cross has the power to deal with that dissatisfaction if they will go there. Now, I am not saying women should not work; rather, we must examine our motives for working and evaluate the cost to the precious lives we have been entrusted with.

As for fathers, the book of Ephesians gives a warning and instructs them on their responsibility with their children:

And now a word to you fathers. Don't make your children angry by the way you treat them. Rather, bring them up with the discipline and instruction approved by the Lord (Ephesians 6:4).

Men too have the responsibility of raising their children; they are not to leave that role solely to their wives or others. It is so easy for fathers to get caught up in their dreams of success or to fill their lives with things that grat- ify themselves rather then affirming those they have brought into the world. Each time a child is born, a great responsibility is also birthed as God entrusts us to care for them. Fathers are entrusted as the providers to make sure their families have a home, food, and clothing. The Bible says that if a man doesn't care for his household, he is worse than an unbeliever is (1 Timothy 5:8). I have met several men who claim to be Christians and yet refuse to pay the child support for their families. Obviously they have little or no understand- ing of the work of the Cross.

5. We Must Encourage and Love One Another

As we meditate on the Word, we will become full of Him and able to give to others the love and encouragement they need. Wherever I go, I point those who are discouraged to the Cross and share about its unlimited love and power. I am so thankful when I think of what He has done, and I know that in the Cross lie the answers to the hurts of man. It is the message of the Cross that we are to encourage and love each other with!

When I see the Cross, I always remember why I am serving Him. It is not for the accolades of man, but for what I owe Him because He won my heart by what He did for me. And the love I owe Him He wants me to lavish on the people I am called to minister to, to the best of my ability. When I stray from the Cross, I turn my focus on myself and fail at loving and giving to others. Hebrews 10 says it so well, telling us that we must encourage one another with *"outbursts of love and good deeds"*:

> *Think of ways to encourage one another to outbursts of love and good deeds. And let us not neglect our meeting together, as some people do, but encourage and warn each other, especially now that the day of his coming back again is drawing near* (Hebrews 10:24-25).

This scripture beautifully shows how we need one another and must take that responsibility seriously by being faithful to our commitment to meet together and bless one another with good deeds. I can only love others to the degree my heart is where it belongs. Jesus urges us to love each other over and over in His Word. It is what He has desired for us from the beginning. It is His heart's passion, and He died to enable us to live that way.

Whenever my heart bursts with love for Him, I try to find someone to express it to. That is how He desires us to live. Whether it is simply a phone call, a small gift, or a prayer, we all need the love that He desperately wants to pour out on us through His body.

6. We Are to Pray, Worship, and Thank God at All Times

It is so easy to pray, worship, and thank God when we see the Cross. Thankfulness is an attitude of the heart. If we always keep ourselves aware of the incredible gift of the Gospel and the fact that we didn't get what we deserved, it is easy to be grateful. When we love someone, it is easy to communicate with that person. My prayer life flows easily into God's presence now that I am in love with Him. Keeping the Cross before me ignites the fire of that love burning in my heart. I won't let it diminish, and when it begins to, I set time aside and rehearse with thanksgiving what He did for me—every painful step of it, thinking through how I put Him there and how He identified with my pain in every way. Each time I do this my heart is captured again. This is the most important thing. The book of Colossians says that I am responsible to live in peace and always be thankful:

And let the peace that comes from Christ rule in your hearts. For as members of one body you are all called to live in peace. And always be thankful (Colossians 3:15).

In other words, we lose our peace if we are ungrateful and murmur and complain.

Always be thankful, always be thankful, and always be thankful. This message permeates the Word. Why? *It must be for the work of the Cross.* We will always have that to be thankful for, and that is enough! Everything we will ever need was accomplished there, and we must be thankful for the responsibility He gives us. It is an honor, not a burden, to serve Him.

If the Cross is not at the center of our heart, serving Him will feel like a weight instead of a joy. It is only difficult when we lose our focus. First Timothy says we should be thankful that He considers us trustworthy! Now that can be an attitude adjustment for some of us!

How thankful I am to Christ Jesus our Lord for considering me trustworthy and appointing me to serve him (1 Timothy 1:12).

215

How could we not be? Thanking Him comes easily when I think of what He has done for me.

7. We Are to Care for the Widows, the Orphans, and the Poor

I have dear friends who run a large ministry in Africa. At the time of this writing, they feed approximately 450,000 children daily and preach the Gospel in mass crusades throughout Africa. They have literally led millions to the Lord. They have birthed an amazing ministry that fulfills this mandate, which God has placed on them, in ways that would seem impossible. I am blessed to know and serve on the ministry board of such faithful, humble, diligent people. We make sure that we support them and other ministries like them around the world that help those who cannot help themselves.

> *The Cross is about character and responsibility.*

The book of James tells us that we all have the responsibility of taking care of orphans and widows. Whether we can give a little or a lot, we are called by God to meet these needs.

> *Pure and lasting religion in the sight of God our Father means that we must care for orphans and widows in their troubles, and refuse to let the world corrupt us* (James 1:27).

We cannot love God and neglect those whom He loves so much.

Jesus did not neglect His responsibility for His mother, even up to His death.

Jesus set the example as He looked at His precious mother and His closest friend John. He took His last responsibility and passed it on to John when He said, *"Woman, he is your son,"* and *"She is your mother."* Once again He demonstrated in His greatest need that it is all about "others."

Chapter Twenty-one

Forsaken on the Cross

At noon, darkness fell across the whole land until three o'clock. At about three o'clock, Jesus called out with a loud voice, "Eli, Eli, lema sabachthani?" which means, "My God, my God, why have you forsaken me?" (Matthew 27:45-46)

Forsaken by God. I cannot think of anything more horrible. In my earlier years as a Christian, because of my insecurities and personal history, I feared being forsaken by God. I literally had nightmares about it at times. I was desperate for God to stay with me, feeling that I was falling into an abyss of desolation and loneliness, left alone. Panic and sweat accompanied these horrid bouts of fear as I wrestled with understanding the nature of God. To be forsaken by God had to be the worst conceivable position to be in, and I could not even stand to think about it. To forsake means to entirely give up on or renounce.[41] It is similar to being abandoned, but much worse. I can't imagine what it would be like to be entirely given up on and left with the feeling of worthlessness.

Many people feel forsaken by others they have relied on and trusted in, but I could never conceive what it would be like to be abandoned by my friends and left by my people, my church, and my God all at once. That is what happened to Jesus.

There is eternal significance in the moment when He cried out, *"My God, my God, why have you forsaken me?"* Jesus, who was innocent of all evil, was now being forced to see and experience all the forces of sin and hell, the absolute terror and desolation of untold evils, culminating in complete intensity with all wickedness and destruction—and God had turned His face. Like the scapegoat bearing the sin of all, He was sent out into the outer darkness, banished from all that is good, to bear the wrath of God alone. He tasted the sorrow and hopelessness of separation from God for all mankind. He was deserted by all in heaven and on earth; God had to turn from Him when Jesus experienced His greatest fear: becoming the object of His consuming fire. The fullness of God's wrath permeated His tortured body and soul…unspeakable suffering to be uttered in one cry at the ninth hour, as Matthew recorded:

> *At noon, darkness fell across the whole land until three o'clock. At about three o'clock, Jesus called out with a loud voice, "Eli, Eli, lema sabachthani?" which means, "My God, my God, why have you forsaken me?"* (Matthew 27:45-46)

Darkness in the middle of the day descended as evil upon evil was poured out and He was abandoned to consummate the complete suffering as the Passover Lamb. He absorbed it all completely, determined to set you free. He took your hatred so that you would love. He took your selfishness so you would give. He took your wrath so you could enter the presence of God. He emptied Himself so you could be full and never be separated from God again.

He was forsaken for all the times you cried and heaven seemed silent.

He was forsaken for you, for all the times you cried out, "God, where are You? Please do something! I can't take it anymore!" and heaven seemed silent. There have been those times in my life when God seemed to not care, when the crushing agony of my heart didn't move Him to rush to my defense and change the nightmare I was living.

Night after night, day after day, the gut-wrenching cries of mankind pierce through the darkness of evil that has enveloped them with circumstances too great to bear. Around our world people are forsaken, left without food, left without homes, left without their needs met. Homeless orphans, mutilated bodies, corrupt governments, and movements of hatred where man destroys man circle our globe. Added to the corrupted hands of man are the natural disasters that descend like looming forces of darkness ready to attack their unassuming victims without notice. The tsunami of Christmas 2004 destroyed untold lives, ripping them apart in a brief moment in time. People were forever changed; they were left feeling abandoned and fearful in a world jarred from its foundation.

The darkness descends and the curse of sin perpetuates as man turns his back on God. We live in a fallen world that is under a curse from the sin of man. All sin by its very nature breeds the curse of death and destruction. Unfortunately there are many children, even in North America, who have been forsaken—but not by God.

Forsaken, But Not Forgotten

Bill Wilson is a mighty man of God who runs one of the largest Sunday school programs in the world. His ministry is in the dregs of society in Brooklyn, New York. The motivation behind Bill's desire to help the helpless and forsaken children of society was birthed out of his own personal experience. When he was 12 years old, his mother brought him to a street corner in Pinellas Park, Florida, and told him, "I can't do this anymore. You wait here." He waited until the sun went down, wondering what she meant when she said she couldn't take it anymore. He waited fearfully all night, wondering where she was and when she was coming.

The night turned to day, and in fear and loneliness the hours passed. He thought about his life, his parents' divorce, his sick father who had moved away, and his alcoholic mother who was raising him. She worked at a bar and frequently brought home different men. Bill would fall asleep listening to cursing, fighting, and carousing. *Surely she'll be back soon,* his desperate thoughts reasoned.

Another day and night passed. And then another. He sat for three days in the hot Florida sun with nowhere to go and no one to go to. He had never felt loved, barely knew his dad, and now was forsaken by his mother, never to return. After three days, a Christian man finally stopped to help him. He had noticed Bill there and finally realized that something was wrong. Divine providence had stepped in as this kind man Dave Rudenis, took him and brought him to a youth camp. The rest is history, as Bill Wilson found faith in God and grew up to become a pastor and pioneer in inner city ministry.[42]

You may not have been forsaken by your parents and left all alone, but each one of us throughout our lives has probably faced some level of feeling forsaken.

I remember my first day in kindergarten when, due to a communication problem, no one came to pick me up. My mother was working a full-time job and had assigned someone to get me, but there was a misunderstanding in their communication and no one came. We had just moved to that area and I had no idea where I lived. I was left sitting outside the school for a while feeling afraid, forgotten, and all alone. The feelings of that day stuck with me and haunted me for years. I cannot imagine what Bill must have felt after three days.

Being forsaken leaves you feeling empty, isolated, and terrified, and it is crippling to your sense of self-worth. Many of you have been forsaken and left feeling that no one cared. Some of you even felt that God was distant and unreachable, never seeming to show up when you needed Him. You may have forsaken others yourself and broke their hearts as they cried out for you while you turned your back on them with a hard heart.

Many believers live in a fantasy world. They are oblivious to what is going on throughout the world. However, as I write this, I believe that we are getting a taste of the desperation that is rampant around our globe. Between natural disasters and war-torn countries, we have seen and heard the desperate cries for help and witnessed the atrocities that can occur in the worst of circumstances. The feeling of being forsaken has smacked us in the face and its pain has brought many of us to tears.

The cry of man was uttered from the lips of Jesus, forsaken because of sin. The Father and the Son separated in fellowship, yet not in the oneness of who they are. No longer could Jesus feel the presence of His Father. He felt alone, abandoned, forgotten, and left to die. His world of total peace and goodness was ripped from Him by the forces of darkness and hissing demons. He was shaken to the core of His heart, with nowhere to go but into the utter darkness of horror and hopelessness.

Several years ago, Rick and I were staying with missionaries in the Philippines when we awoke early one morning to our beds shaking violently. Panic struck our hearts for a moment as the reality sunk in that we were in an earthquake. There was nowhere to go; when the earth shakes, you are at its mercy. A tsunami followed the earthquake, and thousands died just a few hundred miles away from us. We thought of all those people who went to bed that night and were swept out to sea in their sleep.

Where is God in all of this? Does He not care? Has He left us all to die at will to whatever calamity assails us? Daily we hear in the news of the murders, rapes, bombings, wars, robberies, child abuse, and all the other atrocities that happen. Each time a new victim is left wondering, *Why me? Where was God when I needed Him?* Hearts are hardened with seemingly unanswered prayers.

Jesus Knows What It Is Like

Believe it or not, God knows what it is like when heaven is silent and emptiness, abandonment, loneliness, and horror engulf you with the darkness of hopelessness and grief of all that is evil. Psalm 22 contains the prophetic account of Jesus' crucifixion—of that cry permeating the heavens with desperation, pleading for mercy:

> *My God, my God, why hast thou forsaken me? why art thou so far from helping me, and from the words of my roaring?...But I am a worm, and no man; a reproach of men, and despised of the people. All they that see me laugh me to scorn: they shoot out the lip, they shake the head, saying, He trusted on the LORD that he would deliver him: let him deliver him, seeing he delighted in him....Be not far from me; for trouble is near; for there is none to help. Many bulls have compassed me: strong bulls of Bashan have beset me round. They gaped upon me with their mouths, as a ravening and a roaring lion. I am poured out like water, and all my bones are out of joint; my heart is like wax; it is melted in the midst of my bowels. My strength is dried up like a potsherd; and my tongue cleaveth to my jaws; and thou hast brought me into the dust of death. For dogs have compassed me: the assembly of the wicked have inclosed me: they pierced my hands and my feet. I may tell all my bones: they look and stare upon me. They part my garments among them, and cast lots upon my vesture* (Psalm 22:1, 6-8, 11-18 KJV).

Wow. This is the heart cry of Jesus, God in the flesh, suffering the pain of the curse of sin fully for us. My God suffers. That cry of being forsaken did not mean He was no longer the deity that He was; rather, at that moment the darkness of sin completely veiled the light. Christ had to experience the full impact of judgment and that meant God had to turn from Him. Jesus was forsaken by His Father.

Eternal truth was revealed on the Cross: the truth that God suffers with us for the evil that prevails. Why can't He stop it? He loves us enough to give us freedom of choice, even though He knows that with it comes what He came to destroy.

The suffering of Jesus was the suffering of God.

Jesus was sent so the world could see what God Himself feels about the sin that abounds in the heart of men. The suffering of man is not God's desire for man, but He will use it to destroy the works of darkness. That is what Jesus did on the Cross. The very evil of Satan himself that was set against Jesus was what God used to destroy his power!

Just think of taking an atomic bomb that an enemy unleashes on you and those you love, and with the power you possess you absorb it onto yourself to explode and turn it into the very weapon that destroys your enemy. You come out of the explosion free from harm, along with everyone who stuck by you, and your enemy is destroyed by his own bomb. When Satan devised his evil plan to take out Jesus, he did not realize that God was taking his hatred and turning it into the greatest love story that ever existed. And God planned it before the devil did.

The devil was just a pawn—still with a free choice—but a tool used by God to implement His ultimate destruction. Wow! God is so powerful that everything that happens works toward the intended end that He has planned since the beginning! Because of His foreknowledge of us and the decisions we make, He is able to orchestrate a perfect plan using even the choices of His enemies. When our mistakes are mixed with faith, God can make them weapons against the devil.

We must understand that God is infinite and all-knowing. In contrast, we are finite and have limited knowledge. We are incapable of understanding everything God does, but we must have faith in His character. The Cross gives proof that we can trust His intentions for us.

Our human pride is so impressed with itself that we often dare to question the wisdom of the Almighty! Who are we to think we can challenge the knowledge of God? I trust in His goodness, and once I make that choice He proves it over and over to me.

So because of His immense love for me, I know that in the big picture of eternity all things are for my best when I trust in Him. He has given me power and authority to overcome the darkness, and nothing can keep me from His love and plan for me.

The Power Is in Us

The power that Jesus possessed because of His total holiness and righteousness is more powerful than any weapon known to man. Because of Him, we possess that same power. The book of Romans says that the same power that actually raised Jesus from the dead is the power that is in us:

> *The Spirit of God, who raised Jesus from the dead, lives in you. And just as he raised Christ from the dead, he will give life to your mortal body by this same Spirit living within you* (Romans 8:11).

It is incredible to think that we have that much power through His Spirit! The power of the Spirit of Christ is utterly complete and amazing. We actually possess Him inside us, but He is only released to the degree that we see who we are in Him and conform to His image and likeness. Jesus went through His passion so we could possess and utilize the same Spirit He had!

The Cross is the ultimate weapon.

The Cross wiped out the forces of darkness from our lives forever. It is the place of our complete victory over our separation from God. Forsaken no more, divine wrath and divine grace met and united us with the Godhead.

We are back to where we were *before* the fall of man, only now we have chosen it. To accomplish our full redemption and justification, Jesus had to go to the lowest of lows, the darkest of dark, and the worst of evil to eliminate their power. In the moment of His greatest need, He cried out as He felt the horror of all that He hated and had come to destroy.

We have already been set free from the power of sin, and when we see and believe it, we overcome the curse of this world. Those who understand the fullness of their redemption will have the power to find victory in the sting of the suffering in this world, and, like Jesus, be able to take what attacks them and use it for the glory of God. We glorify Him when we respond like He did in the midst of evil. This turns our pain into a powerful weapon that destroys the effects of sin and produces a glorious work, bringing us through to the other side.

Suffering will either harden our heart toward Him or cause us to see the very hand of God at work to beat evil. We decide at the Cross.

At the Cross, unbending justice and love without measure were married forever.

Only at the Cross can you see the worst of evil and the greatest of righteousness accomplishing the same goal. The redemption of man was released through a gut-wrenching cry from the heart of the God-man who bore it all.

Erwin Lutzer says in his book, *Cries from the Cross*:

"Here all the forces of the universe converge: Man did his work by killing the Son of God and revealing the evil of his heart. Satan did his work by bruising the seed of the woman and displaying his foolish hostility: Jesus did His work, for He died, 'the just for the unjust, that He might bring them to God' and finally, God did a work by exhibiting His justice and love when His wrath was poured out on His Son."[43]

Jesus was forsaken, and there was nothing more horrifying than that. Hell could not have been fiercer or hatred more real. To witness God forsaking God is a demonstration of how God feels when we turn our backs on Him. It is not an easy thing for God to be easily rejected and forsaken bu the creation He loves so passionately.

Parents of a rebellious child can relate to this when the child they love with all their heart and desire to see safe, runs away to a life of sex and drugs. As a parent you know the dangers that seek to destroy the very soul of your loved ones, and there is nothing you can do to stop them. Your son or daughter will do what he or she wants, and love must let that child go. But love also waits in hopeful desperation for the prodigal to come home.

So God waits for us, the object of all He has done, to run into His arms, leaving Him no more. Are we forsaken by God? The Cross shouts *No!* Jesus Christ was forsaken so we would not be. We are made one with God, and if we ever feel alone, we need only to look at the Cross and see He is with us. God became forsaken so we would never be left by Him. Whatever comes He has given us the ability to glorify Him by His power that defeated the darkness in our life. His darkest hour was our brightest. His despair became our hope, and His tortured body became our healing. What more could He have done to prove His faithfulness to us? Everything in our life must end and begin at the Cross.

We judge Him not by what happens to us, but by what He did for us and what that does in us! A God who suffered and knows the despair of our being forsaken is a God who is *always there*.

He was forsaken by God so we would never be.

Chapter Twenty-two

Thirsting for the Cross

After this, Jesus knowing that all things were now accomplished, that the scripture might be fulfilled, saith, I thirst (John 19:28 KJV).

Jesus, after sweating great drops of blood in the Garden, after being beaten, imprisoned, scourged, crowned with thorns, and nailed and left to hang on a cross for nine hours, would have been totally dehydrated from all the blood loss. It was no surprise, then, toward the end that He cried out, *"I thirst!"* And with those words He fulfilled yet another prophecy.

Jesus knew that He was fulfilling the Scriptures as He uttered these words in desperation of His plight, words so real to Him yet representing powerful truth. Nothing He said or went through was in vain. We can read this prophecy spoken hundreds of years earlier in the Psalms that describes the state of dehydration the Messiah would experience:

My strength has dried up like sunbaked clay. My tongue sticks to the roof of my mouth. You have laid me in the dust and left me for dead (Psalm 22:15).

Jesus, who is crying out with unquenchable thirst, felt His strength drying up. When He took on human flesh, He had emptied Himself of equality with God and was born as a baby who thirsted for His mother's milk. Think about it. This is God, who created all things and knew no need! First He was born to thirst as an infant, and now He thirsted in misery and agony to share in the suffering of the unquenchable thirst of man separated from His Creator. Jesus went to the Cross to thirst so that we could be filled!

The Living Water Experienced Thirst

God shares with every part of our humanity; He joined us to cry out for the needs we desperately have. His pain is real as His cry resonates with every human cry of pain, grief, hunger, and thirst. Jesus is fully man and fully God—the frailty of flesh and the fullness of deity—joined together in His life and now His death to satisfy all the questions known to man. Everything He did in life and death has relevance to our life and our death. He hung on that Cross as the Living Water that would satisfy every craving of the human psyche.

The book of Colossians tells us that He is the visible image of the invisible God. Seeing Jesus is seeing God Himself; there is no difference.

Christ is the visible image of the invisible God. He existed before God made anything at all and is supreme over all creation (Colossians 1:15).

This scripture says that He is *"supreme over all creation."* That means He is the greatest in power, authority, and rank.[44] Jesus is literally God—a God who stripped Himself of all His rights in order to completely identify with us. He is all-powerful but not unapproachable; all-knowing yet sits with us in our pain, whispering softly, "I know what you feel. I am with you always; trust Me."

Believing has to do with seeing and embracing the work on the Cross, yet here *on the Cross, the One who satisfies our thirst is thirsty.* As He cried out He bore the sin of mankind and the fiery impact of God's wrath. The wrath of God is a consuming fire and the Living Water cannot flow where the soul is corrupt with sin. He took our thirst so that we could have the Living Water that only He can provide. What is that Living Water? In the gospel of John we read that Jesus, at the climax of the Festival of Shelters, cried out to all who would hear about the rivers of living water that people could receive from Him. He was referring to the outpouring of His Spirit from His death on the Cross when He said, *"If you believe in me, come and drink!"*

On the last day, the climax of the festival, Jesus stood and shouted to the crowds, "If you are thirsty, come to me! If you believe in me, come and drink! For the Scriptures declare that rivers of living water will flow out from within." (When he said "living water," he was speaking of the Spirit, who would be given to everyone believing in him. But the Spirit had not yet been given, because Jesus had not yet entered into his glory) (John 7:37-39).

Notice that He shouted this out at the Festival of Shelters. This was a festival that would begin on the fifth day after the Day of Atonement[45] and would be celebrated for seven days. To celebrate it, the Israelites would rejoice before the Lord for seven days, offering sacrifices with fire each day. The word *shelter* means a refuge, cover, or protection.[46] This festival taught about God's nature and what He had done for the Israelites when He protected them in the wilderness after they escaped from Egypt. It was a time of renewed commitment to God and commemorated His goodness, protection, and guidance in the wilderness. All of this was a type of the work of the Cross that covers and protects us as we live in this world.

The work of the Cross is a continual guide that leads to wholeness!

At the Cross He thirsted and at the Cross His Spirit was released as He bridged the separation from God to satisfy our thirst for Him. There is something fulfilling in knowing our

God suffered with us—and not just suffered, but also gained victory over the sufferings' intended harm. What an incredible God that He would take on our thirst so we could be filled with His Living Water and never thirst again! Our thirst for God will always be satisfied at the Cross, for it is there that we see Him as He is in all love, humility, and victory over flesh. When we move from the Cross, we become dry.

He has given us His Spirit, the same Spirit of Christ that brought Christ to the Cross. As we see the Cross we see Christ and His Spirit, and that serves as our guide, resulting in wholeness.

Desperately Thirsting for God

On July 19, 2000, NBC's "Dateline" featured a story on Robert Bogucki, an American from Alaska who, on a quest to find God, went on a six-week trek in the dangerous Australian desert. He covered more than 250 miles alone in the Great Sandy Desert, going without food or water for 40 days. He had been participating in a cycling tour when he simply chose to disappear into the desert with some personal belongings, the clothes on his back, and thong sandals for footwear. Driven by an incredible need for water, he eventually dug six feet into the sand with his bare hands to find it. But his real quest was spiritual thirst.

In his desperate need to discover God, he lost 50 pounds and traveled relentlessly in the wilderness, reflecting on life and why he was here. During this time he read his Bible and pressed into knowing more about God and His love for him. He was thirsting to know the truth, and he was determined to find it. During his absence a search team tried to find him to no avail. They spent two weeks looking diligently before they gave up, assuming him dead. His parents, however, did not lose hope. Convinced that he had the skill to survive, they requested help from the 1st Special Response Group. These people responded, and they tracked 40,000 square miles of desert until he was finally found.

In spite of his ordeal, his strength only weakened toward the end, and then he was reunited with his family. When questioned why on "Dateline," Robert replied, "Going without food and water simply to show God that you believe in Him isn't necessary. He would much prefer showing kindness and mercy."

Robert was a man who truly thirsted for more of God and went to the extreme to find Him. As I write this book, I am drinking glass after glass of fresh clean water, and I take it for granted. My garage is full of cases of purified water; I have a water purifier on my kitchen sink, along with a water dispenser on my fridge. At the time of this writing, it is nearing the end of an abnormally hot summer for Canada, and the need for water has increased. My lawn and flowers need watering more frequently, and the evidence of neglect is dried-up, dead vegetation.

Everything must have water to have life. Water is what nourishes and feeds that which grows and produces. We can live for a long time without food, but not without water. It is interesting to note that along with the curse on the ground is the great lack of clean water. In fact, over a billion people do not have clean drinking water, and each year millions of children die of diseases related directly to unsafe water. It is the leading cause of death in the world today.

Water is absolutely necessary for the survival of man, and we live in a world with a water crisis. In the next two decades the average water supply per person will drop by one-third, leaving millions more without this necessity of life. The spiritual often coincides with what is happening in the natural realm. God made enough water for man to survive, but the sin of man has cursed and abused what God has given, and millions are dying as a result.

After Hurricane Katrina I watched in horror on television the thousands of Americans who were left without food or water in 95-degree weather while waiting to be rescued. As slow as it may have seemed, help was on the way, but there are millions who have no help coming soon. The people in New Orleans were dying of dehydration; their thirst was driving them crazy. How must the millions feel who live that way all the time?

The Word of God uses water to describe the fulfillment of God Himself. We can read in the following verses in the gospel of John how the water He gives us completely takes away our thirst. Here Jesus was referring to the rivers of living water that flow out from Himself and satisfy our greatest needs forever:

Jesus replied, "People soon become thirsty again after drinking this water. But the water I give them takes away thirst altogether. It becomes a perpetual spring within them, giving them eternal life" (John 4:13-14).

This passage also says the water He gives will become a perpetual spring inside us. A perpetual spring is a source of water that never ends. In other words, it is a satisfaction to all thirst that would last. This water that He gives not only satisfies our thirst but also gives us eternal life. Unclean water causes disease and death, as we can see throughout our world, but pure clean water produces life. In comparison, the corruption of sin produces unquenchable fire and death while the Living Water satisfies all thirst for all eternity.

It is imperative that we discover what this living water is and how to get it. Again we can read in John's gospel that when we believe in Him, we will never thirst:

Jesus replied, "I am the bread of life. No one who comes to me will ever be hungry again. Those who believe in me will never thirst" (John 6:35).

If that is true, then it is critical that we know what He is talking about when He says *"those who believe in me."* Believing in Him is the key.

However, to get this water that satisfies all thirst through believing in Him, what must we believe about Him?

An Inherent Thirst

The history of man is full of the search for truth, especially for truth about God. To find the truth, you must thirst for it, for it is when you thirst that you will seek. Unfortunately, some do not really want the truth, but a reality that satisfies their need to gratify self.

We tend to create our own realities and allow that perception to control our life. When I was growing up, because of my upbringing, I was convinced that what I needed to make me happy was the perfect man. I thought that meeting and marrying the right man would fulfill the deep needs in my heart. Many young women look for their prince to come and sweep them off their feet in the belief that they will live happily ever after. It doesn't take a long time in to a marriage to realize what an illusion that is. Others try to fill the void with money, power, drugs, or other facsimiles, never reaching true satisfaction.

The key is to know what we are really thirsting for.

The incredible thirst within us craves to be filled and constantly drives us to quench it. When we thirst for something, it means that we have an insistent desire or craving for satisfaction to meet a particular need. Like Robert, if that thirst is intense, we will go to great measures to gratify it.

As babies we are born thirsty, and it is a natural thing to satisfy a need inside us for survival. It is not just the need for food that man is born with; we also need love, validation, and purpose. When God created us, He made us in His image and likeness and inside of us all there is a place only God can fill. When man separated from God because of sin, a great void was created in our heart. After all, we were made to glorify Him. When something is created for a specific reason and then fails to accomplish its purpose, it has no real value. So in our ignorance we try to fill our need for Him with counterfeits. We are born with physical, emotional, and spiritual thirsts, and we gratify those needs with whatever we think will help. No matter who we are or where we live, we will thirst, and we will seek to quench that thirst.

The words, *"I thirst,"* uttered by Jesus spoke volumes for the unmet needs of man. Deep within His soul, He was not only being tormented with the need for a drink of water, but He also felt the dry and empty void of man in the grip of evil and despair.

His cry of thirst was your cry for all the unfulfilled needs, unhealed hurts, and areas that remain in pain. What have you used to try and satisfy those needs with? In my earlier years it was drugs, parties, and artwork. Later I got caught up in materialism, then the need to be accepted by others, and finally the need to succeed. All these things led to futility as only He can complete me. Jesus shared in my suffering and my thirst so that I could share in His power and His life and be with Him forever. Jesus is the revelation of God, the source of all purpose and power, and He demon-strated that revelation completely on the Cross.

As I focus on the Cross, my thirst is satisfied!

The book of Hebrews says that Jesus tasted death for every man. As His tongue was parched with the fire of thirst, He tasted death:

> *But we see Jesus, who was made a little lower than the angels for the suffering of death, crowned with glory and honour; that he by the grace of God should taste death for every man. For it became him, for whom are all things, and by whom are all things, in bringing many sons unto glory, to make the captain of their salvation perfect through suffer-ings* (Hebrews 2:9-10 KJV).

This scripture also says our salvation was made perfect through His suffer-ing. His thirst was the climax of that suffering; it was the cry of "I need!" His crucifixion was a slow process of dehydration and suffocation that brought Him to unbearable limits. The Cross helps us see the ugliness of the great thirst that sin created. His thirst was burning and ravaging like a furious sandstorm that sucks up every bit of life in its path. Without God, man will thirst and never experience the refreshing waters that He has for us. Without His life there is sor-row and death; Proverbs describes how a broken spirit dries our bones:

> *A merry heart doeth good like a medicine: but a broken spirit drieth the bones* (Proverbs 17:22 KJV).

This verse indicates that our spiritual condition affects us in every way. To have dry bones is to be in pain. But it also says a merry heart is like medicine, which means it brings healing.

A merry heart is a happy heart, one that is full of joy. There is great joy in understanding the work of the Cross. It brings a joy that runs so deep and sat-isfies so powerfully that life is produced even when the darkness threatens.

When Jesus said, *"I thirst,"* it was to satisfy the deep void in you. Ask Him to reveal how you are trying to satisfy that thirst. Is it with the accolades of man? With success and power? With an addiction you can't control? Whatever it is, you must surrender your thirst to Him and drink in the rivers of living water that flow from the Cross. Only then will your pursuit of the things of this world cease to grip you. As I allow the Cross to satisfy me, my desire for other things decreases, and it is easy to let go of them.

On the Cross Jesus shows us how to respond to suffering with love instead of hate, faith instead of fear, and forgiveness instead of bitterness. It was the power of His righteousness that raised Him from the dead, and that same power will cause you to thirst no more.

Just as there are millions who thirst for clean drinking water, there are millions who thirst for the true living water and don't know where to find it. Who will give it to them? Are we willing to let His rivers of living water flow from within us to them? Only at the Cross will we find the One who cried *"I thirst!"* and who satisfies our soul so we, in turn, can give to those dying of a thirst for something more.

Chapter Twenty-three

It Is Finished at the Cross

Jesus knew that everything was now finished, and to fulfill the Scriptures he said, "I am thirsty." A jar of sour wine was sitting there, so they soaked a sponge in it, put it on a hyssop branch, and held it up to his lips. When Jesus had tasted it, he said, "It is finished!" Then he bowed his head and gave up his spirit (John 19:28-30).

One of the most powerful cries Jesus uttered on His Cross was, *"It is finished!"*

This was Jesus' sixth cry on the Cross. He died knowing that He had completed the work the Father assigned Him to do.

The word *finished* means accomplished, done, fulfilled, and brought to an end.[47] Verse 28 of John 19 reads that *"Jesus knew that everything was now finished."* The important thing to know is just exactly what "everything" is that was finished!

The meaning of this one phrase, *"it is finished,"* is immeasurable. The list of what was finished is a truth that echoes on for eternity, breaking the power of darkness over the hearts of men in the ages of time. The Cross was the fulfillment of the whole Word of God!

The Cross is the final answer to our slavery to sin and the curses that come with it. It is the fullness of judgment and the completion of our salvation. Our condemnation is finished; our righteousness is complete. Finished is the law of the Old Covenant and the bloody sacrifices of the priesthood. Finished is the power of the curse and the chains that bound us up. Finished is our separation from God and the pain that goes with it. *Finished for all time is our justification, redemption, and sanctification.* At the Cross was victory, triumph, and conquest over the enemy of our soul. Many look at the Cross as a place of death and defeat, and it was; but not for God. It spelled defeat for Satan and all his followers. The book of Colossians explains that on the Cross the Lord disarmed the evil rulers and authorities.

In this way, God disarmed the evil rulers and authorities. He shamed them publicly by his victory over them on the cross of Christ (Colossians 2:15).

Notice that it says the victory was won *on the Cross*. That means a great battle had raged for our soul—a battle between good and evil, God and Satan.

Christ won us back on the Cross! It was His humility and obedience that defeated the pride and disobedience of Satan and released man from his chains.

Jesus won back the world at the Cross.

The enemy of our mind is defeated! It is not something that *will* happen, but something that is *already finished!*

God created the world and everything in it. Because of the sin man chose, however, the world was lost to Him. *At the Cross He won it back.* He ripped it from the devil's hands, and now it is up to us to decide which world we want to live in. Satan can no longer keep us from God. We belong to Him, and we are not of this world anymore.

Our redemption is complete. That means we can break forth and tear off the chains of sin and bondage that have held us captive. Why believe the lies of the devil that bombard us with thoughts like, "you are no good"; "you can't do it"; and "you will fail," if the Cross destroyed those things?

The Definitive Defeat of Satan

Can you imagine how shocked Satan must have been when Jesus defeated him, shamed him, and publicly displayed him openly? He thought he was destroying Jesus, but Jesus decreed "it is finished" to the devil and destroyed his power in the moment Satan thought he'd won. Satan must have been gloating in evil delight as he saw the God of glory hanging naked, bleeding, beaten, and dying. He and his demonic cohorts must have danced in a frenzied flurry of assumed victory—only to be stopped dead in their tracks. In the midst of their pit of desecration and unending darkness burst forth a light so brilliant they tried to flee in terror, but they could not escape the grip of its surge of power. From the heights of heaven to the depths of hell came a victory cry so complete that no evil could hide. Satan was rendered powerless and defeated by the God-man whose nature of righteousness took him out.

Now Satan's only victims are those who do not know the weapon that won. It is imperative that we know what was finished on the Cross and stand firm against Satan's lies. We are called to resist the devil through the Cross because it is what he is most afraid of. It destroyed and shamed him for all the principalities and powers to see.

What was Jesus thinking as He paraded the murderer of those whom He loved so much? Was He overcome with joy because He knew our defeat was over and our pain would end? Did He feel the joy that would possess our heart as we see Him and fall down at His feet with eternal adoration? Did He see the multitudes that would look at His Cross and know they have won because the work is finished? I must identify with the work of the Cross as it shows me the truth over the contradictions of my flesh.

The words of Jesus in Luke declare that Satan has no power over us. He has fallen from heaven, and we have been given the authority from Christ to rule over him and all his power!

> *"Yes," he told them, "I saw Satan falling from heaven as a flash of lightning! And I have given you authority over all the power of the enemy, and you can walk among snakes and scorpions and crush them. Nothing will injure you. But don't rejoice just because evil spirits obey you; rejoice because your names are registered as citizens of heaven"* (Luke 10:18-20).

Jesus did not think even this was as much to rejoice over where we are heading. He knew our destiny was sealed in heaven and what awaits us there. That is what He told us to rejoice over! We are registered as citizens of heaven. When you are a citizen of a country, you have the rights to all the benefits of that country. We have been given exceeding great and precious promises, and they are ours forever. It is at the Cross that our life here is finished and a new life begins. It was finished when the kingdoms of the world became the kingdom of our God. In the spiritual realm it is already done. It is like paying for something that you now own, but you are just waiting for the right time to take possession of it.

The entire future of the world, where it is headed, rests in the finished work of the Cross. The deal was signed at the Cross, and it was sealed and delivered by the Spirit.

As God's holy people and members of His family, what He has belongs to us! This promise in Ephesians says that He Himself lives in us by His Spirit!

So now you Gentiles are no longer strangers and foreigners. You are citizens along with all of God's holy people. You are members of God's family. We are his house, built on the foundation of the apostles and the prophets. And the cornerstone is Christ Jesus himself. We who believe are carefully joined together, becoming a holy temple for the Lord. Through him you Gentiles are also joined together as part of this dwelling where God lives by his Spirit (Ephesians 2:19-22).

The Cornerstone of Our Foundation

We are built on the foundation of all that the Old Covenant prophesied and talked about, and Jesus is the cornerstone through the Cross. The cornerstone is the indispensable and fundamental basis of something.[48] Several years ago I built a house and had to hire each trade in a specific order for the construction. I started with the foundation. The foundation is the base on which something is established. The cornerstone is where that foundation begins. Whatever the foundation is will determine the stability of what is built on it. To move away from the foundation will bring sure destruction.

We can read here in 1 Corinthians that Jesus laid the complete foundation for the church. That foundation is the work of the Cross; there is no other foundation that we can build on.

Because of God's special favor to me, I have laid the foundation like an expert builder. Now others are building on it. But whoever is building on this foundation must be very careful. For no one can lay any other foundation than the one we already have—Jesus Christ (1 Corinthians 3:10-11).

It says here that we must build on the foundation of Jesus Christ. To build means to develop or give form to something. Our walk of faith, which is the way we are to live our lives, must be on the foundation at all times or it will topple, just as a building would.

We are finished and are being transformed into the image of Christ. How? Like an egg that has been fertilized in our mother's womb, we are growing and maturing with every part we need already within our genetic makeup. Like a pregnancy that cannot be stopped, we will be birthed into the fullness of light and power because we are finished!

When Jesus said, *"It is finished!"* our consummation was done and our life began. Like a baby forming in the womb, what has begun is finished. His job is complete; now we have a responsibility, as citizens of heaven, to start building the kingdom on the foundation of the Cross.

> *What an awesome foundation we have in the Cross!*

The book of Colossians says we are complete through our union with Christ:

> *For in Christ the fullness of God lives in a human body, and you are complete through your union with Christ. He is the Lord over every ruler and authority in the universe* (Colossians 2:9-10).

We must see ourselves as complete in Him. As I press into the Cross, I can see the work He has done for me and can be who He has called me to be. It is there that He healed and delivered me and transformed me into righteousness and holiness. He empowered me with His Spirit and gave me the ability to produce life.

Facing the Fiery Trial

A few years ago I had the opportunity to interview an amazing woman who had been kidnapped by terrorists and faced the trial of her life. I first heard about her and her husband as I watched a national TV broadcast of a missionary couple who had been kidnapped by the Abu Say-yaf, a Moslem terrorist group with ties to Osama bin Ladin. My heart went out to them in this rare interview by a Filipino reporter as Martin and Gracia Burnham pleaded for their lives. They were forced to live in deplorable conditions as captives in a marshy jungle. They looked like they were starving to death and unable to enjoy even the most basic of sanitation. I wept as I watched them and heard the ordeal they were experiencing. After viewing that show, I prayed for them, along with many others, for months, never realizing that one and a half years later I would have the privilege to meet and interview Gracia.

Martin and Gracia Burnham were serving God in the Philippines and enjoying a well-needed brief vacation at an exotic island getaway in May of 2001 when the unthinkable happened. Three terrorists with M-16s burst through the door of their room in the middle of the night and ordered them to leave immediately. These three men herded the Burnhams to a waiting speedboat where they joined 17 other hostages. Thus began the horrific ordeal that would change their lives forever.

They, along with their fellow hostages, were held captive, and for the next year were on the run in the Philippine jungle. Shortly into their captivity the Armed Forces of the Philippines made a reckless rescue attempt that resulted in random gunfire. The Burnhams, along with the other hostages, were caught in the crossfire. Fearing for their lives, they dropped to the jungle floor. That was just the first of 17 more horrifying gunfights that would eventually take some of their lives. They were constantly held at gunpoint by their captors and many nights forced to sleep on the cold jungle ground or chained to trees to prevent their escape. Adequate food and clean drinking water were luxuries. Even the simplest of things, like having a bowel movement, was a horrendous humiliating ordeal without washroom facilities or toilet paper.

Their captors continually bargained with authorities for ransom money for the release of their prisoners. To prove they meant business, they beheaded one of them, an American businessman, and the terror of their nightmare magnified. Gracia ached relentlessly as her body seemed to age under the duress of her plight. It was becoming increasingly difficult to keep her faith and not lose hope. At her most difficult time, Martin would encourage her, demonstrating incredible strength and faith, and finally Gracia chose to believe the Word of God over her circumstances. That was a turning point for her, and God proved faithful to her in the midst of the ordeal.

Then the attack of September 11, 2001, occurred. They watched mortified as their captors rejoiced and partied at the news. They prayed for the victims of their homeland, feeling the pain even in their own.

Many times Gracia just wanted to give up and die, but the thought of her children kept her going. Finally she and Martin came to terms with their ordeal and named their situation "Camp Contentment." With many relentless hardships, it seemed like the torment was never going to end. Finally, one year and five days after their captivity began, another rescue attempt from the Philippine Armed Forces resulted in Gracia's freedom and Martin's death. The ordeal of their captivity was over, but a new one was beginning with Gracia losing her best friend, husband, and father of her children.

One of the most incredible parts of this story I'll quote is from her book, *In the Presence of My Enemies.* Martin said to her, "Here in the mountains I've seen hatred; I've seen bitterness; I've seen greed; I've seen covetousness; I've seen wrongdoing." Gracia nodded her head vigorously, thinking of her captors, but then Martin surprised her by adding, "I've seen each of these things in myself."[49] Martin wasn't condemning his enemies who tormented them; rather, he was recognizing the condition of his own heart before God. His humility saw his righteousness only in the Cross.

> *The Cross is the beginning and end of all things.*

Whenever we go through a difficult time, it is always liberating when the trial is finished. For Gracia it was bittersweet, as she was free to go home and see her children and family, yet without the man she loved so much. The kidnapping ordeal had ended for her, but for Martin it really was finished as he entered into the presence of God.

Whatever fiery trial we may go through, we can trust with absolute confidence that the Cross is the place where every need we could ever have was taken care of completely. Even in the face of death we do not lose, but instead manifest the fullness of His living Word in us for an eternity of bliss. What could be better than being with Him, freed from the flesh that holds us from the manifestation of the hope of what He finished?

The work of the Cross makes all things new. The book of Revelation declares:

> *And the one sitting on the throne said, "Look, I am making all things new!" And then he said to me, "Write this down, for what I tell you is trustworthy and true." And he also said, "It is finished! I am the Alpha*

and the Omega—the Beginning and the End. To all who are thirsty I will give the springs of the water of life without charge!" (Revelation 21:5-6)

On the television show called "Who Wants to Be a Millionaire?" the contestants often are asked, "Is that your final answer?" That answer would determine whether or not they won. God is saying to us, "The Cross is My final answer."

The Cross is God's final answer to all who believe it.

I once heard a well-known journalist say that there is no absolute truth in the world. He is wrong; there is one absolute truth, and that is the work of the Cross. In a world of no absolutes, nothing can be seen as certain. With no certainty, there is no solid foundation. The world would not survive without a hope that is real and absolute.

It tells us the truth about how to live and how to die and it finishes the work for both. Finished are our hurt, betrayal, fears, and lack of purpose.

May we be like the apostle Paul and say before we die, *"I have finished the race."* Paul knew that he had done all that he needed to do for the cause of Christ, as he wrote in 2 Timothy:

As for me, my life has already been poured out as an offering to God. The time of my death is near. I have fought a good fight, I have finished the race, and I have remained faithful (2 Timothy 4:6-7).

We all have a race to run as we reach out and share Christ, and we will be faithful as Paul was so that when we die, we have finished our course.

Nothing that ever existed has finished as much as the Cross. Its complete work is ever working in us as we recognize that in it we are entire and lacking nothing.

The Cross is the culmination of the Word of God, forever declaring that "It is finished!"

Let that be your cry.

Chapter Twenty-four

Surrendering to the Cross

Then Jesus shouted, "Father, I entrust my spirit into your hands!" And with those words he breathed his last (Luke 23:46).

Trusting is difficult for many of us, especially if we have experienced many broken promises in our life. Trust is a major factor in the disintegration of marriages, since many men do not trust women, and vice versa. Infidelity is rampant; spouses lie to each other all the time about money, jobs, and family. Many relationships actually start with dishonesty since each is out to impress and win the other's heart with deception during courtship. At the Cross, Jesus teaches us to trust.

Jesus submitted to His Father in the Garden and went down a path that destroyed and humiliated Him beyond reason. He had just cried out, *"My God, my God, why have you forsaken me?"* and *"I thirst!"*—both indicating that God had turned His back on Him. Then Jesus, with His dying breath, uttered one last thing: *"Father, I entrust my spirit into your hands!"*

It is amazing that this commitment of faith follows the desperate cries of being deserted and forsaken. Despite such abandonment and pain, Jesus still chose to trust His heavenly Father. He knew that no matter what happened to Him or how He felt, His Father was trustworthy. That is how well He knew the Father and desired to please Him.

At the moment of His death, Jesus fulfilled the blood sacrifice for the sins of man. He faced the fiercest desire to rebel from the will of God but demonstrated true submission to Him so we could too. Faith and absolute trust is the inner nature of Jesus Christ. It is with that nature that all the fullness of God's grace can be received and enjoyed. Jesus had one purpose in His life: to do the will of God. The book of Hebrews says,

"Then I said, 'Look, I have come to do your will, O God—just as it is written about me in the Scriptures.'" Christ said, "You did not want animal sacrifices or grain offerings or animals burned on the altar or other offerings for sin, nor were you pleased with them" (though they are required by the law of Moses). Then he added, "Look, I have come to do your will." He cancels the first covenant in order to establish the second. And what God wants is for us to be made holy by the sacrifice of the body of Jesus Christ once for all time (Hebrews 10:7-10).

It is the sacrifice of Jesus on the Cross that makes us holy. As we submit to the message of the Cross, we will see its power overtake the works of our flesh. The Old Covenant of animal sacrifices was ended when Jesus died and established a new one. The New Covenant was established by the nature of Jesus, who desired to do the will of the Father at whatever cost to Himself. That is the type of faith God is looking for in us, and His grace is the divine enablement to do what His will is.

I find it easy to submit to the will of the Father when I look at the Cross; I know that His plan is better than mine. There are times when we may feel like God is not there, and that feeling can cause us to waver and try and save ourselves. However, we must come to a place where we know to do His will no matter what.

Trusting God—No Matter What

Many years ago I read a story of a Romanian minister who had been put in solitary confinement for five years for his faith. To keep from going insane, he continually preached sermons to himself. Often he felt the desperation of his plight and questioned God—until one day he made a decision and prayed something amazing. He told God that even if God Himself turned His back on him and deserted him, he would still choose to serve Him. Of course God would not ever leave him, but this man had to come to that place in himself to keep from giving up in despair. As a result he had a spiritual breakthrough in his cell that empowered him to keep going. Eventually he was released and preached the Gospel around the world.

Trusting God in a world of sin is not always easy, but we must learn to do as Jesus did and surrender to the Father no matter what is happening around us. To trust in someone is to have firm reliance in that person's integrity and character. Many struggle in this area when it comes to God.

Mike is a young man who attends our church (and who also happens to be my hairdresser). Recently he had an experience with God that took him from an inability to trust to full surrender. Mike along with his wife Jen had been in our church for several years, but he never seemed to connect. He had difficulty trusting God due to some experiences with his father during his childhood. His father left when he was four or five years old and moved out west. With the exception of two years, when Mike was eight and nine, he lived with his mother.

As a young child he had a hunger for God and was always praying. Many considered him an "angel." Being raised a Roman Catholic, he had a strong desire to become a priest. As he grew up, people continually enforced the fact that he was a good kid and that being good was enough. Mike began to credit himself with his ability to behave. When he did see his father, he was constantly told to "do as I say, not as I do." His father also told him to trust in good, not in better, causing Mike to believe he was good enough. His father, although affectionate toward him, continually broke his promises. He also convinced his son not to trust women, though he himself was a womanizer.

Mike, without realizing it, was steeped in pride, believing that he was a pretty good person. And he trusted only in that. Then he met Jen, fell in love, and got married. Jen was born out of wedlock to her 16-year-old mother and was left without a father. Her mother married someone else when Jen was one year old, and her new stepfather adopted her. Her adopted father was an alcoholic, and she had always felt that he treated her differently than her siblings. This led to a great need in her for acceptance. During this time her aunt brought her to church, and she gave her heart to the Lord.

As problems mounted at home, Jen left when she was just 16, got involved in drugs, and became promiscuous. By the time she turned 19, she was pregnant. Left alone with a baby on the way, she was prompted to return to church and get her life right with God. She delivered a healthy baby boy and shortly afterwards went to hairdressing school were she met and eventually married Mike.

Mike was willing to take on the responsibility of Jen's child, but deep inside he resented her past. Soon she became pregnant again. Over time Jen shared her faith with Mike and began to push him to attend church. Upon the dedication of their son they started frequenting our services. Mike, however, seemed to lack passion for God and still relied on his ability to live a reasonably good life in his own strength. His philosophy was to trust no one and as he witnessed hypocrisy in some people in the church, it affirmed his belief. Due to his difficulty in trusting others, he also felt he could not trust the church leadership. He thought that perhaps the church was just a big scam.

His resentment toward his wife continued to grow as he thought her past had forced him into marriage and going to church. Slowly thoughts of infidelity began to creep in. The more he felt that his wife was responsible for tying him down, the more he toyed with the temptation of getting into an affair. He had always relied on his own strength to do right, and soon he realized that he was beginning to get drawn into something he knew was wrong. He was becoming like his father.

Still his resentment toward his wife and the church grew, and he started slipping. It wasn't long before he was on the verge of going too far. His struggle with trusting God, his wife, and the church was leading him down the wrong path. Then God intervened. Through a series of events, Mike was coerced into going on a men's encounter weekend. He really did not want to go—and in fact tried to get out of it several times—but God had set him up.

On the weekend, Mike discovered the Cross in a way that he had never known before. He had always taken it for granted, but there he experienced a revelation of the love that was poured out for him. It was at the Cross that he found the healing he needed from his father, along with the forgiveness and the ability to trust that he desperately lacked. The Cross became real to him like never before.

Mike came back from that weekend a changed man. God had gotten hold of him in the nick of time before he destroyed his marriage. Jen shared with me that prior to Mike's seeing the work of the Cross, he could never really love her the way she needed to be loved. She knew the trust wasn't there and that he resented her. Now he loves his wife deeply, and he has confessed and dealt with his inappropriate behavior and is now the spiritual leader in their home. Mike has a passion for God, and he along with his wife are actively winning people to Christ.

Mike summed up his change to me in this one statement: "I now trust God because of the Cross."

The Cross Is All About Character

If I can't trust someone who would drink the cup of my sin and take the wrath of God for me, along with my betrayals, desertions, guilt, shame, beatings, humiliation, pain, suffering, and every conceivable nightmare known to man, then who can I trust? My criteria for trusting God does not depend on what He may or may not do for me now, but on what He has *already* done for me.

In order to experience the power of God, I must trust Him. That is what faith is all about. Jesus told us in the gospel of John that to trust in God we must trust in Him. We need to have confidence in His character, and that is easy to do when we look at the Cross.

> *Don't be troubled. You trust God, now trust in me* (John 14:1).

The work of the Cross reveals what He has already done.

Notice it says here, *"Don't be troubled."* That means do not be in an emotional state of anxiety, worry, or distress. There is something about the Cross that, when I focus on it, takes away the emotional fears that may be overtaking me. Life is full of things we can be anxious about, but peace is found at the Cross. It is there I can trust in the love of God and know that He is in control no matter what happens in my life. If I surrender it to Him, it will turn out.

We also can read in John's gospel that no judgment awaits those who trust in Him. This means faith in His Cross removes God's judgment.

> *There is no judgment awaiting those who trust him. But those who do not trust him have already been judged for not believing in the only Son of God* (John 3:18).

To distrust or not believe in Christ means we are already judged. Therefore we need to see daily the place where we put our trust so that our faith will increase and not be shaken. We must trust and surrender ourselves completely to

God's love like Jesus did on the Cross. He knew that the Cross was God's plan for Him, and He knew that He had to take the full wrath of God. Yet, in spite of all that He chose to completely surrender and trust His spirit to Him.

Jesus knew the character of God, and He knew that the Father's love for Him would not fail. He had complete confidence in God's love even though all the circumstances around Him were screaming, "He doesn't care about You!" Jesus knew what He felt like, but He did not base His faith on His feelings or on what He saw. He kept His focus on the truth about His heavenly Father and believed that He would conquer in spite of all He endured.

Real Trust in Bad Times

It is easy to trust God and surrender to Him when things go the way we think they should. It is when God seems far away that we see what we really believe about Him. I have made a decision to put total confidence in God's love for me. The Cross makes that simple because I can't deny His proof of love. The key to our faith is to be rooted and grounded in the love of God.

The Cross deepens our awareness of His immense love for us. There is nothing like it, and understanding every aspect of the Cross makes that a strong assurance. We really must ask ourselves what we are trusting in if it is not the love of God. Is it our good works? Some are depending on themselves to earn "brownie points" with God. Do we trust in our money? Many think the answer lies in what they have or can accumulate in this life. First Timothy, however, warns that to trust in money is foolish, for it will not last:

Tell those who are rich in this world not to be proud and not to trust in their money, which will soon be gone. But their trust should be in the living God, who richly gives us all we need for our enjoyment (1 Timothy 6:17).

I have learned over the years that if I put my faith in God, He definitely takes care of my needs. I do not have to figure it out or find ways to bless myself. My job is to bless others, and when I do so, I trust Him to bless me. I give because I believe in His promises that if I surrender my finances to Him, He will take care of my needs. Instead of seeking the One who blesses, many people get caught up seeking the blessing, which is really a lack of faith. I would rather have His presence and love and peace flowing through me than all the money in the world. So many believers have lost their faith by putting their need for the blessings before their love and trust for God. It will not work that way.

I also am amazed at how easy it is for all of us to try and do God's job because we don't trust Him. Then when things don't work, we get mad at Him. Yet, all the time we were the ones stopping His hand from moving because we believed more in ourselves than in Him! For example, someone might be believing for a loved one to get saved and harass that loved

Whenever we trust God for anything, we will be tested.

one, relentlessly preaching to him or her, trying to make it happen instead of loving the person, blessing him or her, sharing at the Spirit's leading, and trusting God with the outcome.

Many throw away their faith in Him during a trial. This aborts what God wants to do. There is a warning about doing this in the book of Hebrews. It says that *"no matter what happens,"* we must keep our trust in the Lord!

> *Do not throw away this confident trust in the Lord, no matter what happens. Remember the great reward it brings you!* (Hebrews 10:35)

Wow! We receive a great reward when we have confident trust in Him no matter what happens. That means nothing should shake our faith in Him. No matter what comes, no matter how bad it looks, even if God seems to have disappeared, we need to trust Him. We either believe or we don't. God does not honor faith that is based on what we see and feel.

In order to have unshakeable faith, I have to have somewhere to put it. I can't put trust in an abstract concept of God; I put it in a real God who reveals what He is like. In 1 Peter it says that we love Him even though we can't see Him. How can we love someone we can't see? By seeing what He did for us! We do not see Him, but we do see the work of the Cross, and that enables us to trust Him. The Cross gives me the glorious inexpressible joy that these verses so wonderfully declare:

> *You love him even though you have never seen him. Though you do not see him, you trust him; and even now you are happy with a glorious, inexpressible joy. Your reward for trusting him will be the salvation of your souls* (1 Peter 1:8-9).

I must trust Him for the salvation of my soul, as this scripture says. That is a daily process. Every day I thank Him for the work of the Cross in my life and trust its power to continue to form me into the image and likeness of God. *I must become what I am in Him.* My job is to feed from the Cross—the tree of life—and not the tree of the knowledge of good and evil.

When I think my salvation is based upon how much I pray, read the Bible, attend services, or give, then I am feeding from the tree of the knowledge of good and evil. I will never be able to love my husband enough, pray enough, or do enough good works. No matter what I do, the tree of the knowledge of good and evil says it is not enough. I will always come up shorthanded. Trusting in that is futile. If I trust in the tree of life, then I am feeding from Him and everything I do will be right. If I pray 15 minutes one day, and that is the best I can do, it is enough. If I pray five hours, it is enough. If I bless my husband, it is enough. Whatever I do that is motivated by the tree of life is enough. One produces life, the other death. One satisfies; the other condemns. One desires to win the lost, and the other resents that it has to.

When Jesus cried on the Cross, *"Father, I entrust my spirit into your hands,"* He was completely trusting the Father with His eternal destiny. So must we.

When I am centered on the Cross, I am choosing to live in Him. I will love Him immensely and see His unfailing love for me. It is then I am united in His love! Can you look at the Cross and say, "Father, I entrust my spirit into Your hands"? Or will you continue to choose to take matters into your own hands? The choice is simple for those who see what was accomplished. Take an inventory of your life and commit it all into His hands. Commit your marriage, your children, your job, and your destiny to Him. Jeremiah prophesied that His plans for us are good!

> *"For I know the plans I have for you,"* says the LORD. *"They are plans for good and not for disaster, to give you a future and a hope"* (Jeremiah 29:11).

We may face disasters and things may look hopeless, but when we surrender ourselves and trust Him, it all will turn out to be glorious!

Like Jesus, you can say, "Father, I entrust my spirit into Your hands."

Only then will you truly be safe.

Chapter Twenty-five

The Cross and the Bride[50]

One of the soldiers, however, pierced his side with a spear, and blood and water flowed out. This report is from an eyewitness giving an accurate account; it is presented so that you also can believe. These things happened in fulfillment of the Scriptures that say, "Not one of his bones will be broken," and "They will look on him whom they pierced" (John 19:34-37).

After Jesus breathed His last breath, the soldiers pierced His side, and blood and water flowed out. This was one of the most powerful and significant events that transpired before His resurrection. Jesus had done it all; He had finished His work—a work in which His beaten and battered body was given to take His unfaithful creation back into His heart. The fruit of His work on the Cross was poured out in total commitment for those whom He loved from a broken heart. It was the moment that married us to Christ, making us one with Him forever.

We Are His Body

The Word of God says that we are His body. The custom of crucifixion was to break the legs of the condemned men to ensure their swift suffocation. Not one bone of Jesus' body was broken, indicating that every part of His body was connected. There was no breach that could disqualify any man from receiving His life. He was fulfilling the prophecies that none of His bones would be broken and that His side would be pierced.

To understand the significance of this detail, we must go back to the beginning in Genesis and see what God did when He created man and woman.

So the LORD God caused Adam to fall into a deep sleep. He took one of Adam's ribs and closed up the place from which he had taken it. Then the

LORD God made a woman from the rib and brought her to Adam. "At last!" Adam exclaimed. "She is part of my own flesh and bone! She will be called 'woman,' because she was taken out of a man" (Genesis 2:21-23).

Jesus died to birth His bride and to demonstrate how much He loved her.

The woman was taken out of the side of man and formed from one of Adam's ribs. This symbolized that the man and woman were to walk side by side, together to rule and reign and multiply the earth with their offspring.

Now in 1 Corinthians we read that there were two Adams, the first and the last; one a living person and one a spiritual. Jesus is called the last Adam and is a life-giving Spirit:

The Scriptures tell us, "The first man, Adam, became a living person." But the last Adam—that is, Christ—is a life-giving Spirit. What came first was the natural body, then the spiritual body comes later. Adam, the first man, was made from the dust of the earth, while Christ, the second man, came from heaven (1 Corinthians 15:45-47).

This passage is very significant as it give us God's perspective for mankind. We all came from one man, and just as the natural man came from Adam, so the spiritual man comes from the last Adam, Christ.

Born to Be His Bride

When Jesus was pierced and the blood and the water flowed from His side was the release of His Spirit to birth His church, the bride of Christ.

Just as God took Eve out of the side of Adam, so He took the bride of Christ out of His side. The church was born to be one with Him as a woman is to be with her husband. The piercing of His side released the birth of the Spirit to man, and we became one with Him. Interestingly enough, there is a prophecy in Isaiah that states God would bring man back from the forsaken and desolate state of being separated from Him to become His bride, and that He has claimed us as His own:

Never again will you be called the Godforsaken City or the Desolate Land. Your new name will be the City of God's Delight and the Bride of God, for the LORD delights in you and will claim you as his own. Your children will care for you with joy, O Jerusalem, just as a young man cares for his bride. Then God will rejoice over you as a bridegroom rejoices over his bride (Isaiah 62:4-5).

This is the promise that Christ fulfilled when His side was pierced and His blood and water poured out to the earth. Fallen man has been like the wife who committed adultery and left for someone else. Through His death we are brought back to Him so He can love and cherish us. We have been chosen as the bride of Christ and have all the benefits and privileges as His bride.

When you are in love with someone, you want to set yourself apart for that person. That is what God expects of us. He is jealous for us and is devastated when we run after other lovers. In 2 Corinthians the Word says that He desires us to be pure for Him:

I am jealous for you with the jealousy of God himself. For I promised you as a pure bride to one husband, Christ (2 Corinthians 11:2).

Never did a bridegroom deserve more from a bride. Just think of what He went through to win your heart. He took all the punishment for all your sins, was betrayed, beaten to a pulp, stripped naked, and humiliated and shamed for you. He was mocked and ridiculed, deserted and falsely accused; He bore your burdens and pain, was crushed to destroy all that could destroy you, and ultimately allowed Himself to be tortured to death so that you would be His bride. Never has any groom so loved His bride, nor gone to such extremes to win her heart and lavish His love upon her in immeasurable amounts.

The Wedding of the Century

All that Christ has done for us points to a day when there will be an incredible wedding feast that will make even Prince Charles and Lady Diana's wedding pale in comparison. I remember the day the world tuned in on July 29, 1981, to watch the wedding of the century. It seemed to have everything fairytales were made of, and few wanted to miss it. My daughter Melissa (who was 11 at the time) and I woke up early and watched with anticipation as Lady Diana and Prince Charles exchanged their vows at St. Paul's Cathedral. The absolutely stunning Lady Diana had mounted a beautiful glass coach in princess style at the Clarence House and rode to the church with masses of spectators admiring her every move. She wore a wedding gown that took your breath away. The dress had been the most guarded secret in fashion history and had a 25-foot train, the longest in royal history. It was a romantic gown made of ivory silk, taffeta, and lace, and was hand embroidered with more than 10,000 tiny mother-of-pearl sequins and pearls. It was called the dress of the century, just like the wedding. Her prince was dashing royalty as he waited at the front of the packed cathedral. Thousands spilled outside the church doors in sheer joy and excitement at the monumental covenant that would impact their lives.

Prince Charles was the heir to the throne of England, and his bride was absolutely beautiful. They had every royal trapping any romantic could dream of. As I watched the wedding, I recalled growing up loving the story of Cinderella, the poor abused girl who was swept off her feet by a prince. It was such a romantic dream for so many young girls, and of course in the end they lived happily ever after. Isn't that the way it is supposed to be?

I could see my daughter Melissa's eyes captivated by the magnificent spectacle of such a royal event, and our hearts were warm as we watched the adored couple ride off in a traditional royal coach drawn by majestic horses amid cheers and ringing bells that echoed through the city. What a celebration! It made so many believe that maybe fairytales do come true. This storybook couple road off for their honeymoon in Hampshire aboard the royal yacht *Brittania* in the Mediterranean Sea—to live happily ever after.

On August 28, 1996, 15 years later, they were officially divorced. The following year in the late summer of 1997, Princess Diana and her new fiancé Dodi Fayed were killed while being chased by paparazzi. Their chauffeur-driven Mercedes, traveling 80 to 85 miles per hour, crashed in a tunnel along the Seine River at the Pont de l'Alma bridge, less than a half mile from the Eiffel Tower in Paris, France.

What went wrong? Obviously many rumors have run rampant as media and fans speculate, but we do know this much: Diana never had the heart of her prince. Right from the engagement she had a feeling that a woman named Camilla played too great a role in Charles' life. Diana suffered terrible jealousy; thus their marriage began with serious problems. The popularity of Diana only added to their stress as the world's obsession with her beauty, smile, and fashion splattered every magazine cover around the globe. The fairytale had turned into a nightmare, and eventually it ended in death. The world mourned, not just for the loss of their princess, but also for the loss of a dream that maybe could have been.

Married to Jesus

Weddings are all such grand events, and we do many of them in our church. Usually years or months of planning and large amounts of money are spent by the couple as they anticipate with great excitement their special day. It is always exciting to see the faces of a radiant bride and groom as they exchange their vows and bestow the promise of love "till death do us part" to one another. Because of experience and statistics, people often wonder where their new life together will take them. Marriage today is high risk with the odds against us for the happily-ever-after ending we so anticipate. Even many marriages that do make it are often between two people who have learned to tolerate each other at a level they can live with. Only a small percent actually enjoy the bliss of being madly in love with their spouse.

> *The Cross is the most amazing masterpiece of God marrying man to become one with him.*

God intended for marriage to be two people becoming one so that together they would be a blessing and accomplish God's will for them on the earth. Unfortunately, because of sin, what was meant to bless for many has been a curse. But there is a wedding feast like no other that awaits us. We look forward to the marriage supper of the Lamb when we will be with the lover of our soul forever.

This marriage supper will be so grand and awesome that we are incapable of even comprehending it with our natural minds. The fairytale of our dreams will come true; our Prince will come and we will live with Him happily ever after. Everything Jesus did was for this purpose. Even the first miracle He performed was symbolic of what He had planned for us. When Jesus attended the wedding in Cana and they ran out of wine, His mother told Jesus. He responded with, *"How does that concern you and me?…My time has not yet come,"* referring to His crucifixion. She then said to the servants, *"Do whatever he tells you"* (John 2:4-5).

Under the Old Covenant it was customary for the parents to arrange the wedding, and it was always necessary for their blessing on it. The wedding in Cana was symbolic of the covenant where the old wine of the Old Covenant had run out and the new wine was introduced. Mary, as Jesus' mother, was involved in having Jesus change the water into wine, which represented the blood of the New Covenant. The best was saved until last. This was the official beginning of the ministry of Christ, symbolizing that He was to bring in the new and do away with the old. It was meant to happen at a wedding because that is the intimacy of our relationship as we come to Him. Jesus referred to Himself often as the groom. For example, the gospel of Mark tells the story when the Pharisees got upset that Jesus and His disciples were not fasting:

Jesus replied, "Do wedding guests fast while celebrating with the groom? Of course not. They can't fast while they are with the groom" (Mark 2:19).

Jesus, while still on the Cross, birthed His life, His nature, and His Spirit into His bride, the church. As He breathed His last breath, He poured all of Himself out for us. He triumphed over all the works of darkness to redeem us for His bride, to be eternally His. He thought of us as any bridegroom would. He couldn't wait for the moment when the vows were exchanged and the prize of His heart would be secure in His arms of love, to have and behold.

When He left us with holy communion through the bread and the wine, He left us with the reminder of what He had consummated at the Cross; we were to remember that we are married to Him and will be with Him always. We were washed with the regeneration of His Holy Spirit by the new man birthed from His side. His church came from His side as Eve did from Adam, close to His heart to walk along beside Him, together as one to do the will of God.

The life of the Spirit lives in the faith of the church, for it is there that the rivers of His life are given to His spouse. This is an incredible sign of the power of the Cross. We now have communion with Him, in Him, and through Him. The pierced body of Jesus stood between the Old Covenant prophecy that waited expectantly for the Cross and the promise that waits for those who believe in it. Flowing from Him is the saving grace that He already achieved for us as well as the glory that was yet to come.

Whoever touches the Cross will be made fresh, pure, alive, and healed. This is the true work of the Cross of Christ. Those who are touched by it will produce fruit and be instruments of healing. What an incredible promise has been released as the living water flowed from the body of Jesus along with the blood that sealed us as His own.

The Coming Feast

The book of Revelation talks a lot about the marriage feast that will take place at the time God has appointed. All that Christ did on the Cross was in anticipation of the day when He would be completely united with His bride, and He provided the robe of righteousness for her to wear.

"Let us be glad and rejoice and honor him. For the time has come for the wedding feast of the Lamb, and his bride has prepared herself. She is permitted to wear the finest white linen." (Fine linen represents the good deeds done by the people of God) (Revelation 19:7-8).

This scripture passage refers to a specific time when we will celebrate the wedding feast. As we allow Him to do His work in us, we will be ready for the day when we will be with Him in heaven. Just as a bride adorns herself for her special day, so we adorn ourselves by the good deeds we do for others. If Christ is the new Adam, then we are the new Eve and as such His help-mate. We share in the responsibility of the marriage union. The church is one with Him, not to be divided, but to be His undivided body.

> *The church is one with Him to be His undivided body.*

Our good deeds do not save us; rather, they demonstrate how much we want to be as beautiful and pure as we can for our groom.

We also are called to reproduce by reconciling others to Him. We are told that we are ministers of reconciliation; the Word says many will know that we are His by our love for one another. This is a testimony to the world. So much of the body of Christ is in strife and division with one another because they have so little revelation of the Cross. When a married couple consummates their marriage out of their love for one another, they will have children. The same takes place with us. As we love Christ through understanding the Cross, our intimacy with Him grows and with the love we share we will win the lost. When I think about the wedding feast, I want everyone I know to be there, just like I did when I got married to my husband Rick.

Revelation 19 continues in verse 9 about how those invited to the wedding feast of the Lamb will be blessed beyond their wildest dreams. As we are in complete oneness with God, no longer bound to our fleshly bodies, we will be in an unspeakable joy, peace, and love unimaginable here on earth. We can experience it now to a certain level, but then we will be captured by all the glory and fullness of His love that He waits to lavish on us.

We are married to Him now; the ceremony took place at the Cross.

And the angel said, "Write this: Blessed are those who are invited to the wedding feast of the Lamb." And he added, "These are true words that come from God." Then I fell down at his feet to worship him, but he said, "No, don't worship me. For I am a servant of God, just like you and other brothers and sisters who testify of their faith in Jesus. Worship God. For the essence of prophecy is to give a clear witness for Jesus" (Revelation 19:9-10).

Notice the angel added, *"These are true words that come from God."* And in verse 10 it says that *"the essence of prophecy is to give a clear witness for Jesus."* The clear witness is the work of the Cross! Everything prophesied and written in the Word of God was to magnify and point out the work of the Cross.

The Cross is the altar of the sacrifice *and* the altar of the wedding. These scriptures do not say that we will have a wedding in heaven, but a wedding *feast*. A wedding feast takes place after the wedding itself.

Our Happily-Ever-After Ending

In Revelation 21 the Word says that at the time appointed we the bride will live with God without the limitations of our flesh. Then we will be in that place of no sorrow, death, crying, or pain. All evil will be done away with and all things will be new, as He accomplished on His Cross. It is in us to desire the happily ever after in a love relationship because that is what we were created for!

Then I saw a new heaven and a new earth, for the old heaven and the old earth had disappeared. And the sea was also gone. And I saw the holy city, the new Jerusalem, coming down from God out of heaven like a beautiful bride prepared for her husband. I heard a loud shout from the throne, saying, "Look, the home of God is now among his people! He will live with them, and they will be his people. God himself will be with them. He will remove all of their sorrows, and there will be no more death or sorrow or crying or pain. For the old world and its evils are gone forever" (Revelation 21:1-4).

The birth of the New Covenant, a new heaven and a new earth, the birth of the bride, man reconciled to God, and no more death, sorrow, or pain—all these were accomplished on the Cross. That is the happily-ever-after ending we dream about!

Every bride thinks about her groom and waits in great anticipation for the day they will be together forever. We too wait for our coming Prince, and He will be greater than royalty, greater than all power; His majesty and glory will take our heart away as we are enthralled with Him. The Bible describes what He will be like when we see Him come for us to rescue us from all that is evil!

Then I saw heaven opened, and a white horse was standing there. And the one sitting on the horse was named Faithful and True. For he judges fairly and then goes to war. His eyes were bright like flames of fire, and on his head were many crowns. A name was written on him, and only he knew what it meant. He was clothed with a robe dipped in blood, and his title was the Word of God. The armies of heaven, dressed in pure white linen, followed him on white horses. From his mouth came a sharp sword, and with it he struck down the nations. He ruled them with an iron rod, and he trod the winepress of the fierce wrath of almighty God. On his robe and thigh was written this title: King of kings and Lord of lords (Revelation 19:11-16).

He will come for us with the armies of heaven, and we will see Him as He is. He created us, but we fell away and became filthy and sinful, not fit for Him. Yet, in His immense love for us, He became filthy and took our sin. Then He gave us His robe and made us one heart with Him, to love Him, represent Him, and receive the unlimited blessings that a groom desires to bestow on the one who has captured his heart.

We were not brought back to the place where we were first created in Eden, for that could be lost again just like it was with Adam and Eve. Instead we were brought to the tree of life, the Cross, which we can never lose. It is there we are made one with Him, never to be separated again, and it is there we are brought into His inner chambers, the Holy of Holies, as He makes us righteous and pure. We have been presented to Him as His bride because the

> *The Cross is Jesus' victorious symbol of His love for you.*

Cross is more powerful than our sin! We have been reconciled back to God as a couple would be after a long separation. The blessings can now flow freely between us as everything that belongs to God now belongs to us. Just as in marriage when we inherit the assets and liabilities of our spouse, so God took our liabilities and gave us His assets.

Because of His immense love for us, Jesus Christ did not run from the Cross in terror. He loved us more than He hated it.

Christ is now seated on His throne in the place of all power, omnipotent, so He can shower you with blessings. Those who embrace Him as their own at the Cross will be the object of His unlimited love and affection as He reveals more and more of His glory to them. He lives to bestow His nature on you, the nature of the Lamb of God who would stop at nothing to save you and win you. When they pierced His side, the blood flowed out from His heart to yours and then returned to Him as He took possession of you. He ever lives in you to complete the work He started because of His endless love for you.

His desires, His motives, His choices, and His character flowed from Him into us to consummate us into the marriage He died to have. We are His most glorious possession because of the Cross, and His blood sealed us in the power that He possesses. He sanctified us unto Himself, and we are one with Him always. The Cross fills you with His passion for you and yours for Him.

As at any wedding, promises are made and a dying to self takes place in order to meet the needs of the one you marry. The book of Ephesians explains how the work of the Cross sets the example of the way the husband is to love his wife. Jesus, as the husband of the church, loves us more than we will ever be able to fully comprehend.

And you husbands must love your wives with the same love Christ showed the church. He gave up his life for her to make her holy and clean, washed by baptism and God's word. He did this to present her to himself as a glorious church without a spot or wrinkle or any other blemish. Instead, she will be holy and without fault (Ephesians 5:25-27).

His desire is that we be holy and pure as He is; He will present us to Himself without spot, wrinkle, or blemish. Only the Cross has the power to do that. The more I love Him, the more I long for the day when I will see Him without the limitations of my flesh. That is what I live for, and I can't wait for the day we read about here in Revelation:

Look! He comes with the clouds of heaven. And everyone will see him— even those who pierced him. And all the nations of the earth will weep because of him. Yes! Amen! "I am the Alpha and the Omega—the beginning and the end," says the Lord God. "I am the one who is, who always was, and who is still to come, the Almighty One" (Revelation 1:7-8).

All the nations of the earth will weep because of Him, and He is, always was, and is still to come! He is my bridegroom, and we were married when His blood and water flowed from His side. We met at the altar, the Cross, and exchanged our lives forever in the blood covenant of marriage. You and I are one with Him always!

Chapter Twenty-six

The Resurrection of the Cross

He made himself nothing; he took the humble position of a slave and appeared in human form. And in human form he obediently humbled himself even further by dying a criminal's death on a cross. Because of this, God raised him up to the heights of heaven and gave him a name that is above every other name (Philippians 2:7-9).

The body of Jesus was wrapped in a cloth and placed in a tomb sealed with a stone. His fate appeared to be shame and defeat, and by all natural appearances He was gone.

Jesus died a slow, torturous death, enduring it to benefit us; now He was buried for three days as the Scriptures say. The body that was taken down from the Cross was the physical body that God inhabited as a man—a body that was so beaten and mutilated He was unrecognizable. After they pried the nails from His hands and feet, they would have lifted down His lifeless body. To look at Him as God at that point would have seemed incomprehensible. A dead God—who would have thought of that? Where was the power? Where was the victory over the enemy? To judge by sight would have been disastrous, for nothing appeared to be as He claimed.

Looking Beneath the Surface

Jesus died on the Cross, was pierced in His side, and His body taken down from the Cross and buried in a rich man's tomb. The gospel of Mark gives the details:

An honored member of the high council, Joseph from Arimathea (who was waiting for the Kingdom of God to come), gathered his courage and went to Pilate to ask for Jesus' body. Pilate couldn't believe that Jesus was already dead, so he called for the Roman military officer in charge and asked him. The officer confirmed the fact, and Pilate told Joseph he could have the body. Joseph bought a long sheet of linen cloth, and taking Jesus' body down from the cross, he wrapped it in the cloth and laid it in a tomb that had been carved out of the rock. Then he rolled a stone in front of the entrance (Mark 15:43-46).

Unknown to the natural eye, something more powerful than anything that had ever happened was brewing. Jesus had descended into the pit of hell and was destroying all that was meant to destroy us. There was a power in Him that was greater than all the powers of the earth put together, and it was *His nature that ignited it!*

When those who were present at the Cross looked at His desecrated body, they had no idea what was transpiring. They had no clue what was going to change the destiny of man forever. The Scriptures say that people could barely tell that He was a human. The wounds He bore were horrendous to see, and He was without life completely. At that time all the disciples were devastated. They believed it was all over, even though Jesus had told them many times that He would be crucified and rise from the dead. Somehow they had not heard or understood what He meant.

We may think the disciples were slow or ignorant because they missed this, but I cannot tell you how many Christians I know who don't seem to understand that we too are going to be resurrected and get a new body. Many live as though eternity really does not exist; they put all their hope in this life. The resurrection of Jesus Christ is so important because it is the proof that Jesus is who He said He is. Because of His suffering He proved that doing the right thing in the midst of every contradiction will produce supernatural life and power. Much like the churning and brewing of a mighty volcano, something far greater was about to erupt from the earth and spill out a hope that no other could.

All four gospels recount the story of the resurrection. Let's look at the one in the gospel of Matthew:

Suddenly there was a great earthquake, because an angel of the Lord came down from heaven and rolled aside the stone and sat on it. His face shone like lightning, and his clothing was as white as snow. The guards shook with fear when they saw him, and they fell into a dead faint. Then the angel spoke to the women. "Don't be afraid!" he said. "I know you are looking for Jesus, who was crucified. He isn't here! He has been raised from the dead, just as he said would happen. Come, see where his body was lying. And now, go quickly and tell his disciples he has been raised from the dead, and he is going ahead of you to Galilee. You will see him there. Remember, I have told you" (Matthew 28:2-7).

Verse 1 tells us that Mary and Mary Magdalene went to the tomb, only to find that He had risen. Can you imagine how shocked they were to see that Jesus was not there?

The women ran quickly from the tomb. They were very frightened but also filled with great joy, and they rushed to find the disciples to give them the angel's message. And as they went, Jesus met them. "Greetings!" he said. And they ran to him, held his feet, and worshiped him. Then Jesus said to them, "Don't be afraid! Go tell my brothers to leave for Galilee, and they will see me there" (Matthew 28:8-10).

They were frightened, which would be a natural reaction if you saw someone alive whom you just buried, but they also were filled with great joy! This passage of scripture says they actually held His feet and worshiped Him.

Jesus rose from the dead on the third day as He had predicted, and when it happened they were stunned. *"He is alive! He is alive! He is alive!"* would have been resounding throughout the region as word spread quickly the following days. Soon Jesus appeared to His disciples and proved to them that He was actually alive, as state in the book of Acts:

During the forty days after his crucifixion, he appeared to the apostles from time to time and proved to them in many ways that he was actually alive. On these occasions he talked to them about the Kingdom of God (Acts 1:3).

Jesus had only one thing to talk about when He did appear to them: the kingdom of God! I am sure that He explained to them the whole meaning of the Cross and how perfectly He had satisfied God's wrath, dealing with our sin completely. He would have explained to them the purpose of His death and the promise of resurrection life that comes with dying to self. It was after that the disciples went from hiding in fear to feeling privileged and blessed to suffer for Him. They would have listened intently as He explained how He went down to the lowest place to bring us to the highest. They would have been captivated as they learned how they were exalted to be with Him on the throne of glory.

His Nature Is Our Power

Romans chapter 6 says that death could not keep Him down, as revealed by His resurrection!

And since we died with Christ, we know we will also share his new life. We are sure of this because Christ rose from the dead, and he will never die again. Death no longer has any power over him (Romans 6:8-9).

It was the very nature of Christ that flowed in His blood that produced the power to rise from the dead. The nature of Christ is where the power of the Cross is because it was that nature that led Him to the obedience of His death. If we want the power, we must understand His nature.

> *The nature of Christ is where the power of the Cross is.*

The blood of Christ that carries His divine nature never stops working in us. The blood of Christ and the Spirit of Christ are inseparable. The blood was on the Cross and the Spirit was released from the Cross, and the resurrection was the result. His blood was not dead, but powerful and able to make all things new, including His body. He Himself has life that is independent of time, for He is ever present. The book of Revelation tells us that we overcome by the blood of the Lamb, and the Holy Spirit will always glorify the blood of the Lamb, which is the work of the Cross.

The Cross got its power from the One who died on it, from the nature He possessed. It is His desire that we conform to that nature. His nature is that of total love and humility, and that is power. Heaven cannot receive or trust us with new bodies when we are steeped in human pride.

There was not a selfish bone in His body; He emanated divine love and holiness, purity and righteousness. He was all that man is not.

The Cross makes no room for selfishness and pride. It cannot live in the midst of that; it destroys the "I" in us. We are crucified; nevertheless, we live in the Spirit. The weakness and death of the Cross is married to the life and immense power of God. We must not just glory in the Cross that He died on, but also in that *we* died there and are made alive there. *In meekness He overcame, and in meekness we will too!*

The Cross revealed His nature, manifested His divine character, and inspired all that He did.

Our heart should desire His meekness to abound in us because it was that nature that caused Him to become the greatest. Jesus told the disciples when He washed their feet that the leader must wash the feet of those he or she leads (my paraphrase), and then He set the example for them to follow. He did not just set it through washing their feet, but also through the Cross. It is only when I make the Cross the center of my life that my need to be humble becomes obvious. It is in true humility that the resurrection power of God is released. This powerful scripture in Philippians explains how it was the nature in Christ that exploded the forces of God and caused Him to rise from the grave and ascend into the heights of heaven:

> *He made himself nothing; he took the humble position of a slave and appeared in human form. And in human form he obediently humbled himself even further by dying a criminal's death on a cross. Because of this, God raised him up to the heights of heaven and gave him a name that is above every other name* (Philippians 2:7-9).

His humility was willing to submit unto death for the benefit of others, so He was not messing around when He said He would show us by example. In humility we will find rest as it is difficult to always try and prove ourselves. Humans run around trying to impress one another; most only care about how they themselves look. Pride always has to jockey for position and calculate evil in order to promote self. Pride caused the fall of the devil and is the root of evil, self-will, self-love, and self-gratification. The way of the Cross is self-denial and selflessness, and that is the very character and essence of God Himself. The way up to the throne room of God is the way down to self.

THE CROSS

One of the people I most admire is my husband Rick. He is a man with a lot of authority, and over and over again I see him humbly take the abuse of those who are jealous or disagree with him. Often, these people say things that are very unkind. He has learned to always respond with true humility and love. As a result, God keeps promoting him. I am very appreciative of this quality in him, and I know that he truly desires to serve others.

Another person I greatly admire I met unexpectedly. We attend the Christian Booksellers Association annually to conduct most of our TV interviews and pre-book most of our guests. Every year we leave a few slots open for "divine appointments"—people whom we believe God would have us interview. A few years ago, while taping in Anaheim, California, I met a beautiful young lady who blessed me and impressed me like none other. Renée Bondi was one of the most uplifting, optimistic, and dynamic people I have had the privilege to meet. She has been pushed to the limits and beyond, yet she demonstrates a positive attitude that is second to none. She literally radiates the love of Jesus and blesses many with her testimony and trust in God even in devastating circumstances.

The Last Dance

At the age of 29 Renée had a bright future. She was recently engaged and sang like a melodic bird. On May 15, 1988, her fiancé was in town on business and took her out for a romantic dinner and presented her with a beautiful engagement ring. She was on cloud nine! They danced together that night, and they enjoyed celebrating their upcoming wedding. It was the last time she would ever dance.

The following night, the unthinkable happened. Renée was sleeping in her room in the condominium that she shared with her roommate Dorothy and Dorothy's 12-year-old daughter. She woke up suddenly in the middle of the night in midair and landed on the floor on the top of her head. She heard her neck crack. When she tried to move, she couldn't. Helpless and in excruciating pain, she tried to call out and could only utter a faint cry. So she began to pray. The words that flowed were unusual and prophetic as she kept saying, "I'm Your instrument; I'm Your tool; use me."

Fortunately Dorothy woke up. Thinking she heard something, she went to check on Renée, only to discover Renée lying helpless and unable to speak except in a small whisper. Dorothy's daughter Jenn stayed with Renée while she went for help, and soon Renée was whisked off to the hospital. Everything was a blur for her as the doctors and nurses worked diligently on saving her. The next day a neurosurgeon told her the tragedy that had occurred that would change her life forever. Dr. Palmer told her, "Your neck is broken, and your entire body beneath your neck is paralyzed. You are a quadriplegic." Renée's life as she knew it had ended. Now she faced a long recovery of learning to live completely dependent on others for everything she needed.

> *"If you stand before the power of hell and death is at your side, know that I am with you through it all."*

Renée's stay in the hospital was difficult; everywhere she looked she saw braces, wheelchairs, and people with desperate needs in their bodies. It took compassion to look past the immense need in others and see the people who were trapped in bodies that would not function for them just like her own. Her fiancé Mike stayed by her side every day and learned how to take care of her needs. His love for her never failed, and, in spite of the seriousness of her handicap, he was determined to live the rest of his life with her. Renée told me that the love in his heart was seen in how he loved her, and she trusted him because of it.

Renée had many sleepless nights in the hospital and times of great despair and depression. With much difficulty she would try to pray, until one night she had a breakthrough. She always knew that God was there, but she prayed desperately for answers. On this particular night a song dropped into her head with the words, "Be not afraid; I go before you always. Come, follow Me, and I will give you rest. If you pass through the raging waters in the sea, you shall not drown; if you walk amid the burning flames, you shall not be burned. If you stand before the power of hell and death is at your side, know that I am with you through it all."

"Music had been my lifeline to God, and now He was speaking to me through it," she told me with a twinkle in her eyes and a radiant smile. "If Jesus cared enough about me to die on the Cross, I had to trust that He cared enough to take care of me in this situation." Renée had ups and downs throughout the long process until she could finally leave the hospital and go home. She had to battle depression and feelings of insecurity, especially feelings of unworthiness of her fiancé's love and commitment to her. She and her family had given him permission to walk from the relationship, but Mike refused.

Renée struggled with the reality of never walking again, driving a car, signing her name, or doing even the simplest of tasks. She had become an enormous, time-consuming burden. She never dreamt that she would be a wife who could do nothing for herself. The most difficult humiliation she endured, she told me, was having someone bathe and clean you up. She could not even go to the bathroom or brush her teeth without someone's help. No longer would she have the privacy that so many of us take for granted. She felt helpless and vulnerable and spent months trying to be strong and keep a good attitude while inside she was spiraling into despair.

Then one day she broke and wailed at the death of her body, the death of her career, and the end of all her future dreams. It was a pivotal moment as she grieved the loss of so many things. Never did she blame God or feel that He was the problem, but releasing her grief to Him began her healing. In fact, at one point, as part of her rehabilitation program, she had to be in counseling with a therapist who also was paralyzed and bitter at God because of it. Renée refused to work with her, telling her that her attitude toward God was not something she would tolerate. She knew her relationship with the Lord was her only hope, and she would not allow anyone to infect her with negativity toward Him. Trusting in God was her priority. How many believers allow their bitterness toward God to infect their mind and plant those seeds in the heart of others?

In spite of Renée's feelings of unworthiness, she and Mike were married. He had assured her that her body was broken, but not her. She was the woman he had fallen in love with and he chose to marry her because of the love he couldn't let go of. How wonderfully Mike represents Christ as He loves His bride's broken body and chooses to be one with us. Mike and Renée continued their life together and God began to powerfully use Renée as an inspiration to the body of Christ.

She has spoken nationwide and been a guest at the Crystal Cathedral with Robert Schuller and at the Saddleback church with Kay Warren. She also has made numerous television appearances. God has given back her singing voice, which she had lost, and she ministers mightily in song wherever she goes. Her attitude and smile light up a room, and I know that Renée is anticipating the new body her Savior promised her. It took her years to overcome her embarrassment of being disabled when everything in her wanted to be normal, but her greater desire is to be the servant of Christ no matter what she is going through. God has blessed Mike and Renée with a son, Daniel. The birth of her son was another of God's blessings for her, as that too was said to be high risk and almost impossible.

Renée keeps her positive attitude by focusing on the work of the Cross of Christ. She does not take for granted what Christ has done for her, and she waits expectantly for the day when she will be raised up and freed from a body that holds her captive.[51] The resurrection of Jesus Christ is the hope that we all have as Christians; it is the hope that we too will be resurrected and completely free from the flesh that holds us and works contrary to the spirit realm we are now created for.

The Promise of a New Body

The work of the Cross reveals the power of God in ways beyond our imagination. I want to focus, however, on the one thing that we all should be excited about and keep alive in us: the hope of the promise of our new bodies. We are blessed to have the bodies of flesh that God has given us, but no matter how hard we try to stop the process, they will slowly deteriorate and eventually die. In 1 Corinthians the Word describes the new bodies we will have and how they will be different than the weak bodies we now possess:

There are bodies in the heavens, and there are bodies on earth. The glory of the heavenly bodies is different from the beauty of the earthly bodies. The sun has one kind of glory, while the moon and stars each have another kind. And even the stars differ from each other in their beauty and brightness. It is the same way for the resurrection of the dead. Our earthly bodies, which die and decay, will be different when they are resurrected, for they will never die. Our bodies now disappoint us, but when they are raised, they will be full of glory. They are weak now, but when they are raised, they will be full of power. They are natural human bodies now, but when they are raised, they

271

will be spiritual bodies. For just as there are natural bodies, so also there are spiritual bodies (1 Corinthians 15:40-44).

What is so exciting is that when we get our new bodies, they will be eternal and *full of glory and unlimited power!* I am looking forward to the new body God has for me because, like everyone else, I am limited by my fleshly one.

Can you imagine having a body that never gets sick, tired, or run down? It will be so awesome to feel free and perfect in every way. To have the life of Christ pulsating through every part of your being with a power that flows without limits. Then you will be finally rid of all that is perishable and take on immortality! That is what awaits you and I when we die!

Every human being has an earthly body just like Adam's, but our heavenly bodies will be just like Christ's. Just as we are now like Adam, the man of the earth, so we will someday be like Christ, the man from heaven. What I am saying, dear brothers and sisters, is that flesh and blood cannot inherit the Kingdom of God. These perishable bodies of ours are not able to live forever (1 Corinthians 15:48-49).

Flesh and blood cannot enter the kingdom of God. I am sure that when Jesus taught His disciples between the resurrection and His ascension into heaven, they were seeing His imperishable body and were amazed that they too would have one. First Corinthians continues on and tells us that we must be transformed, or given a different form or appearance:

For our perishable earthly bodies must be transformed into heavenly bodies that will never die. When this happens—when our perishable earthly bodies have been transformed into heavenly bodies that will never die— then at last the Scriptures will come true: "Death is swallowed up in victory. O death, where is your victory? O death, where is your sting?" For sin is the sting that results in death, and the law gives sin its power. How we thank God, who gives us victory over sin and death through Jesus Christ our Lord! (1 Corinthians 15:53-56)

When it says that we will have victory over death and that death is the last enemy to be conquered, it means we must die in order to have that victory. But in dying we will live because of the resurrection of Jesus Christ. It is so important that we do not base our lives on what we see right now. We are to live for what awaits us in eternity, doing what He has called us to do, reaping the massive harvest of souls that He died for. We must focus on the great joy and rewards that await us when we enter into the eternal realm.

Scripture emphasizes in 2 Corinthians that planet Earth is not our final destination. I love this portion of scripture that so beautifully explains how we can have confidence in knowing that being away from these bodies will be incredible, for we will be completed in every way in our oneness with God:

> *Imagine having a glorious body that never gives you a hard time!*

> *For we know that when this earthly tent we live in is taken down—when we die and leave these bodies—we will have a home in heaven, an eternal body made for us by God himself and not by human hands. We grow weary in our present bodies, and we long for the day when we will put on our heavenly bodies like new clothing. For we will not be spirits without bodies, but we will put on new heavenly bodies. Our dying bodies make us groan and sigh, but it's not that we want to die and have no bodies at all. We want to slip into our new bodies so that these dying bodies will be swallowed up by everlasting life. God himself has prepared us for this, and as a guarantee he has given us his Holy Spirit. So we are always confident, even though we know that as long as we live in these bodies we are not at home with the Lord. That is why we live by believing and not by seeing. Yes, we are fully confident, and we would rather be away from these bodies, for then we will be at home with the Lord (2 Corinthians 5:1-8).*

I am so excited that I know, no matter what happens here, there will be even greater blessings awaiting me as I take on immortality.

You will be so in tune with God because you will no longer have to battle the voice of your flesh. The book of Philippians talks about how the power that He uses to conquer everything, everywhere, is the same power that changes your weak body into a powerful one.

> *He will take these weak mortal bodies of ours and change them into glorious bodies like his own, using the same mighty power that he will use to conquer everything, everywhere (Philippians 3:21).*

So often we Christians complain about our bodies. They are too tall, too short, too thin, too wide, too old, too young, etc. We tend to look at ourselves in the mirror and see all the flaws and things we dislike about our appearance. Even the most beautiful people are not happy with how they look and are very concerned about aging. I believe too much time and emotional well-being is consumed by the condition of our bodies. I believe we have a responsibility to take care of them, but much of the world is obsessed with having perfect bodies.

When we allow our flesh to dictate our self-worth, then we are actually worshipping it. This corruptible flesh is important, but it won't be around for long. We show a lack of faith when we allow the temporal to rob us of our love, peace, and joy. When we look at the Cross, we see the eternal truths, and those truths help us keep our eyes on what really matters. Nothing can be taken away from us. Jesus went to hell and back for us because He knew that He was the only way man can experience His resurrection life. The gospel of John relates what Jesus said about this prior to His crucifixion:

> *Jesus told her, "I am the resurrection and the life. Those who believe in me, even though they die like everyone else, will live again"* (John 11:25).

Jesus knew who He was, and in this verse He did not just say that He would rise again; He said that *He is the resurrection and the life.* As we die, we will live. First Corinthians tells us that if Christ had not been raised from the dead, then everything we believe about Him is useless and we are still condemned in our sins:

> *If there is no resurrection of the dead, then Christ has not been raised. And if Christ has not been raised, then your faith is useless, and you are still under condemnation for your sins* (1 Corinthians 15:16-17).

All that Jesus suffered and died for, He did so that you and I would have the hope of the resurrection. He did it so that no matter how difficult things get here, we have the power to die to self and live to new life, and eventually be resurrected with new bodies that will be perfect and eternal.

What a promise we have from Him! We owe it all to what He so willingly endured for us. How can we not be thankful when we keep these truths before us? When we live like mere mortals, we have moved far from the work of the Cross. But when we see it, we live in amazing joy and excitement for what is to come, along with what we already have. Our passion for Him will automatically spill over onto others, and the world will see that our God is alive. The Cross produced the resurrection of Christ and made the way for ours.

Oh, how our heart should yearn to honor the Cross and the resurrection life it promises, for it is our complete salvation!

Chapter Twenty-seven

The Cross Is the Altar of Exchange[52]

The altar from which God gives us the gift of himself is not for exploitation by insiders who grab and loot (Hebrews 13:10 MESSAGE).

The Cross is the altar of God. It is the only place we can go to and exchange death for life and sin for righteousness. To exchange something means to turn it in for replacement; it is giving one thing for something else.[53] Our lives are a series of exchanges. We give time for money and money for things like shelter, food, clothing, etc. We exchange news with friends, we trade on the market, and we choose one thing for another in our jobs and education. We even at times trade friends. The whole world operates on an exchange system.

Every decision we make is an exchange of valuing one thing over another. In churches around the world, vows and rings are exchanged in the covenant of marriage. Men and women give up the benefits of a single life for a married one. When it comes to our spiritual life, we may exchange watching television for time with God, immorality for purity, and sleeping in on Sunday morning for attending church. Unfortunately, most people do not know what they really want. As a result, they exchange what they need for what they think they want out of a desire for immediate gratification.

There have been times in my life when I really wanted to purchase a particular item, but because I didn't want to wait until I had enough money I bought something inferior—and regretted it later. I've seen some who really want to get married, so they settle for someone who is not Godly and miss out on what the relationship could have blessed them with. We have counseled many who live with the consequences of their poor decisions. Whenever you accept what is wrong, you give up what is right as well as the blessing that comes with it.

The Cross: Our Altar

God has established the Cross as the altar we can go to and we can go and lay down the wrong desires that lead us astray. It is there that we can be empowered to make right choices as we exchange our wrong motives for His.

The altar is the door to God; we cannot get to Him without going through it.

The word *altar* in the Hebrew language means the place of slaughter or sacrifice.[54] In the Old Covenant the altar was the place where animals were sacrificed to atone for the sins of the people. It also was occasionally used as a place of refuge, as a reminder to the Israelites of their heritage, and something that called attention to a major event. The New Testament contains no reference to a physical altar, but in Hebrews chapter 13 the altar from God is referred to as the work of the Cross, the place where the *"the gift of himself"* is given:

> *The altar from which God gives us the gift of himself is not for exploitation by insiders who grab and loot. In the old system, the animals are killed and the bodies disposed of outside the camp. The blood is then brought inside to the altar as a sacrifice for sin. It's the same with Jesus. He was crucified outside the city gates—that is where he poured out the sacrificial blood that was brought to God's altar to cleanse his people. So let's go outside, where Jesus is, where the action is—not trying to be privileged insiders, but taking our share in the abuse of Jesus* (Hebrews 13:10-13 MESSAGE).

When this scripture says *"taking our share in the abuse of Jesus,"* it is stating that we bear the responsibility for putting Him on the Cross; that we acknowledge it was our sins that put Him there. We need to realize that the altar is the door or entranceway to God; we cannot get to Him without going through it. Under the Old Covenant something always had to die in order to cleanse the people of sin because the shedding of blood represents the total giving of self.

We could not worship God under the law without an altar; under the law of grace He has established the Cross as the altar that gives us access to His throne. This altar is separated and sanctified by God for the sacrifice of ourselves that we offer to Him. It is the place of death and consecration to God, and it is the altar by which everything in our lives must be surrendered. It was on the Cross that Jesus reached the climax of His purpose and perfection, forever establishing His love for us, providing victory over our enemies, and sealing us with His blood. Whatever is put on the Cross becomes holy because of the holiness and sanctity of what was accomplished there on our behalf.

> *Nothing can change people as dramatically as the Cross.*

It is always important to have a focal point as a reminder to keep our perspective right. God has given us the Cross for that purpose. In New York City, on the site of the twin towers destroyed on September 11, 2001, there is a monument that represents the tragedy that transpired there. Many who visit it bow their heads in silence, remembering and honoring those who died on that tragic day. How much more should we go to the place where Jesus was tortured for us and remember and honor what He did?

On my own I can never measure up to Him, but at the Cross I can believe that every part of me is sanctified and made holy. It will always make the difference as I lay every part of me on the altar in exchange for what completes me. I must mentally, spiritually, and emotionally submit to its power to transform me.

Recently my husband and I met with Nicky Cruz, who is well known for his famous conversion to Christ in the 1960's. A bold preacher by the name of David Wilkerson went into the streets of New York and confronted Nicky and his violent street gang with the Gospel. Rick and I sat riveted as we listened to the incredibly compelling testimony that he unfolded to us. As a new believer I had heard of his conversion and seen the subsequent movie, *The Cross and the Switchblade*, which had been released at that time.

Tears welled up in our eyes as he shared with us parts of his story that we had never heard. With great emotion he disclosed the severe abuse from his mother, a practicing witch, and his father, a satanic priest. As a young boy he endured severe beatings, broken ribs, and devastated emotions as he was repeatedly told he was a child of the devil and hated by his parents. He shared with us one of his lowest points when he was about to commit suicide by hanging himself from a tree and his younger brother intervened and begged him to stop. However, the continual abuse inflicted on him had taken its toll. He was a mass of unhealed pain—inside and out—and his life as a gang leader was subsequent to the rejection and need to feel nothing for anyone in order to survive.[55]

In the movie that told the story of his dramatic encounter with God, one of the most powerful moments transpired at a service David Wilkerson was conducting. Nicky showed up with his fellow gang members. Suddenly the Spirit of God moved powerfully and a weeping Nicky rushed up to the front to meet David and exchange his knife for a Bible. That exchange was momentous in that it amplified the absolute truth of what the Cross does. It takes our weapons of death in exchange for His weapons of life!

The Great Exchange

Each chapter in this book covers a part of our life as it pertains to the suffering of Jesus Christ. The work that He accomplished was His decision to exchange all our faults, disappointments, and pain for all that He has in the eternal riches of His kingdom. Every day I take an inventory of my life, my heart, and the choices I make and bring them to the Cross. It is the altar that removes all my garbage in exchange for the endless riches of His glory! I recall the aspects of His passion that relate to me as I suffer things that would cause me pain and sorrow.

If I am facing great temptation, I think of His in the Garden and call on Him for a way out so that I will not fall. If I am facing a fear that is tormenting me, I exchange it for the courage and faith He had to obey His Father as He wrestled with His fear. If I am facing betrayal that has deeply wounded my heart, I exchange it for His faithfulness and unending love for me that promises a better day. If desertion is my pain, then I think of that night when all of His companions fled in fear when He needed them the most, and I trade mine for the comfort of knowing He is always with me. When I am falsely accused and the anger and desire to retaliate rise up, I think of the great contradiction that Christ withstood humbly and obediently as lies were assailed on Him, and I lay mine down and receive His humility.

When I have been cut deeply with shame and humiliation that want to torment my mind, I meditate on Him as He stood before 200 Roman soldiers who stripped and mocked Him, beating Him relentlessly. Then I can thank Him for the privilege of going through my shame as I receive His dignity and grace for me. As I face ridicule and mockery that strip me of my self-worth, I look to Him and receive the confidence of who He is and who He has made me to be. When I feel beaten down and am suffering with pain, I remember His scourging and think about those deep gashes of

Whatever I lack, I must seek for it at the Cross.

mutilated flesh that He bore in exchange for my healing. When oppression grips my thoughts, I see Him with the crown of thorns and the purple robe and lay down my negative lies to receive the authority and titles He has so richly purchased for me. In my suffering, I see His and exchange mine for the strength and faith He gives me to continue on and receive my breakthrough.

Sometimes I feel stuck in a situation unable to do anything but trust in Him, and I thank Him for the nails that held Him on the Cross that my hands and feet deserved. It is then that He gives me His power to move mountains by my faith. At times I struggle with forgiveness. When everything in me wants to retaliate and get even, then I hear His cry of forgiveness from the Cross and run to Him, surrendering my bitterness in exchange for mercy and love toward my enemies. I recall His words to the thief dying beside Him of a promise in paradise, and remember my destiny is sure. Sometimes I feel overwhelmed with the responsibilities that I have and feel like running, but then I see Him dying a torturous death, yet reaching out to His mother to meet her needs, and my selfishness is quickly changed for His selflessness. When I thirst with dissatisfaction and a need to be fulfilled, I know where to drink from pure rivers of living water that satisfy my soul.

At the Cross, He has given me all that I need to face every day and conqueror my emotions and flesh. When I have nothing to give, I reach my arms up to His outstretched ones of love and take all I need to touch another life that needs His hope. It is there that I am called to make the exchanges and find the power to overcome in my mind, will, and emotions. At the Cross He never leaves me without a way to break through and enter His heart.

Honoring the Cross

I love and admire Him so much for the incredible character He demonstrated in every situation, and I desire that same power and self-control in my life. I am more than willing to exchange all that I am for all He is and receive His life-giving power to destroy what could destroy me! The Cross is the altar of my death to all the things I must overcome, and it is the place of incredible resurrection life as I possess His power that takes me where I could not go without Him.

Everything I lay on the altar of the Cross is made perfect by His blood—blood that now runs through my veins as a child of the living God. It is there that I consummate the full fellowship of glorious communion with Him. The revelation of the Cross has birthed in me a strong desire to partake of the bread and cup of communion whenever I fellowship with Him. I have discovered there is something supernatural that satisfies my longing for Him as I celebrate what He has done!

God desires us to cherish the Cross in our heart. Every time we have communion, we are announcing His work on the Cross until He returns. Because He wants His greatest work to be remembered at all times, He established the communion table to keep it before us. He opens our eyes and unfolds the eternal riches of our inheritance and satisfies our parched heart with living water. It is also the place of rest where we exchange all our works for what He has done. Every time I get caught up in anything that robs me of my peace and causes me stress and turmoil, I need to remember the Cross.

It is awesome to know that there is a place we can find rest and the desire to obey because we are His beloved. Jesus our high priest finished His work, sat down in heaven at God's right hand, and now ministers on our behalf.

Here is the main point: Our High Priest sat down in the place of highest honor in heaven, at God's right hand. There he ministers in the sacred tent, the true place of worship that was built by the Lord and not by human hands (Hebrews 8:1-2).

Notice this passage also says that our place of worship is not built with human hands. In other words, it is not by our works. Therefore we must *continue to rest in the work He has done for us.* It is so wonderful to know that we can never earn it yet trust in the fact that our salvation is complete!

Verses 16 to 19 of Hebrews 9 state that the New Covenant was established when Jesus shed His blood. This refers to the fact that you do not receive the benefits of a person's will until the person has died.

The Cross is proof of the New Covenant.

Now when someone dies and leaves a will, no one gets anything until it is proved that the person who wrote the will is dead. The will goes into effect only after the death of the person who wrote it. While the person is still alive, no one can use the will to get any of the things promised to them. That is why blood was required under the first covenant as a proof of death (Hebrews 9:16-18).

The blood shed on the Cross was the proof of death that released the will or benefits of God toward us. To get these benefits, we must acknowledge the blood of Christ and go to the place where they are released. In the same way that I shop at a store and exchange my money for the goods I want to buy, I can go to the Cross and exchange the junk in my life for the blessings waiting for me that His death provided. The Cross proves that the blessings belong to me; it is at the altar that I lay down all the stuff that robs me from receiving them.

The Cross does not lie; He is making us holy. It is a process, and *He* is doing it, not us. He also said "It is finished." How can He say that? He is a God of faith who calls those things that be not as though they were, and His faith will never fail.

Whatever touches the altar is made holy. The book of Joshua says there is only one true altar of the Lord our God:

If you need the altar because your land is defiled, then join us on our side of the river, where the LORD lives among us in his Tabernacle, and we will share our land with you. But do not rebel against the LORD or draw us into your rebellion by building another altar for yourselves. There is only one true altar of the LORD our God (Joshua 22:19).

THE CROSS

The great exchange of all time took place on the Cross of Christ, and it is open every day of our life, just waiting for us to exchange our garbage for His endless glory. Just as we would leave behind everything we owned if we found a map to a buried treasure, we must leave everything at the Cross. It is the way to the endless treasures that never fade away. There is no better deal.

Chapter Twenty-eight

Remembering the Cross

Remain in me, and I will remain in you. For a branch cannot produce fruit if it is severed from the vine, and you cannot be fruitful apart from me. Yes, I am the vine; you are the branches. Those who remain in me, and I in them, will produce much fruit. For apart from me you can do nothing (John 15:4-5).

To remain in Him is to remember Him.

Jesus told us to remain in Him and He would remain in us. I have discovered that my awareness of His work on the Cross keeps me in the place of continual abiding in Him. It is summed up in the knowledge that all I am and all I have are a result of what He has done for me.

A diminished passion for Him is a good indication that we have forgotten the magnitude of what He has done for us. We must never forget that justice and love were married at the Cross, giving us freedom and eternal life in exchange for condemnation and death. As time goes on, many Christians lose their first love for Christ because they do not purpose to keep alive the memory of what He did for them. We quickly become apathetic and forget when tribulation and trials come, thus allowing them to rob us of the foundation of our faith. How often do we give in to murmuring and negative thoughts, and take things into our own hands rather than trust in His finished work? The book of Hebrews warns us to never forget what we first learned about Christ, regardless of what we face:

Don't ever forget those early days when you first learned about Christ. Remember how you remained faithful even though it meant terrible suffering (Hebrews 10:32).

The first thing we learn as Christians is what He did for us on the Cross.

As we honor the Cross, we grow in the knowledge of its power to save us. Abiding in His crucifixion and resurrection life is where our flesh will die and our spirit will soar. Remembering the Cross releases the power that changes us into the image of Jesus Christ. As we conform to His death, His dynamic nature empowers resurrection life in us, and we will desire to live in the awareness of being crucified with Him and made alive forevermore. The Cross will always loom larger than our weakness when we are fixed on its power! That power is found in His love for us; it is the Cross that proves that love.

We must never forget that our entire salvation begins and ends at the Cross.

As humans we have difficulty keeping our passion burning; we quickly take things for granted. Regardless of what we have in life—our spouse, our children, a job, church, a new home, a car—before long the excitement that we had when those things were new, ebbs.

I love the scripture in Leviticus that emphasizes how the fire must always keep burning on the altar and never go out. As we read this passage, we must remember that the fire is the passion in our heart and the altar is the Cross.

Remember, the fire must be kept burning on the altar at all times. It must never go out (Leviticus 6:13).

We must keep the fire burning brightly and never let it fade or die. His passion must be our passion since we are married at the Cross and live for Him.

Remember the Passover

God called the Israelites to remember the Passover every year as a major celebration of their faith.

When God was dealing with the Israelites while they were in slavery in Egypt, He did amazing and supernatural things to free them of their bondage. We read in Exodus 12 that God gave instructions for each family to choose a lamb or young goat for a sacrifice. He told them to smear the lamb's blood on the top and sides of the doorframe of the house where the lamb was to be eaten with bitter herbs and bread made without yeast. They were instructed to consume the entire sacrifice, burning anything that was left, and to prepare for a long journey. That night the Lord would pass through the land of Egypt and kill all the firstborn sons and firstborn male animals. The blood on their doorposts was a sign; God told them, "Where I see the blood, I will pass over you." The plague of death could not touch them.

Always remember where God has brought you from.

This event is called the Lord's Passover, and the Israelites were instructed to remember this day

and celebrate it forever. This was the Lord's deliverance of His people from slavery in the land of Egypt. As we study God's Word, Egypt is used in reference to the fallen world that held us in slavery to our sin. We must remember that the Cross is the true Passover that delivered us from the slavery and death of this world.

The blood over the doorposts represented the blood of the Lamb of God that was shed on the Cross. Just as God passed over the Israelites, sparing them from His wrath, so those who embrace the work of the Cross also will be passed over when His judgment falls upon man.

After the Israelites left Egypt and God supernaturally opened the Red Sea, sparing them from the angry armies of Egypt, they celebrated with great joy. However, it didn't take long for them to start complaining. All too quickly they forgot what God had done for them. In the book of Hosea, the prophet mentioned that God spoke to the people about how they had forgotten Him and reminded them of all He had done to rescue them:

> *I am the LORD your God, who rescued you from your slavery in Egypt. You have no God but me, for there is no other savior. I took care of you in the wilderness, in that dry and thirsty land. But when you had eaten and were satisfied, then you became proud and forgot me* (Hosea 13:4-6).

"You became proud and forgot me" still cries from the One who never forgets us. God does not like being forgotten anymore than we would. He desires that we always keep before us a reminder of His unending love for us.

He also warned the Israelites in Deuteronomy to be very careful not to forget *what* they had been rescued from.

Be careful not to forget the LORD, who rescued you from slavery in the land of Egypt (Deuteronomy 6:12).

This means we are not to forget we have been delivered from the slavery of the sin that is in this world and the curse that it brought.

We can read further on in Deuteronomy that it is usually our pride that causes us to forget; we become self-sufficient when times are good. Once again God reminds us to remember all that has been done for us:

That is the time to be careful. Do not become proud at that time and forget the LORD your God, who rescued you from slavery in the land of Egypt. Do not forget that he led you through the great and terrifying wilderness with poisonous snakes and scorpions, where it was so hot and dry. He gave you water from the rock! (Deuteronomy 8:14-15)

The rock that flowed with water is a type of the Cross. It satisfies our thirst with His rivers of living water and protects us from the poisonous snakes and scorpions of sin that permeate this world.

Forgetting what God has done leads to unbelief, fear, and the deception of self-sufficiency. It amazes me to see how man neglects God until a tsunami or a hurricane hits and everything is taken away. When our resources are limited, man either becomes bitter or recognizes he needs Him. What our pride continually forgets is that without Him we would not even exist and that only He deserves all our honor and respect as our Creator. How could we ever think anything is worth more than Him once we understand the Cross?

Remember the Sabbath

One of the most important instructions in the Old Covenant was to remember the Sabbath. In fact, it is one of the Ten Commandments and carries the death penalty if ignored.

Exodus 31 contains what God told Moses about the Sabbath:

The LORD then gave these further instructions to Moses: "Tell the people of Israel to keep my Sabbath day, for the Sabbath is a sign of the covenant between me and you forever. It helps you to remember that I am the LORD, who makes you holy. Yes, keep the Sabbath day, for it is holy. Anyone who desecrates it must die; anyone who works on that day will be cut off from the community. Work six days only, but the seventh day must be a day of total rest. I repeat: Because the LORD considers it a holy day, anyone who works on the Sabbath must be put to death. The people of Israel must keep the Sabbath day forever. It is a permanent sign of my covenant with them. For in six days the LORD made heaven and earth, but he rested on the seventh day and was refreshed" (Exodus 31:12-17).

> *The people of Israel were commanded to remember the Sabbath. To remember the Cross is to remember the Sabbath.*

This tells us several things about the Sabbath that we need to know. First, it is a sign of the covenant between God and man. Second, it would help them remember that He is the Lord who makes us holy. Third, the Sabbath itself is holy. Fourth, to work on it is to desecrate it and cuts us off from the community. Last, to ignore it results in our death. The purpose of the Sabbath was to remember what God had delivered them from.

Now let's look at how the Sabbath relates to the work of the Cross.

In the New Covenant, it is the work of the Cross that reminds us of our covenant with God. It is the Cross that reminds us that God is the One who makes us holy. It is also holy itself as the altar of God; to desecrate it cuts us off from the kingdom of God and we remain in death. And, just as the Sabbath was, the Cross is our reminder that we have been delivered from the slavery of this world.

The word *Sabbath* means a day to rest from our labors.[56] The book of Hebrews shares that there is a rest from our labors that we are to enter into by faith; we must do our best to enter into that rest:

> *For all who enter into God's rest will find rest from their labors, just as God rested after creating the world. Let us do our best to enter that place of rest. For anyone who disobeys God, as the people of Israel did, will fall* (Hebrews 4:10-11).

The Cross is the place where we cease from our own works and completely depend on what He has done for us. To move from that place is to fall away from God. Its purpose is to destroy our pride and show us His contempt for all human greatness. In the gospel of Mark is the account of Jesus telling the Pharisees the true purpose of the Sabbath after they accused the disciples of violating the Sabbath by breaking off some heads of wheat to eat.

> *The Cross is the Sabbath that we are to rest in.*

Then he said to them, "The Sabbath was made to benefit people, and not people to benefit the Sabbath. And I, the Son of Man, am master even of the Sabbath!" (Mark 2:27-28)

To be the master is to be the owner and keeper of something; it is to be the original of what copies are made of. It also means to defeat and overpower.[57] Jesus is the real Sabbath, and all that was done under the law represented what He fulfilled.

In the book of Colossians it says we should not be condemned about the Sabbath; it was just a shadow of the real thing, which is Christ Himself:

> *So don't let anyone condemn you for what you eat or drink, or for not celebrating certain holy days or new-moon ceremonies or Sabbaths. For these rules were only shadows of the real thing, Christ himself* (Colossians 2:16-17).

It is still important for believers to meet together and fellowship in church; after all, the Word does tell us not to forsake the assembling of ourselves together since it is necessary for our spiritual growth. It is important that we be plugged into a local church to work within a community at spreading the Gospel and helping to meet the needs of saints.

The true Sabbath, however, is the work of the Cross. We must rest in what was accomplished there and stop believing that any of our works have anything to do with our redemption. As soon as we start to think we have anything to do with it, we are desecrating the Cross and breaking the Sabbath. To depend on our works for our righteousness is the same as working on the Sabbath. The result is death and is an abomination to the work He has done for us. The Sabbath was about remembering what God had done, just as the Cross is.

Remember the Bread and Wine

Jesus looked forward with deep longing to what we call "the last supper" on the night of Passover. It was then that He called the elements of bread and wine His body and blood and sealed our covenant with Him. He had waited in anxious anticipation to eat this Passover meal with them; in fact, He had been longing for this moment since the beginning of time. He had carried it in His heart like a groom dreams of the day he can finally take his bride! History was made on the night of the Passover as the famous last supper and the first communion unfolded.

It was to be an eternal reminder of all the Cross accomplished as we were begotten of God and married to His Son!

Then at the proper time Jesus and the twelve apostles sat down together at the table. Jesus said, "I have looked forward to this hour with deep longing, anxious to eat this Passover meal with you before my suffering begins. For I tell you now that I won't eat it again until it comes to fulfillment in the Kingdom of God." Then he took a cup of wine, and when he had given thanks for it, he said, "Take this and share it among yourselves. For I will not drink wine again until the Kingdom of God has come." Then he took a loaf of bread; and when he had thanked God for it, he broke it in pieces and gave it to the disciples, saying, "This is my body, given for you. Do this in remembrance of me." After supper he took another cup of wine and said, "This wine is the token of God's new covenant to save you—an agreement sealed with the blood I will pour out for you" (Luke 22:14-20).

Jesus knew that every Passover celebration ever held was for what He was about to suffer. He knew that He was the fulfillment of the multitudes of Sabbaths. What was He thinking as the moment finally arrived and He could tell them the secrets of His plan? Did He long with anticipation the fulfillment of being one with man? Did His heart beat faster as He thought of those He loved being with Him always? As He took that bread and wine, did He inwardly tremble at the thought of His broken and mutilated body oozing with blood that would seal our heart? Did He feel the heartache of all the spilled blood of man that would soon be washed by His own? Did His mind fill with the wonder and joy of the beginning of the new and the end of the old? Was He praying fervently within that we would always know His love by remembering His work of the Cross? How could we look into His eyes and disappoint the lover of our soul by forgetting? How could we not remember that neither heaven nor hell could stop Him from His desire to capture our heart?

The Power of Remembering

In the book of Romans the apostle Paul told us that remembering, which is renewing, will bring about the transformation of His perfection in our lives:

And be not conformed to this world: but be ye transformed by the renewing of your mind, that ye may prove what is that good, and acceptable, and perfect, will of God (Romans 12:2 KJV).

He says to think on God's Word and what He has done for us. What we think on is always a choice; whatever we allow our eyes to see and our ears to hear will direct our thoughts. I choose to think on His greatest act of unending love for me. This verse from Philippians tells us the essence of what we should turn our thoughts to:

Finally, brethren, whatsoever things are true, whatsoever things are honest, whatsoever things are just, whatsoever things are pure, whatsoever things are lovely, whatsoever things are of good report; if there be any virtue, and if there be any praise, think on these things (Philippians 4:8 KJV).

I cannot imagine anything more true, honest, just, pure, lovely, and of a good report to praise God about than the work that was accomplished on the Cross of Christ. It is my most important memory and is essential to life like nothing else. Only the living Word of God through His work on the Cross has the power to change how we think and act.

There are many things in my life I choose to remember, and some I'd like to forget. One thing I love to do is keep a record of all the things God has done in my life. I remember clearly the night I gave my heart to the Lord and the following day when He supernaturally began revealing Himself to me.

I love to think about my wedding, the births of my children, and many supernatural provisions from God in my life. I remember the first car the Lord gave me, my first week in full-time ministry, and the first time I ever spoke publicly at a ladies' ministry. I remember the times the Lord supernaturally provided homes and jobs for me. I also think of the numerous mission trips to Russia, the Philippines, Italy, Mexico, and Africa.

One of my fondest memories is of a particular day during a missionary trip we took to the Philippines with our associate pastors, Luc and Christine. We woke up to an earthquake, then flew in a small Philippine ten-seat aircraft to land on a dirt runway that ended abruptly at the foot of a mountain. Next we traveled in a windowless jeepney over dirt roads to stay in a bamboo hotel on the South China Sea. Upon arriving at that hotel I was bitten by a monkey chained to the railing at the top of the stairs on the way to our room. There we dropped off our luggage and boarded a bonca boat (a large canoe with skis attached to the sides) with some natives who took us on the choppy sea for several hours and brought us to the island of Culion, a leper colony.

Remembering the Cross is critical to our spiritual growth.

We spent the day handing out candy to impoverished children and toiletries to the lepers, praying and listening to them share how they pray for us. Then we boarded the bonca boat to head back across the South China Sea in complete darkness, and I witnessed my first falling star. We fell into bed exhausted late that night in the bamboo hotel, where every sound could be heard through the walls, including a loud TV over the bar in the lobby. That was a day of many "firsts" for me, and it is etched in my mind forever.

I have hundreds of memories of the awesome things God has done over the years, but the greatest to me is the day a deeper revelation of the Cross began to sink into my heart and caused me to love God more than I could ever imagine.

When we think of all He has done for us, serving Him becomes an honor and we will make it our mandate. The key is in purposing to remember.

Everything we think and do must be built on the cornerstone that the Cross is more powerful than any sin we could commit, and it alone makes us holy. Everything in creation will give account to the Cross's message of justice and love and what they did with it. Apart from the Cross there is no Gospel; that means there would be nothing…no hope, no salvation, no healing, no deliverance. Always remember that the work of the Cross is the "I am" of the ever-present God. It knows no end to its power and forever speaks of the mercy of God.

It is the rod of Moses, the fire by night, and the pillar by day. It is the rock that flowed with water and the fulfillment of the law. It forgives, heals, delivers, and sets free, making holy whatever it touches. It is the blood of the Passover Lamb and the Sabbath that ends our works, destroying our pride and exalting Him. It took us from the depths of hell to the heights of heaven, giving us the riches of His glory. It is the altar of our marriage to our conquering Bridegroom, who died to win our heart. It made all things new! It gives us the breath of life, a song to sing, and a dance in our step. It is the altar of God that overwhelms our heart with the desire to worship Him forevermore. The Cross is the culmination of all that He is and has done for us, and it equips us to be like Him.

Let your heart cry be what is summed up so well in this prophetic psalm:

Praise the LORD, I tell myself, and never forget the good things he does for me. He forgives all my sins and heals all my diseases. He ransoms me from death and surrounds me with love and tender mercies. He fills my life with good things. My youth is renewed like the eagle's! The LORD gives righteousness... (Psalm 103:2-6).

Never forget the power of the Cross, as God does exceedingly abundantly above all we can ask or think. He continually outdoes even Himself as He started with one lamb for one man when He cut a covenant with Abraham. Then He outdid Himself when He offered one lamb for each family on the night of Passover, when He freed the Israelites from slavery in Egypt. Then His power went beyond that when He offered one lamb for a nation as the high priest sacrificed the offering for the sins of Israel. And again He exceeded Himself by offering one Lamb, Jesus Christ, for the sins of all man.

The blood of the Cross continues to work and grow as its power reaches further and multitudes daily come into the heart of God by its selfless love. There are more people alive today than have ever been since God created man, and there is no limit to what we can do through the power of the Cross. Its power knows no end as it reaps the increasing harvest of souls through those who have been changed by it.

Oh, children of God, always remember to rest in the finished work of the Cross, knowing that Jesus completed you and met your every need, then ascended into heaven and sat down at the right hand of God. The Cross stands as an eternal reminder that *it is finished!*

Endnotes

1. "wisdom," *The American Heritage® Dictionary of the English Language, 4th ed.* (Houghton Mifflin Company, 2000), <www.Dictionary.com>.

2. "concentrate," *The American Heritage® Dictionary of the English Language, 4th ed.* (Houghton Mifflin Company, 2000), <www.Dictionary.com>.

3. "supersede" *Merriam-Webster's Dictionary of Law* (Merriam-Webster, Inc., 1996), <www.Dictionary.com>.

4. C.J. Mahaney with Kevin Meath, *The Cross Centered Life* (Sisters, Oregon: Multnomah Publishers, 2002).

5. C.J. Mahaney with Kevin Meath, *The Cross Centered Life* (Sisters, Oregon: Multnomah Publishers, 2002), pp. 20-21.

6. For more on the concepts in this chapter, read William P. Farley's book, *Outrageous Mercy* (Grand Rapids, Michigan: Baker Books, 2004), pp. 40-46.

7. William P. Farley, *Outrageous Mercy* (Grand Rapids, Michigan: Baker Books, 2004), p. 41.

8. "implode," *The American Heritage® Dictionary of the English Language, 4th ed.* (Houghton Mifflin Company, 2000), <www.Dictionary.com>.

9. "character," *The American Heritage® Dictionary of the English Language, 4th ed.* (Houghton Mifflin Company, 2000), <www.Dictionary.com>.

10. "justice," *Merriam-Webster's Dictionary of Law* (Merriam-Webster, Inc., 1996), <www.Dictionary.com>.

11. "awesome," "awe," *The American Heritage® Dictionary of the English Language, 4th ed.* (Houghton Mifflin Company, 2000), <www.Dictionary.com>.

12. "sin," *The American Heritage® Dictionary of the English Language*, 4th ed. (Houghton Mifflin Company, 2000), <www.Dictionary.com>.

13. You can read Carrie McDonnell's complete story in her book, *In the Face of Terror* (Integrity Publisher, 2005).

14. Richard Booker, *The Miracle of the Scarlet Thread* (Shippensburg, Pennsylvania: Destiny Image Publishers, 1981), p. 53.

15. "horror," *The American Heritage® Dictionary of the English Language*, 4th ed. (Houghton Mifflin Company, 2000), <www.Dictionary.com>.

16. "The Cross—Jesus in China," a documentary film © 2003 by China Soul for Christ Foundation, <www.chinasoul.com>.

17. "betrayal," *The American Heritage® Dictionary of the English Language*, 4th ed. (Houghton Mifflin Company, 2000), <www.Dictionary.com>.

18. "abandonment," *The American Heritage® Dictionary of the English Language*, 4th ed. (Houghton Mifflin Company, 2000), <www.Dictionary.com>.

19. "deny," *The American Heritage® Dictionary of the English Language*, 4th ed. (Houghton Mifflin Company, 2000), <www.Dictionary.com>.

20. "guilty," *The American Heritage® Dictionary of the English Language*, 4th ed. (Houghton Mifflin Company, 2000), <www.Dictionary.com>.

21. "atonement," *The American Heritage® Dictionary of the English Language*, 4th ed. (Houghton Mifflin Company, 2000), <www.Dictionary.com>.

22. Not her real name.

23. Not her real name.

24. "strip," *The American Heritage® Dictionary of the English Language*, 4th ed. (Houghton Mifflin Company, 2000), <www.Dictionary.com>.

25. "despise," *The American Heritage® Dictionary of the English Language*, 4th ed. (Houghton Mifflin Company, 2000), <www.Dictionary.com>.

26. "reject," *The American Heritage® Dictionary of the English Language*, 4th ed. (Houghton Mifflin Company, 2000), <www.Dictionary.com>.

27. "oppress," *The American Heritage® Dictionary of the English Language*, 4th ed. (Houghton Mifflin Company, 2000), <www.Dictionary.com>.

28. "dart," *The American Heritage® Dictionary of the English Language*, 4th ed. (Houghton Mifflin Company, 2000), <www.Dictionary.com>.

29. "take," *The American Heritage® Dictionary of the English Language, 4th ed.* (Houghton Mifflin Company, 2000), <www.Dictionary.com>.

30. "remove," *The American Heritage® Dictionary of the English Language, 4th ed.* (Houghton Mifflin Company, 2000), <www.Dictionary.com>.

31. "Barabbas," *Easton's 1897 Bible Dictionary* (public domain), <www.Dictionary.com>.

32. "insurrection," *The American Heritage® Dictionary of the English Language, 4th ed.* (Houghton Mifflin Company, 2000), <www.Dictionary.com>.

33. "excruciating," *The American Heritage® Dictionary of the English Language, 4th ed.* (Houghton Mifflin Company, 2000), <www.Dictionary.com>.

34. "grace," *Easton's 1897 Bible Dictionary* (public domain), <www.Dictionary.com>.

35. "denial," *The American Heritage® Dictionary of the English Language, 4th ed.* (Houghton Mifflin Company, 2000), <www.Dictionary.com>.

36. "cover," *Wordnet 2.0*, (Princeton University, 2003), <www.Dictionary.com>.

37. Concepts in this section were based on Erwin Lutzer, *Cries from the Cross: A Journey into the Heart of Jesus* (Chicago: Moody Press, 2002), pp. 57-65.

38. "stumble," *The American Heritage® Dictionary of the English Language, 4th ed.* (Houghton Mifflin Company, 2000), <www.Dictionary.com>.

39. Charles Swindoll, *The Darkness and the Dawn: Empowered by Tragedy and the Triumph of the Cross* (Nashville: Word, 2001), pp. 153-154, as quoted in Erwin Lutzer, *Cries from the Cross: A Journey into the Heart of Jesus* (Chicago: Moody Press, 2002), pp. 73-80.

40. Erwin Lutzer, *Cries from the Cross: A Journey into the Heart of Jesus* (Chicago: Moody Press, 2002), p. 80.

41. "forsaken," *The American Heritage® Dictionary of the English Language, 4th ed.* (Houghton Mifflin Company, 2000), <www.Dictionary.com>.

42. You can read more about Bill Wilson and his ministry in his book, *Whose Child Is This?* (Creation House, 1992).

43. Erwin Lutzer, *Cries from the Cross: A Journey into the Heart of Jesus* (Chicago: Moody Press, 2002), p. 90.

44. "supreme," *The American Heritage® Dictionary of the English Language, 4th ed.* (Houghton Mifflin Company, 2000), <www.Dictionary.com>.

45. The Day of Atonement was the day the high priest made the annual animal sacrifice for the sins of the nation of Israel.

46. "shelter," *The American Heritage® Dictionary of the English Language, 4th ed.* (Houghton Mifflin Company, 2000), <www.Dictionary.com>.

47. "finished," *The American Heritage® Dictionary of the English Language, 4th ed.* (Houghton Mifflin Company, 2000), <www.Dictionary.com>.

48. "cornerstone," *The American Heritage® Dictionary of the English Language, 4th ed.* (Houghton Mifflin Company, 2000), <www.Dictionary.com>.

49. Gracia Burnham, *In the Presence of My Enemies* (Wheaton, Illinois: Tyndale House, 2003), p. 214.

50. For more on the concepts in this chapter, see Oliver Treanor, *This Is My Beloved Son: Aspects of the Passion* (London: Darton, Longman and Todd, Ltd., 1997), pp. 184-186.

51. You can read more about Renée Bondi's story and ministry in her book, *The Last Dance But Not the Last Song: My Story* (Fleming H. Revell, 2002).

52. For more on the concepts in this chapter, see Andrew Murray, *The Blood of the Cross* (New Kensington, Pennsylvania: Whitaker House, 1981), pp. 37-52.

53. "exchange," *The American Heritage® Dictionary of the English Language, 4th ed.* (Houghton Mifflin Company, 2000), <www.Dictionary.com>.

54. "altar," *Vine's Expository Dictionary of Old Testament Words*, <www.Dictionary.com>.

55. To find out more about Nicky Cruz's testimony and ministry, you can read his book, *Soul Obsession: When God's Primary Pursuit Becomes Your Life's Driving Passion* (Waterbrook Press, 2005).

56. "Sabbath," *Eastons 1897 Bible Dictionary* (public domain), www.Dictionary.com.

57. "master," *The American Heritage® Dictionary of the English Language, 4th ed.* (Houghton Mifflin Company, 2000), <www.Dictionary.com>.

About the Author

Cathy Ciaramitaro is an inspiring teacher in the body of Christ. Her practical and applicable approach to the Word of God is refreshing, challenging, and life-changing as her desire is to see the body of Christ grow up in the Lord. She is also the host of a weekly television production, "Life Inside Out," where she brings insights and solutions through her practical teachings of God's Word.

Cathy has spoken nationally as well as internationally alongside her husband, Apostle Richard Ciaramitaro, Senior Pastor of Windsor Christian Fellowship in Windsor, Ontario. Together they pastor a growing and radical congregation of 1,700 and love to see souls come into the kingdom of God and into the full knowledge of Christ. Cathy has ministered at numerous conferences and seminars around the world and is widely recognized for her expertise in leadership training.

The mother of six children and grandmother to ten grandchildren, Cathy understands both the joys and struggles of being a busy woman. She is a dedicated and creative homemaker who is generously given to hospitality and mentoring women.

Cathy Ciaramitaro
c/o Windsor Christian Fellowship
4490 Seventh Concession
Windsor, Ontario
Canada N9A 6J3

email: wcf@2windsorchristianfellowship.com
website: www.windsorchristianfellowship.com
phone (519) 972-5977